RANGERS

NEW YORK RANGERS
SEVENTY-FIVE YEARS

NEW YORK RANGERS
SEVENTY-FIVE YEARS

by John Halligan

Foreword by Wayne Gretzky

TEHABI BOOKS

Over the course of their seventy-five seasons, the Rangers have forged some terrific rivalries. One of the first was with the Boston Bruins, against whom Phil Goyette, above, celebrates a 1967 goal that eluded Boston goaltender Gerry Cheevers in the third Madison Square Garden.

Following the Bruins, the Rangers' greatest rivalries were with their nearest neighbors, the New York Islanders, the New Jersey Devils, and the Philadelphia Flyers.

The "Canyon of Heroes," as special a place as there is in New York, welcomed the Stanley Cup champions on Friday, June 17, 1994. Lower Broadway was awash with ticker tape and "Rangers fever." The most popular float, quite naturally, was the captain's. Mark Messier, again and again brandishing the Stanley Cup, was joined by teammates Kevin Lowe, Brian Leetch, Steve Larmer, Mike Richter, and Adam Graves.

MESSIER
11
9

99
NEW YORK RANGERS

In a bird's-eye view of a New York–New York face-off, the "Great One," Wayne Gretzky, met Joel Otto of the Philadelphia Flyers.

AUTHOR'S ACKNOWLEDGMENTS

I would like to acknowledge, more than anyone, my wife Janet, the only female Ranger. If she had a number, it would be "99." I would also like to honor my parents and my brother Edward, who started my love affair with hockey—and the Rangers—in 1949 by bringing home a copy of *Inside the Blueshirt.* (Buddy O'Connor was on the cover; some things you never forget.)

Now for the difficult part: saluting the scores of friends and colleagues who have urged me to "just write a book" or who have helped in its writing. Emile Francis, Stan Fischler, Stu Hackel, Paul Kanow, and Matt Loughran have been overly generous with their time . . . and their reminiscences. Kenny Albert, Marv Albert, Tom Barnwell, Hal Bock, Frank Brown, Jim Callahan, Bill Chadwick, Jim Clements, Mike Cosby, Mickey Cotter, Phil Czochanski, John Davidson, Philip Driggs, Dave Freed, Arthur Friedman, John Gentile, Rod Gilbert, Vic Hadfield, Jeff Jennings, George Kalinsky, Dan Leary, Todd Levy, Danny McBride, Jack McCarroll, Sal Messina, Ginger Killian Milbury, Fran and Bob Murray, Don O'Hanley, Ben Olan, Dan O'Neill, Mark Piazza, John Rosasco, Sam Rosen, Stan Saplin, Bill Shannon, Marvin Schleyer, "Ski Ball," and John Totaro have been invaluable.

JOHN HALLIGAN
New York, 2000

Tehabi Books developed, designed, and produced *New York Rangers: Seventy-Five Years*, and has conceived and published many award-winning books that are recognized for their strong literary and visual content. Tehabi works with national and international publishers, corporations, institutions, and nonprofit groups to identify, develop, and implement comprehensive publishing programs. The name *Tehabi* is derived from a Hopi Indian legend and symbolizes the importance of teamwork. Tehabi Books is located in San Diego, California. www.tehabi.com

Chris Capen, *President*
Tom Lewis, *Vice President of Development*
Tim Connolly, *Director of Brand Publishing*
Andy Lewis, *Design Director*
Nancy Cash, *Editorial Director*
Sarah Morgans, *Project Editor*
Thomas Schmidt and **Gail Fink**, *Copyeditors*
Camille Cloutier, *Proofreader*
Ken DellaPenta, *Indexer*
Stan Fischler, *Editorial Consultant*

Special thanks to the staff at the New York Rangers for their contributions in the creation of *New York Rangers: Seventy-Five Years.*

Photography credits appear on page 180.

Library of Congress Cataloging-in-Publication Data

Halligan, John 1941–
New York Rangers: seventy-five years / by John Halligan ; foreword by Wayne Gretzky.
p. cm.
Includes index.
ISBN 0-7607-2298-6 (hardcover) -- ISBN 0-7607-2299-4 (pbk.) --
ISBN 1-887656-34-0 (deluxe hardcover) -- ISBN 1-887656-35-9 (limited collector's edition)
1. New York Rangers (Hockey team)--History. 2. New York Rangers (Hockey team)--History--Pictorial works. I. Title.

GV848.N43 H24 2000 00-041779
796.962'64'097471--dc21

This edition is printed on acid-free paper that meets the American National Standards Institute Z39.48 Standard.

Printed by Dai Nippon Printing Co., Ltd. in Hong Kong

Contents

MODELL'S
SPORTING GOOD
NYR
99
HESPELER

Foreword

by Wayne Gretzky

When I think back on the three years I spent with the Rangers, I realize how very rewarding that time was for me and my family. It was a privilege to finish my career in New York, maybe the greatest city the world has ever known.

Ever since I was young I have followed the sport of hockey, with its traditions and great players. I admired the Original Six teams, so it was really meaningful to wear the classic Rangers sweater after signing with the team in 1996. At that time, the Rangers had over seventy years of tradition . . . that has now reached seventy-five. Putting on the New York throwback jersey connected me with that rich history.

Playing in New York had so much to offer. First there's the city—there's a buzz in the air, a sense of urgency, that is thrilling. New York quickly became home to me and my family. The diehard New York fans welcomed us and gave me their support with an unrivaled energy, while playing for the Rangers in the fabled Madison Square Garden was incredible.

My time with the Rangers provided some great personal memories. Our run to the 1997 Eastern Conference finals was a tremendous thrill for me. The afternoon of my retirement, when the presentations had been made, the game had been played, and all that was left was for me to circle the ice one last time, was also really memorable. Up until then, everything had happened so fast. As I skated slowly, alone, I savored everything—that day and all the years I had played this great game. Stepping off the ice, I felt myself become part of the rich history that makes this game so very special. Considering the New York Rangers' storied past and time-honored traditions, I felt it was appropriate that it was a Rangers jersey that I wore for that final game.

New York City entered the world of professional hockey in 1925. Within a year, the New York Rangers were formed, creating a thrilling intercity rivalry. It was a serendipitous start for a great team and a great city.

1926

May 15—The Rangers were granted a franchise and joined the National Hockey League. The NHL announced that Chicago and Detroit would also have new teams in November, provided their home rinks were finished. The moves gave the NHL ten teams.

Oct. 27—The Rangers named Lester Patrick as their new coach and general manager. Patrick replaced Conn Smythe.

Nov. 16—Bill Cook scored the first Rangers goal, and Hal Winkler became the first goaltender in NHL history to record a shutout in his first career game as New York won 1-0 over the visiting Montreal Maroons in the first game in Rangers history.

Lester Patrick

1927

Mar. 26—Despite losing 4-3 to the Boston Bruins on the final night of the season, the Rangers won the NHL's American Division championship (with a record of 25-13-6) in their first season in the league.

1928

Apr. 7—Forty-four-year-old coach Lester Patrick replaced injured netminder Lorne Chabot in goal, and Frank Boucher scored at 7:05 of overtime to give New York a 2-1 win over the Montreal Maroons in game two of the 1928 Stanley Cup finals.

Apr. 14—New York beat the Montreal Maroons 2-1 in game five of the finals to become the 1928 Stanley Cup champions. It was the Rangers' first Stanley Cup after only two seasons in the NHL.

1929

Feb. 28—The Chicago Blackhawks were shut out for the eighth straight game, an NHL record, when Rangers goalie John Ross Roach and the Blackhawks' Chuck Gardiner dueled to a scoreless tie in Chicago.

The Original Stanley Cup

The Classiest Team in Hockey

New York City was the self-proclaimed center of the universe when the New York Rangers were born on May 15, 1926, at the height of the Roaring Twenties and three years shy of the Great Depression.

It was the "golden age of sports" in America. Average New Yorkers cared more about Babe Ruth, Jack Dempsey, Red Grange, Bobby Jones, and Bill Tilden than they did about politics or foreign affairs. Secretaries pulled in about $15 a week. Sirloin was 41¢ a pound. The *Daily News*, one of thirteen dailies in the Metropolis, was 2¢ a copy. Charles Lindbergh, who flew the Atlantic, was in the news. So was Gertrude Ederle, who swam the English Channel. Ernest Hemingway's *The Sun Also Rises* and *Winnie the Pooh* by A. A. Milne were hot reads. On the screen, it was Ronald Colman in *Beau Geste*, and on the stage, Lynn Fontanne played Liza in *Pygmalion*.

It was the era of the flapper. Prohibition was in its seventh year and there were an estimated twenty thousand speakeasies in New York, most of them located between 40th and 60th Streets. The Rangers landed smack in the middle, between 49th and 50th, in the brand-new Madison Square Garden, "the world's premiere sports arena."

The man who brought them there was George Lewis "Tex" Rickard. Born in Kansas and raised in Texas, Rickard became a New Yorker, and he looked every bit the part, complete with a jaunty straw hat, a bow tie, and an ever-present cigar. "Part carnie barker, part adventurer, part hustler, but all promoter," as Eric Whitehead described him in *The Patricks,* Rickard was a boxing man who was running the Garden at the time. Tex knew a winner when he saw one, and he liked what he saw in the New York Americans, New York's first hockey team: great box office.

The Americans preceded the Rangers in the National Hockey League by a single season, renting the Garden from Rickard and his associates in 1925. The "Amerks" were an immediate hit, and it took Tex less than a year to get a team of his own. That team would be called the Rangers, as in "Tex's Rangers."

Rickard and his boss, Colonel John S. Hammond, the president of the Garden, wanted to hit the ground running, and they wisely recruited a sage hockey man, Conn Smythe of Toronto, to build the franchise. It was a terrific choice. It was also very short-lived. "I knew every hockey player in the world right then," Smythe boasted years later. "Putting that whole team together, many of whom had never played pro hockey before, cost the Rangers a total of $32,000."

Smythe and Hammond, both iron-willed, inevitably clashed. Hammond won out, and bought

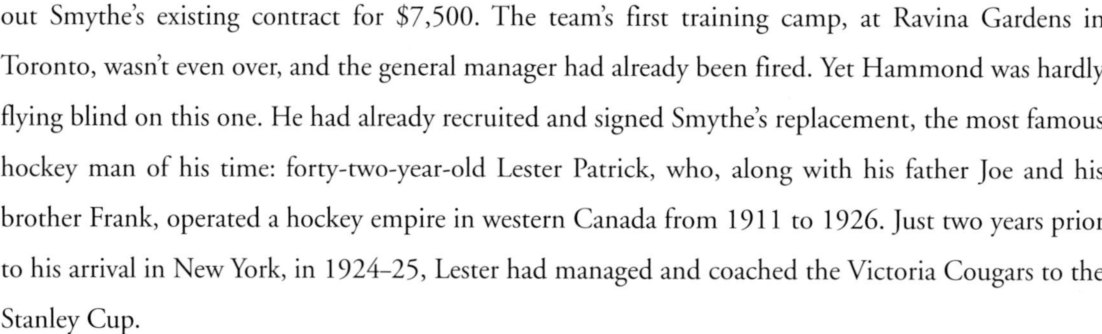

out Smythe's existing contract for $7,500. The team's first training camp, at Ravina Gardens in Toronto, wasn't even over, and the general manager had already been fired. Yet Hammond was hardly flying blind on this one. He had already recruited and signed Smythe's replacement, the most famous hockey man of his time: forty-two-year-old Lester Patrick, who, along with his father Joe and his brother Frank, operated a hockey empire in western Canada from 1911 to 1926. Just two years prior to his arrival in New York, in 1924–25, Lester had managed and coached the Victoria Cougars to the Stanley Cup.

It has been said that Lester Patrick wrote hockey's first rule book, and that Frank didn't like it entirely, so he sat down and rewrote it. So, Rickard and Hammond were hardly getting a neophyte when they signed Lester. In fact, they were getting a legend who, in addition to managing, would also be the Rangers' coach for their first thirteen seasons.

Born Curtis Lester Patrick, of Scottish-Irish descent in Drummondville, Quebec, on New Year's Eve of 1883, Lester Patrick grew to be tall, stately, and almost magisterial in demeanor. He had the appearance of a banker or a lawyer. Well tailored to a fault, he was a gentleman, and a man of presence and dignity. More important, especially to his Garden bosses, Lester knew how to sell the game of hockey. To that end, he courted New York's legendary sportswriters, both individually and collectively, earning him his nickname, "The Silver Fox."

Ed Daley, then sports editor of the *New York Herald-Tribune*, coined the moniker following one of Lester's numerous "hockey information sessions" (press briefings). "Yesterday," Daley wrote, "I spent a fascinating half hour in the lair of 'The Silver Fox' . . ." It was a name that would stay with Patrick throughout his career.

Lester's hockey information panels were very important to the team's development. Historically, New York's greatest and most influential sportswriters and columnists were not enamored of, and certainly not comfortable with, hockey. Through the years, this group included Grantland Rice, Damon Runyon, Jimmy Cannon, Red Smith, and Dick Young. Only Dave Anderson, like Smith a Pulitzer Prize winner, was comfortable with the game, intrinsically liking it and having covered it as a beat writer for the *Journal-American* in the late 1950s and early 1960s. Lester's strategy with the press was a wise one, and it was followed by many of his successors, notably Frank Boucher, Emile Francis, and Neil Smith.

In reality, this was not Patrick's first trip to New York City. Eighteen years earlier, in the spring of 1908, Lester, brother Frank, and a group of Canadian pros that included one of the most famous hockey players of the era, Fred "Cyclone" Taylor, were in town for an exhibition series against the famous amateur team, the St. Nick's Hockey Club. The games were played in the seven thousand–seat St. Nicholas Arena on New York's west side, one of only three artificial ice surfaces in the world at that time. It was New York City's first view of professional hockey.

According to Patrick's biographer, Eric Whitehead, it was this pioneering trip that planted the seeds in Patrick's mind for the dynasty that was to become the Rangers

The Rangers' first general manager and coach, Lester Patrick, brought the Stanley Cup to New York in only his second season, 1927–28. Lester's ability to vigorously sell and promote hockey was a key factor in the success of the game in New York. It earned him his lifelong nickname, "The Silver Fox."

Although he never officially had the title of general manager, it was a hockey-wise Torontonian by the name of Conn Smythe (right) who assembled the first Rangers team, doing so at the direction of Madison Square Garden President Tex Rickard (center). The two men had a falling out before the season even got started, and Rickard quickly brought in Lester Patrick (left) as Smythe's replacement. The changing of the guard took place at Ravina Gardens in Toronto, site of the Rangers' first training camp in October 1926.

Tex Rickard's pen, used to sign documents to join the NHL

The "A Line," one of the greatest lines in NHL history, was named after the subway that ran (but didn't stop) beneath Madison Square Garden on 8th Avenue. Center Frank Boucher is between right wing Bill Cook (left) and left wing Bun Cook (right). The A Line would be the first Rangers line to warrant a nickname, and it started a Rangers tradition of naming lines that continues to the present day. All three members of the A Line were inducted into the Hockey Hall of Fame.

almost two decades later. Recalled Taylor, who passed away in 1979 yet outlived all of the visiting Canadians, "Lester and Frank . . . were by nature intensely curious and observant men, and they got a lot more out of New York than just another hockey experience. In their off hours, they saw all they could of the city, and we saw little of them. They always gave the impression that they were filing away information for future reference. Like the rest of us, Lester was taken with Broadway . . . and the Ziegfeld Follies. Some of the boys wasted time hanging around the Times Square taverns instead of seeing the real sights of New York. Lester, Frank, and myself were teetotalers, so the taverns with their nickel beers and free lunches didn't interest us much." But it was a staunch rival of Lester's—Tommy Gorman, the boss of the Americans—who best described the relationship between Lester and New York City. "Lester didn't adjust to New York," Gorman said, "New York adjusted to him."

So Patrick set about the business of running a hockey team. Despite his short time on the job, Smythe had left behind a starry roster of veterans that included the line of Frank Boucher at center between the Cook brothers, Bill and Bun. They were called the "A Line" after the subway line of the same name that was being constructed directly beneath Madison Square Garden. The line was the most famous of its era. It became one of the greatest of all time, with all three players making the Hall of Fame. To legendary Canadian broadcaster Foster Hewitt, the A Line seemed "like they had the puck on a string."

It is a stretch of almost eighty years—and a span of some four generations—but Frank Boucher was the Wayne Gretzky of his day. Boucher and Gretzky were both mercurial, left-handed shooting centers who thrived on creativity and clean play. "I got an exhilaration out of being able to avoid the checks in a violent game and tried to play it cleanly," Boucher explained. An *artiste sur la glace* or "artist on the ice," as he was called in the French press, Boucher was one of the cleanest players of all time. He won the Lady Byng Trophy so many times, seven in all, that the National Hockey League gave it to him permanently and had a new trophy struck. Sadly, the original Byng Trophy and all of Frank's hockey memorabilia were lost on February 23, 1965, when a fire destroyed Byng Farm, a 160-acre apple orchard Frank ran with his son Earl in Mountain, Ontario, outside of Ottawa.

Boucher drew only one major penalty—five minutes for fighting with Bill Phillips—in his entire career. Ironically, the fight occurred in the Rangers' very first game, a 1-0 triumph over the Montreal Maroons at the Garden. "It was the first and only time I ever had a fight on the ice," Boucher recalled. "I am thankful for that."

Boucher's right wing was Bill Cook, the Rangers' first captain who fittingly scored the team's first goal in the opener with the Maroons. It came at 10:37 of the second period. And as creative as he was stoic, Bun Cook, whose real first name was Fred, was the perfect complement on left wing to his strong-willed brother and the willowy Boucher. Bun, short for "Bunny," came from Fred's habit of hopping like a bunny on his skates to gain momentum.

Left wing Murray Murdoch, an original Ranger and the NHL's first "Iron Man," never missed a game. Number 9 played his entire Rangers career (563 games) without a miss and won two Stanley Cups. When Murdoch reached 400 consecutive games played, baseball's "Iron Man," Lou Gehrig of the Yankees, paid tribute to Murdoch on the Madison Square Garden ice and presented a ring to him.

Following his playing career, Murdoch coached hockey at Yale University for twenty-seven years. He was the first president of the American Hockey Coaches Association and instrumental in getting the NCAA hockey championships started. In 1974, Murdoch was honored for "outstanding service to hockey in the United States" by winning the Lester Patrick Award, which was named for his first Rangers boss.

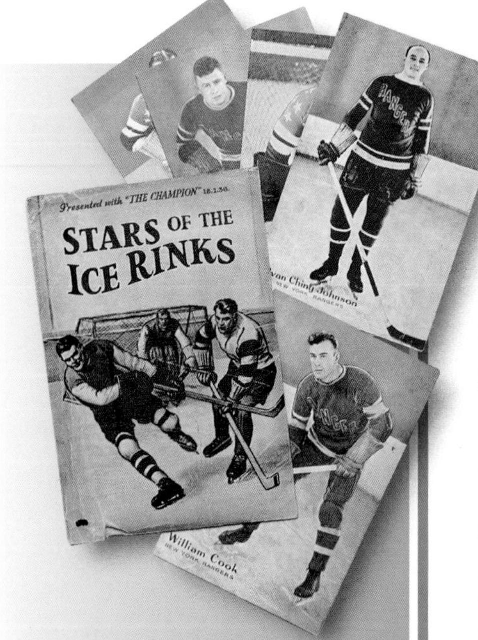

Active years before Bernie "Boom Boom" Geoffrion and Bobby "The Golden Jet" Hull, Bun Cook is sometimes credited with being the first player to utilize a slap shot. It was a maneuver he didn't use often but it had an element of great surprise, even in practice. Cook's claim as the originator of the slap shot is not without challenge. Alex Shibicky, Bun's successor at left wing on the Rangers' first line in 1936, admits he got the idea of the slap shot from watching Bun in practice. The two wingers played together for only one season, 1935–36, Cook's last Ranger campaign and Shibicky's first. "Bun didn't use it in a game," said Shibicky, now eighty-six years of age. "I did."

One of the keenest observers of the Rangers' formative years is Murray Murdoch. He was the Rangers' original "Iron Man," playing in the team's first 563 games without a miss. "Back in those days, all teams were built around the first line," Murdoch recalled. "The first line did exactly as they pleased. The second line did exactly as they were told. The third line was so happy to be there that they never said a word. I was on the second line."

Defensively, Smythe left Patrick with two great players—Ching Johnson and Taffy Abel, a pair of gritty, open-ice body-checkers who delighted Garden crowds with their thumping ways. Johnson, whose real first name was Ivan, was always a mischievous sort. One of his favorite tricks was to hide a puck in his gloves, hardly an easy task given the tight-fitting equipment of his day. During a multi-player scrum along the boards, Ching would release the second puck, causing an immediate whistle and more than a little confusion, not to mention a breather for the wide-grinning defenseman. "I only did it four, maybe five times, but it was great fun," Johnson said. "I even used to do it in practice, and that was tough because Lester used to count the pucks, no foolin'."

Johnson's nickname—the fans would yell "Ching, Ching, Chinaman"—had nothing to do with his ethnicity. It was derived instead from camping trips Johnson and his pals would often take in western Canada. It was common practice on week-long hunting excursions of this sort to hire a man, usually of Chinese descent, to serve as the group's cook. Johnson regularly volunteered for the duty, probably to save money, and the now-unseemly nickname was born.

Abel, whose given name was Clarence, got his nickname because of his fondness for saltwater taffy. The name stuck with him for a lifetime. One of the few American-born players of the time, Abel was born in Sault Sainte Marie, Michigan.

Even though he didn't play in the Rangers' first game in 1926 (Hal Winkler did), Lorne Chabot, a lanky French-Canadian, became the Rangers' first regular goaltender. Chabot gained considerable renown when team publicist Johnny Bruno would routinely change his name to "Chabotsky" in early box scores to appeal to New York's large Jewish-born population. Bruno did the same with Oliver Reinikka, a center of Finnish descent out of Shuswap, British Columbia. Bruno called him Ollie Rocco to appeal to New York's Italian population. Ever the hockey purist, Lester Patrick soon put an end to Bruno's flamboyant "press agentry."

Lorne Chabot, below, was the Rangers' first regular goaltender, and one of the most traveled netminders of his era, playing for six different teams in eleven seasons.

Ivan "Ching" Johnson, opposite, the ever-smiling defenseman—even with a broken jaw—was one of the original Rangers' most popular players. He played eleven seasons for the Rangers before switching to the rival Americans for his final season, 1937–38.

RANGERS

RANGERS
RANGERS
RANGERS
RANGERS
RANGERS
RANGERS
RANGERS
RANGERS

The Rangers of 1927–28, New York City's first Stanley Cup team, trained at Ravina Gardens in Toronto. Front row (left to right): trainer Harry Westerby, Murray Murdoch, Art Chapman (who never played for the team but attended training camp), Leo Bourgault, Laurie Scott, Reg Mackey, Frank Boucher, and Alex Gray. Back row (left to right): Ching Johnson, Billy Boyd, Paul Thompson, Lorne Chabot, coach Lester Patrick, Bill Cook, Taffy Abel, Sparky Vail, and Bun Cook.

The Rangers would become known as "The Classiest Team in Hockey," and were even advertised as such in out-of-town newspapers. Some called them the "Park Avenue Rangers," and the club immediately attracted a notable "dinner jacket" following.

New Yorkers All

As a rule, the Rangers have always been a close team, generally sticking together at home or on the road. "Once a Ranger, always a Ranger" has long been a team touchstone.

The Rangers of the 1950s, below, relax as a team in a fashionable soda fountain of that era. From the right are Andy Bathgate, Guy Gendron, Parker MacDonald, and Lou Fontinato. At the top are Harry Howell and Larry Cahan.

Over the years, Rangers players have lived in all five boroughs of the city—Manhattan, Brooklyn, Queens, the Bronx, and Staten Island. Add Nassau County on Long Island, Hudson County in New Jersey, and, more recently, Westchester and Connecticut, and you have a true Metropolitan Area Baedeker populated by New York Rangers players. Many of the original Rangers lived immediately down the block from Madison Square Garden in the Forrest Hotel on West 49th Street between Broadway and 8th Avenue, "the home of the elite in the sporting, theatrical, and newspaper professions."

"My wife Ag and I and our son, Earl, who was then six months old, spent our early days at the Forrest," recalled former center Frank Boucher. "We found it elegant, though small, and it seemed to be the residence of a number of dark, attractive, well-dressed men with side-brimmed hats and gleaming shoes. Two of the kind and smiling men who so often stopped to admire the baby were Legs Diamond and Dutch Schultz. We were truly astonished when the hotel clerk identified them as renowned gangsters. Of course, the Forrest was owned by Bill Dwyer, who also owned the Americans, and it was widely believed that Dwyer was one of New York's kingpin bootleggers."

The short-term home for many Rangers of the late 1940s and early 1950s was the Belvedere Hotel. Its rear entrance was directly across 49th Street, about halfway between the entrance to the team's offices at 307 West 49th and the employees entrance of the Garden, closer to 9th Avenue. Somewhat infamous in its later years, the Belvedere was quite elegant in its prime. "Outside rooms" went for $3 to $6 a night and the dining room served "the best food in New York." In the 1950s, its decline was evident when one night a cowboy from the rodeo rode his horse in and around

the huge Belvedere bar. By the 1980s, the bar was called "Better Days."

The odd Ranger, and more than a few of their amateur counterparts, the New York Rovers, "came of age" in the Belvedere, being that the establishment was oft-times frequented by female fans. "Stage Door Annies" they were called down the block on Broadway. Translated into sporting lingo, they were "groupies." The "Hook" and the "Crook"—their real names were Joan and Bev—were two of the most famous. The Hook was so named because of the prominence of her nose and the Crook because of her occasional attempts at lifting an amorous player's wallet.

Long Island, specifically Long Beach and Atlantic Beach, became home to the Rangers in the mid-1960s. Prominent signs touting Long Beach as the "home of the New York Rangers" were posted at every entrance to the community, a fact that eventually irked the New York Islanders upon their arrival in the region in 1972. The Rangers rented what for the most part were summer homes for the winter season. About the hardly elegant accommodations, defenseman Rod Seiling once said, "Whenever I lifted the carpet, I knew I would find a pile of sand."

Team members rode the Long Island Railroad. The "Iron Lung," some called it, invoking a term also used to describe team buses. Bernard "Boom Boom" Geoffrion, no doubt more conditioned to the splendor, quietude, and convenience of the Montreal subway system, once cracked about the LIRR, "All I know is that when I die, whether I go to heaven or to hell, I have to change in Jamaica."

"The Beach," as it was called, was geographically isolated from the rest of New York and, ironically enough, even from most of Long Island. "There's nothing to do there," was a common—and accurate—complaint. Phil Esposito, upon his arrival in 1975, settled for a time in Garden City, one of the finest of suburbs. But not for long. The Rangers were heading out, leaving the Island to the Islanders.

Salaries were starting to escalate, and the Rangers' new home certainly reflected that. It was Westchester County, not the "Big Apple" but the "Golden Apple." More specifically, the Rangers settled in and around the hamlet of Rye. Their new home, on the practice ice at least, was Playland, a rink that was older than the team itself and whose narrow ice surface Freddie Shero called "a bowling alley with boards." The Rangers were ecstatic with their new surroundings. The players quickly put down stakes in quaint and tony towns in Westchester and lower Connecticut, where they mostly remain today.

All five boroughs of New York City have been home to the Rangers. The Bronx was home to Eddie Shack and Lou Fontinato, who lived just a cab ride away from the busy intersection of Fordham Road and the Grand Concourse, above. Center Don Raleigh lived for a time in New York's smallest borough, Staten Island. A handful of Rangers lived in Brooklyn, and practically the whole team resided in Queens in the 1960s. Most of the original Rangers lived in Manhattan hotels.

CHEVROLET
Pepsodent
TOOTH PASTE
HOTEL CLARIDGE
CRITERION THEATRE
SMILING LIEUTENANT
CHEVALIER IS AT HIS
CLAUDETTE COLBERT
MIRIAM HOPKINS IS A
CHINATOWN

So, the "Blueshirts," as the Rangers were fondly called, flew into their first season with quite a bit of diversity, somewhat reflective of New York itself. They were an immediate hit. They became known as "the classiest team in hockey" or the "Park Avenue Rangers." This was in marked contrast to their rivals, the Americans. Somewhat swashbuckling, on the ice and off, the Amerks became known as the "Bowery Amerks." True to their nicknames, the Rangers attracted a glamorous, "dinner jacket" crowd. Their games were the place to be seen for celebrities, politicians, and even purported gangsters.

Frank Boucher, in his biography *When the Rangers Were Young*, recalled two celebrities in particular. "Many famous New Yorkers followed us," Boucher wrote, "people like Babe Ruth, who would come into the Garden in his flashy beige camel hair coat and matching cashmere cap, and Lou Gehrig, Babe's running mate on the Yankees, a big, rusty-haired fellow with a huge cheek dimple and a wide smile. He would often come to the dressing room to visit us."

There were other stars as well. Lucille Ball, Desi Arnaz, Humphrey Bogart, George Raft, the Duke and Duchess of Windsor, and Cab Calloway all followed the Rangers. Chief among the rooters was New York's flamboyant mayor, the Honorable Jimmy Walker, who arrived fashionably late at the team's first game on November 16, 1926, a 1-0 victory over the Montreal Maroons at Madison Square Garden. Walker remained a regular at rinkside until the early 1930s, when he fled in self-exile to England after a graft-ridden scandal led to criminal charges against him.

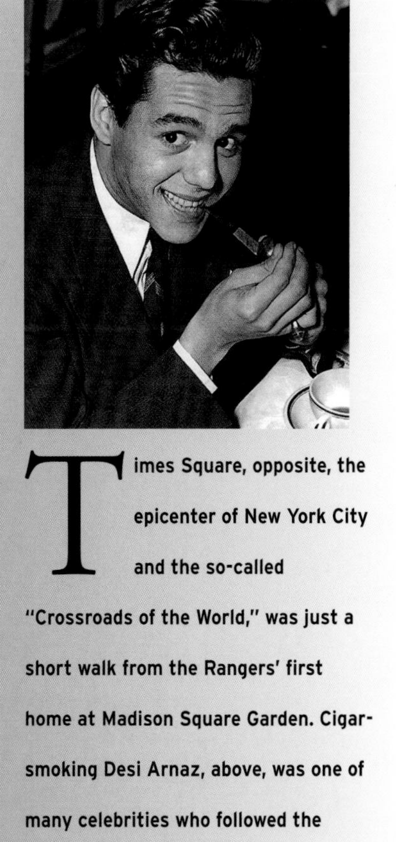

Times Square, opposite, the epicenter of New York City and the so-called "Crossroads of the World," was just a short walk from the Rangers' first home at Madison Square Garden. Cigar-smoking Desi Arnaz, above, was one of many celebrities who followed the "Broadway Blueshirts."

* * *

The Rangers won four of their first five games, finishing the season at 25-13-6 with only five of the losses coming at the Garden. That was good enough to capture the American Division championship. Bill Cook won the Art Ross Trophy as the league's leading scorer with thirty-seven points, thirty-three of them goals, also a league high. And despite being bounced in the opening round of the playoffs by the Boston Bruins, the Rangers had made an impressive beginning, but it was only a beginning. By comparison, the next season was a thunderclap!

The 1927–28 team slipped to 19-16-9, second in the American Division behind the Bruins and fifth in the overall standings. In the playoffs, the Rangers beat the Pittsburgh Pirates and the Bruins, each in two games, to create a matchup in the finals with the heavily favored Montreal Maroons. It was to be an epic. The finals were a best-of-five, and all five games were scheduled at the Montreal Forum since the Garden was hosting the annual Ringling Brothers and Barnum & Bailey circus. The Rangers were flat and lost the opener, 2-0, on April 5. Two days later, the teams met again in a game that has become part of hockey legend. Halfway through the second period, with each team scoreless, goalie Chabot was struck above the left eye by a shot from Maroons ace Nels Stewart. With Chabot unable to continue, Patrick was faced with a dilemma. Alex Connell, a goaltender for Ottawa, was in attendance, but the Maroons quite naturally rejected Patrick's request to use him in net.

So, at forty-four years of age and with a full shock of gray hair, Patrick put himself in goal. An outstanding defenseman in his time, Lester had even played a little goal before, but certainly not on a regular basis. What followed was one of the never-to-be-forgotten games in Stanley Cup history.

Art Ross Trophy

Patrick was inspired in his mission, repelling the Maroons time and again, and his teammates were equally inspiring with their back-checking. Captain Bill Cook snapped the scoreless tie in the third period, but despite two spectacular saves, the Maroons finally beat Patrick. Now the game was tied, and it was on to sudden death—the first overtime game in Rangers history. Just when it seemed the Maroons would prevail, Boucher stole the puck and scored the winning goal at 7:05 of overtime.

The Rangers, in a sea of bedlam, mobbed Patrick and skated him around the rink on their shoulders. The heroics of the game were captured by sportswriter Jim Burchard in a famous poem, *An Ode to Lester's Gallant Stand.* Recalled Murray Murdoch, "Lester's performance was a big deal, don't get me wrong, but it was that poem that made the story bigger and bigger every time it was told and re-told." Universally overlooked in the hoopla surrounding Patrick's heroics in goal is the fact that Lester had played one game on defense a year earlier for the Blueshirts. The date was March 20, 1927, four games before the end of the Rangers' inaugural season. Lester even took a penalty in a 2-1 Garden victory over the Americans.

The Rangers' "first fan" was New York's publicity-wise mayor, The Honorable Jimmy Walker, who made a habit of associating himself with the biggest celebrity names of his time. Walker gladly greeted the 1928 Stanley Cup champs at City Hall.

Buoyed no doubt by Patrick, the Rangers went on to win the series, three games to two. A surprisingly large number of New Yorkers made the journey to Montreal to cheer the Rangers, so the club was hardly without supporters even in the Montreal Forum. The deciding goal once again came off the stick of Boucher. The date was April 14, 1928, and the Rangers had their first Stanley Cup in only their second year of operation. In the custom of the time, hardly any of the Rangers returned to New York to savor their triumph, most of them journeying instead to their permanent homes in Canada. There was one notable exception. "Lester Patrick returned to New York a hero," wrote his biographer, Eric Whitehead, "and nobody embraced him more warmly than did Mayor Jimmy Walker, who loved heroes and their company. Walker was still preening in the afterglow of the colossal tickertape parade he had personally ordered to hail the return of Charles Lindbergh following Lucky Lindy's epic flight to Paris.

"[Walker], of course, was up front with the new American idol all the way through that incredible parade scene, and he was also up front a few months later with congratulations and a handshake for Babe Ruth after the Bambino had hit his record sixtieth homer for the Yankees. And now here he was on the steps of City Hall, . . . beaming and embracing Lester as the crowd cheered and the flashbulbs popped." A city, New York City, had begun a love affair with The Classiest Team in Hockey, the New York Rangers.

The versatile Lester Patrick played one game as a Ranger defenseman, but it was his contest as a Ranger goaltender that prompted sportswriter Jim Burchard to draft *An Ode to Lester's Gallant Stand.*

'Twas in the spring of twenty-eight,
A golden Ranger page,
That Lester got a summons
To guard the Blueshirt cage.

Chabot had stopped a fast one,
A bad break for our lads,
The Cup at stake—and no one
To don the Ranger pads.

"We're cooked," lamented Patrick,
"This crisis I had feared."
He leaned upon his newest crutch
And wept inside his beard.

Then suddenly he came to life,
No longer halt or lame.
"Give me the pads," he bellowed,
"I used to play this game."

Then how the Rangers shouted.
How Patrick was acclaimed.
Maroons stood sneering, gloating,
They should have been ashamed.

The final score was two to one.
Old Lester met the test.
The Rangers finally won the Cup,
But Les has since confessed.

"I just spoke up to cheer the boys,
"I must have been delirious.
"But now, in reminiscence,
"I'm glad they took me serious."

James Burchard
November 1947

RANGERS
RANGERS
RANGERS
RANGERS

The "Forgotten Cup" was presented on November 11, 1933, nearly seven months after it was won on April 13, 1933, at Maple Leaf Gardens in Toronto. Presenting for the National Hockey League is its nattily attired president, Frank Calder. Accepting for the Rangers are (left to right): defenseman Earl Seibert, goaltender Andy Aitkenhead, defenseman Ching Johnson, center Frank Boucher, left wing Bun Cook, and right wing Bill Cook.

The Rangers on the Air

Broadcasting from various frequencies—1410, 1270, and 1350 among them—on the AM dial (FM wasn't even available yet), radio station WMSG provided the very first introduction to hockey for many New Yorkers.

In many ways, the broadcast history of the Rangers is as colorful as the history of the team itself. In 1926 the Rangers were the first team based in the United States to put even partial games on the air. They even pre-dated the now-fabled broadcasts of the legendary Foster Hewitt in Canada. Fans had to either stumble upon the broadcasts or find out about them through word of mouth, because newspapers of the time regarded radio—and later television—as a staunch and bitter competitor. Daily listings were decades away.

The voice of WMSG—and the first voice of Madison Square Garden itself—was a "hockey man," John Harmon "Jack" Filman. A native of Hamilton, Ontario, Filman was known for his rapid-fire, staccato play-by-play delivery. In later years Bill Cook reminisced, "They told me that Jack made 'the world's fastest game' seem even faster." Cook himself, along with brother Bun and their center, Frank Boucher, were Filman's favorites and, on the airwaves at least, he carried their banner with great relish. Of course, the players themselves never heard Filman call a game. They were working when he was working, and tape recorders hadn't been invented.

After Filman in the 1950s, the club's announcers included Bert Lee and Les Keiter, who were no strangers to hyperbole when it came to describing hockey games. "He tickled the twine" and "In again, out again Finnigan" were two Keiter specialties.

In 1940, on February 25, the Rangers and the Montreal Canadiens met at Madison Square Garden. It was the first hockey game ever on television, a widely heralded experimental effort that reached maybe three hundred to four hundred TV sets in New York City, and garnered zero rating points. The Rangers won, 6-2. Years later, the Rangers and the Canadiens battled once again in the first hockey game ever on network television. The CBS-TV affiliate, Channel 2 in New York, carried the game. And in 1969, on October 15, the Rangers and the Minnesota North Stars marked the debut of the Madison Square Garden Network. The Rangers won, 4-3.

Through the years the Rangers have been covered by a cornucopia of the top names in New York sportscasting history. There were Marty Glickman, Ward Wilson, Bud Palmer, Win Elliot, Spencer Ross, Sal Marchiano, Bill Mazer, Mike Emrick, Tim Ryan, Howie Rose, Marv Albert, and Kenny Albert, among others. For a single season, 1959–60, Winnipeg-born Monty Hall of *Let's Make a Deal* television fame, was a Rangers radio analyst.

Two of the most beloved voices in Rangers' television history were Jim Gordon and Bill Chadwick. The twosome, born and bred New Yorkers, struck a delicious balance and gave fans an urban patois with which they could identify, even subconsciously. A career sportscaster and veteran newsman out of Syracuse University, Gordon was the consummate professional, blending amazingly well with Chadwick, who came to the booth following a sterling NHL refereeing career that landed him in the Hockey Hall of Fame. "We were good; we were damned good," Gordon recalled. "I worked with lots and lots of people in my time, but Bill Chadwick was the only partner I ever had."

In terms of sheer games worked, Sal Messina is the "godfather" of Rangers broadcast hockey. First taking his post in 1973, on the recommendation of Chadwick, Messina has endured for more than a quarter of a century. For most of his tenure, the New York City–born Messina teamed beautifully with the Brooklyn-born Marv Albert, giving Rangers fans another dual-voiced "city" edge.

Albert/Messina broadcasts were anything but textbook. Freeform would be more like it, professional to a tee at one moment, approaching slapstick the next. Purists might have thought Albert's wryness, acerbic wit, and near overuse of "Red Light," his nickname for Messina, would have been too esoteric for hockey fans. That was not the case. The fans loved the duo. Albert, ever the workaholic, loved the assignments. Messina, ever the genial co-foil, loved the schtick. Sometimes lost in the mix was Messina's always-incisive commentary. His observations, especially on radio, might be missed by the casual fan, but they were always bang-on.

WOR-TV, Channel 9 in New York, carried Rangers games in a variety of formats through most of the 1960s. Most were road contests, and often they would be shown on tape, but the station was a great boon to Rangers fans wanting to keep a close watch on the action.

Longevity reigned over youth in the years between the Rangers' first and third Stanley Cup victories. The team's aging heroes hit milestones, many of which had not been reached by any NHL team.

1931

Mar. 10—The Rangers recorded the one hundredth victory in team history with a 3-2 win over the visiting Detroit Falcons. The win gave them a record of 100-75-43 in their first 218 NHL games.

1932

Jan. 1—John Ross Roach became the first goaltender to record twenty-five career shutouts with the Rangers, with a 3-0 win over the visiting Detroit Falcons. (It was the thirty-eighth shutout of Roach's NHL career.)

Nov. 10—The Rangers beat the Maroons 4-2 in Montreal to extend their season opening-night record to 7-0-0 since joining the NHL in 1926-27. The streak ended with a loss to Toronto the next year.

1933

Apr. 13—The Rangers won the 1933 Stanley Cup when Bill Cook broke a scoreless tie with a power play goal at 7:33 of overtime for a 1-0 win over Toronto. Rookie goalie Andy Aitkenhead got the shutout as New York won the best-of-five series in four games.

1937

Mar. 9—Center Frank Boucher became the first player in NHL history to amass 250 career

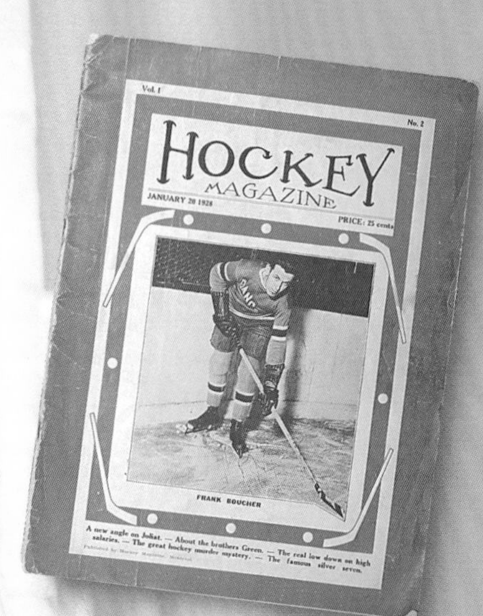

assists. Number 250 came on an Alex Shibicky goal in an 8-7 Rangers win against the New York Americans.

Oct. 30—The Americans and the Rangers played two exhibition games in one day (2 P.M. and 9 P.M.) in Saskatoon, Saskatchewan, to commemorate the opening of a new arena.

The Forgotten Cup

The striking and immediate success of the Rangers—the Stanley Cup in only the team's second season and nine consecutive years in the playoffs—quickly galvanized the club's fandom and just as quickly gave birth to a fierce rivalry with their Garden cotenants, the New York Americans. During its heyday, from 1927 to 1942, the rivalry was every bit as intense as the Rangers versus the Islanders matchups of the 1970s and 1980s. The rivalry was similar, as well, to the epic-like baseball battles between the New York Giants and the Brooklyn Dodgers. Or the bitter World Series clashes between the Dodgers and the New York Yankees.

"Those games were like wars," recalled longtime Amerks boss Mervyn "Red" Dutton years later. "We hated each other. And the crowd was always into it, divided right down the middle, at least in the beginning." Lester's son, Murray "Muzz" Patrick, who played in sixteen Rangers-Americans games, had similar recollections: "When we played each other, it was like a civil war. The landlords against the tenants. The aristocrats against the people's choice. There was electricity in the place." Even socially, the Rangers and Americans refused to mingle. "There was one bar for the Rangers and another for the Americans," said Hall of Fame referee Bill Chadwick. "That line simply wasn't crossed."

Someone should have explained that to Tommy Gorman, the Amerks general manager, who got word that a lot of his players were celebrating at the Green Door, a popular speakeasy down 49th Street between Broadway and 8th Avenue. In a then-routine attempt to curtail his players' imbibing, Gorman corralled two of the Garden's security cops and scurried over to the saloon. What the impromptu posse found were nine or ten of the hated Rangers celebrating Ching Johnson's birthday. There wasn't much Tommy could do about that.

Benny Bennett, a wizened and somewhat crotchety fixture in the Madison Square Garden box office for more than half a century, actually credited the Americans themselves for making the Rangers such a success. "It was the rivalry with the Americans that started fans buying season tickets to the Rangers," Bennett said. "It was intense. The people wanted the exact same seats for the Americans games. In those days, the schedule of home games was printed, linear-style, on index-like cards. Fans would come to the box office with the Americans games circled and ask for four, six, eight tickets, whatever. Only championship fights sold faster than the Rangers and Americans. After the Americans, the two Montreal teams were the hottest. Chicago was the weakest."

RANGERS
MERICANS
DETROIT
N.Y. RANGERS
CHICAGO
BOSTON
CANADIENS
TORONTO
MONTREAL

BOXING FRI NIGHT NOV 20TH
JIMMY MC LARNIN LEW AMBERS
AND ALL STAR CARD AT POPULAR PRICES
MONDAY NIGHT NOV 23 AMATEUR BOXING
HOCKEY TUES NOV 17 AMERICANS CANADIENS
HOCKEY THUR NOV 19 RANGERS DETROIT
GEM BLADES
Cost less per shave
TIME OUT

Americans jersey, circa 1932

Previous spread: By far the most memorable games of the blue-clad Rangers' early years were the ones against the white-shirted New York Americans, their co-tenants at Madison Square Garden. There were ninety-four meetings in all, from the 1926–27 season through 1941–42. The Rangers won fifty-seven, lost twenty-three, and tied fourteen. This game on November 15, 1936, celebrated the tenth anniversary of the Rangers and drew the usual sellout crowd, all of whom faced the 9th Avenue end of the Garden for a specially arranged "house portrait." The Rangers lost, 2-1.

The most epic struggle between the two New York rivals took place on the night (and morning) of March 27–28, 1938. It was the deciding game of the first round of the Stanley Cup playoffs, and the city was in a frenzy. People lined up at dawn hoping to procure tickets to the match, but precious few were available. When face-off time came at 8:30 P.M., no one in the crowd of 16,340 would dare to predict that most would still be sitting there well after midnight. Officially, the game lasted one hundred twenty minutes and forty seconds, more than two full games, and the longest ever on Garden ice.

No doubt, the victory was the biggest in the Americans' history. The hero's mantle fell to Lorne Carr, a diminutive right winger whose shot forty seconds into the fourth overtime period beat Rangers goalie Davey Kerr to give the Amerks a 3-2 triumph. Carr's goal earned him the nickname "Sudden Death" Carr. The game ended at 1:30 in the morning, and was the first hockey game ever to make page one of the *New York Times*. Sadly, for Amerks fans at least, their team was beaten in the next round by the Chicago Blackhawks. The Americans' finest hour came and went in a New York minute.

Gradually, support for the Rangers grew and grew, while the Americans' fan base stagnated. The end was in sight for the Americans when in 1941 Dutton renamed his team the Brooklyn Americans. He hoped to capture the hearts of New York City's largest borough—the "Borough of Churches"—much like their counterparts in baseball, the beloved Brooklyn Dodgers, had done. It didn't work. Even the tabloids did their part, dubbing the team the "Amoiks" in a bit of whimsy that played off the accent of some Brooklynites. But aside from the odd practice session at the Brooklyn Ice Palace, the "Amoiks" remained strictly a Manhattan operation, basically bleeding the bankroll of their bootlegger boss, Bill Dwyer.

Upon the death of the Americans in 1942 and for countless years thereafter, it was the Rangers who were often unfairly blamed for the demise of their predecessors. Then, not unlike today, the Rangers' success came from a philosophy that was unspoken but generally followed: Get the best players. The thinking was, "If we are on 'the world's most versatile stage' [as the Garden would come to be called], then we should get the best actors."

After their first Stanley Cup, the Rangers made the finals three times and the semifinals twice in the next five seasons. One year after Stanley Cup number one, the Rangers and the Boston Bruins met in the Stanley Cup finals and made history. It was the first time that two United States–based teams played for hockey's top honor. The Bruins won, two games to none, outscoring the New Yorkers, 4-1.

On February 27, 1930, the Rangers began a string of four consecutive tie games, a team record that still stands. It began with a 1-1 Garden deadlock against the Blackhawks, and continued with three road knots—3-3 at Toronto, 2-2 at Detroit, and 2-2 at Chicago. "All four of those games went into overtime," Ching Johnson said years later, "but we couldn't buy a goal. The next game, we went to Montreal, and the Canadiens murdered us. I think it was 6-0. We barely limped into the playoffs that year."

The Rangers of 1932–33 reigned as New York's second Stanley Cup championship team. Front row (left to right): Wilfie Starr (never actually played for the team but attended training camp), Carl Voss, Cecil Dillon, trainer Harry Westerby, Art Somers, and Andy Aitkenhead. Back row (left to right): Jimmy Arnott (never actually played for the team), Gordon Pettinger, Bill Cook, Earl Seibert, Oscar Asmundson, coach Lester Patrick, Babe Siebert, Ching Johnson, Bun Cook, Butch Keeling, Murray Murdoch, Ott Heller, and Doug Brennan.

Clarence John "Taffy" Abel, whose nickname came from his fondness for saltwater taffy, was one of the first United States–born National Hockey League stars. The league, at the time, was made up almost entirely of Canadian-born players. Born in Sault Sainte Marie, Michigan, Taffy delighted Rangers fans with his fierce body-checking.

But by and large, the team was a solid one, a contender each season. Stanley Cup number two came in 1933. It is sometimes called the "forgotten Cup," but it was anything but to members of the team. Sandwiched between the 1928 triumph, complete with Lester's "gallant stand," and the epic 1940 Cup, historians have often overlooked the 1933 winners, an aging group of stars who were nearing the end of their hockey careers.

"It was a terrific team," recalled Murray Murdoch. "We were very confident. We thought we had the best players, and we did."

The nucleus of the 1933 Rangers was the same as the first Cup winners. Thinking that the eye injury suffered by Lorne Chabot in the 1927–28 season would have a long-term effect on his play, Patrick dealt the goaltender off to Toronto right before the 1928–29 season. The goalie now was Andy Aitkenhead, a handsome rookie who was born in Glasgow, Scotland, and played all forty-eight of the team's games in his freshman campaign. Taffy Abel, whose biggest fan was actor George Raft, had been sold to the Chicago Blackhawks in 1929. He was replaced by big Earl Seibert, who had been purchased from the Springfield Indians of the Can-Am League in 1931. The team's real stars—the Cook brothers, Boucher, and Ching Johnson—were still on hand. There was also Albert "Babe" Siebert, normally a left wing, who Patrick used on defense, teamed with Johnson.

Midway through the season, just before Christmas, Colonel John S. Hammond resigned as president of the Rangers following a dispute over ticket prices with William F. Carey, president of the Garden. Hammond's replacement, on an interim basis, was Lester Patrick, who was also appointed vice president of the Garden. Patrick was now wearing four hats, a formidable burden indeed, even for a man who thrived on hard work. Carey and Patrick decided to reduce ticket prices, and the Rangers continued to draw large crowds in spite of generally rough economic times.

The Rangers had a so-so regular season, finishing third in the American Division with a 23-17-8 record. Bill Cook, who led the league with twenty-eight goals and fifty points, won the Art Ross Trophy for a second time at thirty-seven years of age.

The opening round of the playoffs matched the Rangers and the Canadiens, the A Line of Cook-Boucher-Cook against Montreal's vaunted "Speedball Line" of Aurel Joliat, Howie Morenz, and Johnny Gagnon. The A Line prevailed hands down: New York won the total goal series, eight goals to five, setting the stage for an intriguing series with the Detroit Falcons (who would not be named the Red Wings until the following season). The series matched goalie Aitkenhead of the Rangers with the man he had replaced less than a year earlier, John Ross Roach, then with the Falcons. Aitkenhead posted a 2-0 shutout in the first game and the Rangers won the series, six goals to three, with a 4-3 win in game two. It was on to the finals against the Toronto Maple Leafs.

As was the case in 1928, the circus would once again preempt the Rangers from the Garden. This time, at least, New Yorkers saw one game, on April 4, 1933, and the Rangers won it handily, by a score of 5-1. The Cooks and Boucher played brilliantly, as did defenseman Seibert, who had really taken over from Johnson as the club's premier defender. Game two, in Maple Leaf Gardens, also went to the Rangers, 3-1. Patrick, generally not known as a boastful man, was predicting a three-game

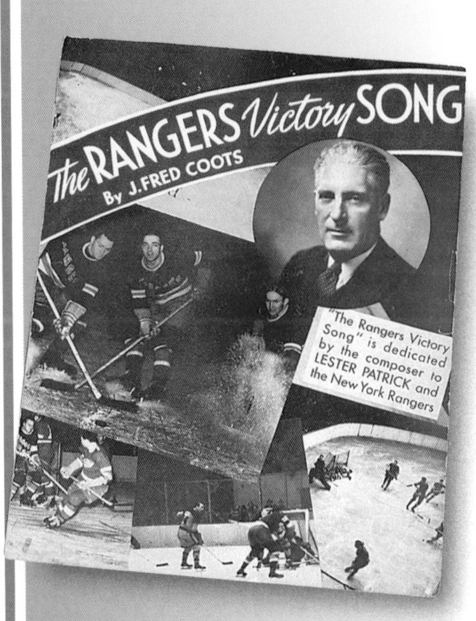

Fans of the Rangers during the 1940s and 1950s certainly have some of the jaunty lyrics to the "Rangers Victory Song" bouncing around in their heads. Written by J. Fred Coots and dedicated to Lester Patrick in 1940, the song was played every time the Rangers took to the ice for the start of a period.

Asked how many times she had played "The Rangers Victory Song," Gladys Goodding, the organist for two generations of Madison Square Garden patrons, replied, "I can't count that high." From her perch in the 9th Avenue and 49th Street corner of the building, Gladys would welcome fans, players, entire teams, even newspapermen with their favorite tunes as she saw them enter the building. Gladys's final song as she echoed into retirement was "Thanks for the Memories."

Butch Keeling slaps the puck toward the net during the first period of the Redwings game, November 8, 1937, below right.

During his tenure as the oldest living NHL player, Murray Murdoch, opposite, had occasion to recount many of the Rangers' historic highs and lows, fondly remembering his teammates from 1926 to 1937.

"I think about those guys all the time," he reminisced. "Sure I miss them. We played together so long, we were like brothers. I love talking about them, and a lot of the other fellows I played against too." Murdoch's former teammates also remember him. Said former mate Alex Shibicky about Murdoch's renowned defensive ability: "When he came on the ice, the other team wouldn't score."

sweep, but game three was a 3-2 Toronto victory, a triumph that proved costly when Toronto star Ace Bailey suffered a torn knee cartilage and was lost to the team.

Game four, on April 13, was a classic. The teams were scoreless after one period, after two periods, and after three periods, so it was on to sudden death overtime. "We were confident, maybe even overconfident," Murdoch recalled. "That's how good we thought we were." As it turned out, the Leafs made it easy for the visitors. Leafs youngsters Alex Levinsky and Bill Thoms, the latter only a rookie, drew penalties in the overtime, and captain Cook, with a two-man advantage, scored the Cup-winning goal on a pass from Butch Keeling at the 7:33 mark. It was a historic goal, the first and only time in Stanley Cup history that a team had won the Cup with a two-man advantage in overtime. If there had been a playoff MVP in those days, it likely would have gone to New York's Aitkenhead, who allowed only thirteen goals in eight games for a squeaky-tight goals-against average of 1.63, and completely shut down Toronto's famous Kid Line of Busher Jackson, Joe Primeau, and Charlie Conacher.

Back in New York, the Rangers were feted at a sumptuous party at the Astor Hotel, the elegant Times Square landmark. Garden president William Carey hosted the bash, and used the occasion to introduce the team to its new president, New York City–born General John Reed Kilpatrick, who would run the Rangers with a "hands-on" management style for most of the next quarter of a century.

So, it was left to Kilpatrick and Patrick (the two quickly became fast friends) to oversee the retooling of the New York Rangers, a painful but necessary task that meant dismantling a team that had not only won two Stanley Cups but had captured the hearts of New Yorkers. As difficult as it was, the breakup of the original Rangers was generally accepted as inevitable by most everyone around the team. "We didn't like it one bit, not at all," Boucher recalled. "We were a family, a happy family for a long time. But it was time. The 1936–37 season was the saddest of all. The old guard had simply grown too long in the tooth."

The symbolic end came when the A Line was broken up on September 10, 1936. Calling it a "very sad day," Lester sold Bun Cook to the Boston Bruins for cash. Brother Bill, by now a shadow of his former self, struggled through a painful final season that consisted of just twenty-one games played, one goal, and four assists. Boucher, too, was struggling mightily, and managed not a single goal and only one assist in his final eighteen games at the start of the 1937–38 season. It was the end of an era.

JOHN MURRAY MURDOCH
90th Birthday Dinner

Yale Hockey Coach
1938-1965

1994 Stanley Cup

Gritty Steve Larmer, who joined the Rangers early in the 1993–94 season, was a key performer in the 1994 Stanley Cup playoffs with sixteen points. Larmer's trademark would be his ability to finish off his checks as he does convincingly, right, against the Madison Square Garden sideboards. Captain Mark Messier, opposite, as determined a player as the Rangers have ever known, blasts a shot past defenseman Jyrki Lumme in game five of the Stanley Cup finals at Madison Square Garden. Messier's goal in game seven would prove to be the Stanley Cup winner for the Rangers.

Hockey's Holy Grail

For New York Rangers fans around the world, the date of June 14, 1994, is forever frozen in time. Like they did with the assassination of John F. Kennedy on November 22, 1963, and the Great Blackout on November 7, 1965, every Rangers fan remembers where they were on that day. They always will.

Telecasters Sam Rosen and John Davidson, integral parts of the Rangers for more than a decade, watched the tableau unfold from their Garden aerie, and no doubt told the widest audience about it. The Rangers had won their fourth Stanley Cup, their first in fifty-four years. "That's it. Fifty-four years of curses are over! No more 1940! The New York Rangers are the Stanley Cup champions! And this one will last a lifetime! Let the celebration begin," screamed Rosen.

Marv Albert—a fixture on the radio side for parts of four decades—took a somewhat lower key approach to the monumental achievement: "Bure and MacTavish with one and six-tenths seconds to go. The puck is dropped, MacTavish controls, and it's all over. The New York Rangers have won the Stanley Cup, something that most people thought they would never hear in their lifetime, and the Rangers pour onto the ice to pound each other. Mike Richter being congratulated. And they are going wild at Madison Square Garden."

Madison Square Garden, packed with 18,200 people (a count that certainly did not include the fire inspector), exploded with excitement as only Madison Square Garden can. It was a love fest more than half a century in the making. Rangers fans of all ages were celebrating. Big time. And who could blame them? The wait was over. The fireworks had just begun.

Scores of New York City police officers, most of them in full riot gear, were at the ready, circling the arena's lowest tier. They weren't needed. There wasn't a single arrest. Not a one. Just joy. "Now I can die in peace" read a sign that popped up on the 7th Avenue end of the pulsating amphitheater. The celebration rocked on.

LUMME
21
CCM
LOUISVILL

CCM

Celebrations erupted after Brian Leetch (left) scored the first goal of game seven against the Canucks at 11:02 of the first period. Sergei Zubov (center) and Mark Messier (right) assisted on the goal.

For the first time in Rangers history, the Stanley Cup was presented to the Rangers on home ice. Right: Mark Messier, ecstatic and excited, came forward to accept the trophy from NHL Commissioner Gary Bettman. That night—and for several days thereafter—fans, below, celebrated the long-awaited victory.

Murray Murdoch, a crisp ninety years of age at the time, was with his old team, not physically but spiritually and emotionally, as he watched the euphoric finish on television at home in Hamden, Connecticut. "I didn't miss a minute, no sir," said Murdoch. "Oh, the memories that brought."

Neil Smith, the winning team's president, general manager, and chief architect, careened giddily through the Garden's rotunda area shouting, "We did it! We did it! We did it!" Smith was en route to a boisterous mob scene at the Rangers bench, a scene that many feared might never happen. Emile Francis, the Rangers' longtime general manager and coach during the 1960s and 1970s, was in the arena as a television analyst that night. "I was in the Zamboni tunnel," Francis recalled. "I didn't even watch the ice as the clock ticked down. I turned instead and faced the fans. I watched their faces. So many of them were crying. It was really something. I'll never forget the noise and the happiness."

Murray "Muzz" Patrick, a member of the team that had captured the Rangers' previous Cup in 1940, hardly watched at all. Muzz was suffering from Alzheimer's disease, and his memory had started to go. "We had hoped the moment might move him, but it didn't," recalled his wife Jessie. "He hardly noticed." Four years later, at age eighty-three, Muzz passed away. But Clint Smith, who was Muzz's teammate on the 1940 squad and the man they called "Snuffy," didn't miss a thing. He watched from his home in Vancouver, British Columbia, and shed a few "tears of joy and tears of memories," as Captain Mark Messier and all of the others toted the Stanley Cup around the Garden ice.

Chuck Rayner, MVP goaltender and bellwether of the team that came within a single goal of the Stanley Cup in 1950, watched from his home in Langley, British Columbia. "The emotion was hard to contain," Rayner confided. "New York was a great part of my life."

Fred Shero, had he been alive, probably would have said something like, "By winning tonight, we will walk together for the rest of our lives." The enigmatic general manager–coach who guided the 1979 team to the finals most certainly would have added, "Once a Ranger, always a Ranger," invoking a long-time team touchstone that was used principally in the 1940s and 1950s but was a favorite of his.

Rod Gilbert, Steve Vickers, Walt Tkaczuk, and Gilles Villemure, stars of the 1970s Rangers teams that "almost did, but didn't," watched along with other members of the Rangers Alumni Association from special seats adjacent to the home team penalty box on the 31st Street side of the Garden.

Did the Alumni guys root hard? You bet they did. "I hurt my hands thumping on the glass," said Gilbert, the club's all-time leading scorer and chief goodwill ambassador. "And I lost my voice in English and in French." The building continued to rock, the noise tumbling in waves from all around the Garden, only

The Rangers were number one. The fans, above, knew it. General Manager Neil Smith, left, knew it as he bench-pressed the thirty-eight-pound Stanley Cup. Even Mayor Rudy Giuliani knew it. His invitation, below, to a victory celebration at his residence, Gracie Mansion, was eagerly accepted by the champions. The reception capped a dizzying day for the Rangers, who earlier had been paraded up lower Broadway and feted at City Hall.

The Mayor of The City of New York
Rudolph W. Giuliani

cordially invites you to attend a

VICTORY CELEBRATION
for the
NEW YORK RANGERS
as the
1994 STANLEY CUP CHAMPIONS

Friday, June 17, 1994
5:00 p.m. – 8:00 p.m.

Gracie Mansion
East End Avenue at 88th Street

Please R.S.V.P. by fax (212) 788-7226

Invitation non-transferable

Key to New York City

With ticker tape fluttering, the Rangers' victory parade slowly made its way up lower Broadway, below. Captain Messier was a human merry-go-round as he displayed the Cup for all to see, north, south, east, and west. Arm-thrusting fans from all over the region came to salute their heroes, many of whom were still feeling no pain, even three days after the championship had been won.

the second home the Rangers had ever known. Messier, his toothy captain's grin aflash and his shaved head already covered with a championship hat, exulted as the cheers continued to wash down. Goalie Mike Richter, sweat-soaked and looking like someone out of a Dead End Kids movie, just grinned and grinned. He looked like he was in a trance. He probably was, and he had a lot of company. All were in dreamland, Rangers dreamland.

Brian Leetch, peerless defenseman and perhaps the team's all-time best player, calmly (as is his way) accepted the Conn Smythe Trophy as the most valuable player of the playoffs. It was the Rangers' very first Conn Smythe Trophy, named after the legendary builder who mostly assembled the original Rangers in 1926 but was fired before the team hit the ice for the regular season. Lester Patrick, the Rangers' patron saint and the man who succeeded Smythe, probably would have smiled sagely during the giddy celebration, had he been alive, and promptly dispatched someone to count the pucks and sticks. "Gentlemen, we have won the Stanley Cup," Lester was said to have told the celebrating New York squad in 1940, "and not one stick is to leave this dressing room. Everything here is the property of the New York Rangers Hockey Club."

That sort of stricture was hardly in effect in 1994. The party, make that parties, had begun. The team—and the fans—would spend the next six months celebrating not only 1994, but seventy years of history, seventy years of memories . . . that have now reached seventy-five. But the Rangers have always been a team of the people, of New York City, and of the region. And nothing demonstrated that fact better than Messier passing the Stanley Cup, hockey's Holy Grail, into the crowd for the fans to touch and savor, while Madison Square Garden continued to bellow, fully twenty minutes after the championship had been secured.

NEW YORK'S LARGEST & MOST COMPLETE
AUDIO • VIDEO • ELECTRONICS
MEGA-STORE
PSION SERIES 3
THE MOST POWERFUL POCKET COMPUTER IN THE WORLD
J&R MUSIC WORLD
the jazz outlet
STANLEY
HARDWARE
THE PAIN IS OVER
NEW YORK RANGERS

A talented group of young Rangers dominated the NHL, garnering attention that had not been focused on hockey before the 1939-40 Stanley Cup-winning team came along.

Davey Kerr

1939

Jan. 31—Davey Kerr became the first goaltender to get one hundred wins as a member of the Rangers, in a 3-2 victory over the visiting Chicago Blackhawks.

1940

Jan. 13—The Rangers extended their team-record winning streak to ten games (and their unbeaten streak to 14-0-5), with a 4-1 win over the Maple Leafs at Toronto. The string ended the next day with a 2-1 loss against Chicago.

Feb. 25—The Rangers faced the Montreal Canadiens in the first hockey game televised in the U.S. The game aired on station WXBS in New York, with one camera in a fixed position to three hundred TV receivers in New York. The Rangers won 6-2 for their fourteenth straight home win.

Apr. 13—Bryan Hextall scored at 2:07 of overtime as New York beat Toronto 3-2 in game six of the finals, to become the 1940 Stanley Cup champions—the Rangers' last Stanley Cup title for fifty-four years.

1941

Nov. 2—Bryan Hextall had a goal and two assists in the final period as New York won 4-1 at Toronto. The win started the Rangers on an NHL record-117 game non-shutout streak.

Dec. 1—Four sets of brothers played in one NHL game: The Rangers' Lynn and Muzz Patrick and Neil and Mac Colville played against the Blackhawks' brother acts of Max and Doug Bentley and Bob and Bill Carse. The Blackhawks won the game 4-1 at Chicago Stadium.

1942

Nov. 7—Bryan Hextall scored the two-thousandth goal in Rangers history during a 4-3 win over the Montreal Canadiens.

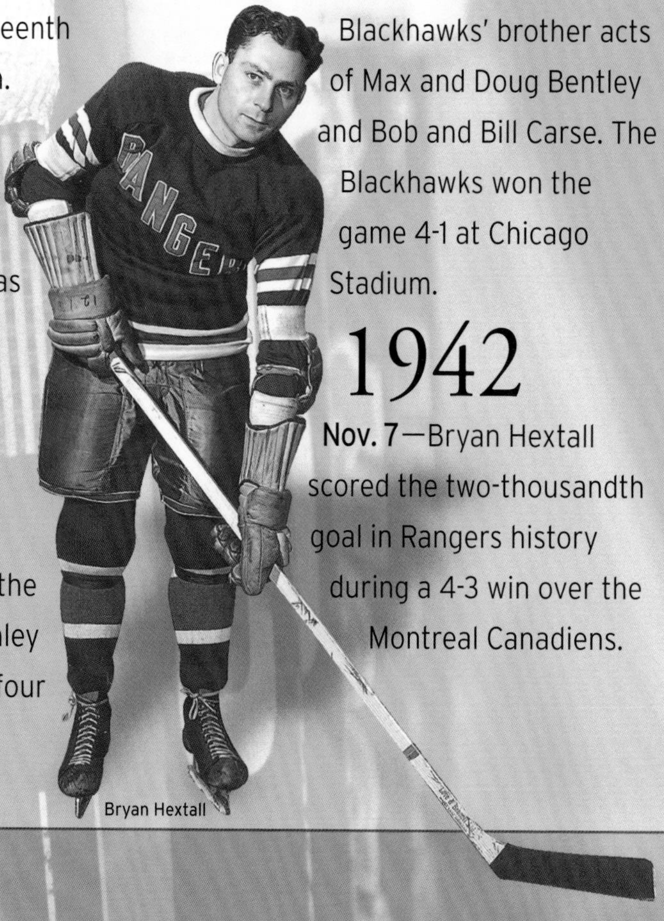

Bryan Hextall

The Best Team I'd Ever Seen

When Frank Boucher took the coaching reins for the start of the 1939–40 season, he knew what he was getting. "What Lester Patrick gave me," recalled the nonpareil retired center iceman, "was the best team I'd ever seen." Of course, the emotional breakup of the original club was considerably lessened for Boucher himself. For several years, he was unanimously expected to succeed Lester when the time was right. Frank greatly anticipated that role, as it would allow him to remain, oft-times to a fault, "one of the boys."

Boucher was the first NHL coach to introduce the "box defense" when his team was shorthanded. The team's four remaining skaters would position themselves in a "box" in front of the goalkeeper, better enabling them to defend against the opposition's five skaters. Eventually, that strategy was universally accepted, and it remains a staple of modern-day penalty killing. Frank also toyed with what he called "offensive penalty killing," in effect turning a disadvantage into an advantage. Recalled Boucher: "When we were a man short, we'd send out three forwards and one defenseman and we'd forecheck like crazy in the other team's end. This worked so well that first season that we scored more goals shorthanded than were scored against us." The Rangers under Boucher were also the first team to remove the goalkeeper for an extra man "on the fly" when a penalty was called on the opposition.

Ever the self-effacing gentleman, Boucher never gloated over his innovative nature or over the innovations themselves. Obliquely, he would often credit them to anonymous players or "coaching by harmony," as he liked to call it. "I used to encourage suggestions from the team," he said. "The boys would come up with them and then we would practice the new ideas. Some worked, and some didn't. History will only remember the ones that worked."

Like most hockey men at the time, Boucher believed in building a team "from the goal out." Unlike the Rangers of the previous decade and a half, whose goalkeeping was mostly unsettled, the 1939–40 team had one—and only one—goalkeeper. He was a diminutive but durable 160-pounder from Toronto by the name of Davey Kerr, who had already been with the team for five seasons after having been purchased from his original NHL club, the Montreal Maroons, on December 14, 1934. Kerr was said to be "as nimble as a squirrel and as sharp-eyed as a hawk."

Besides a fifty-four-year run (1940–1994) as the last Rangers' goalkeeper to win a Stanley Cup, Kerr has a distinction that no other hockey player—forward, defenseman, or goalkeeper—can ever take away from him. Davey Kerr was the very first hockey player to make the cover of *Time* magazine, something no other hockey player would manage until Montreal Canadien Maurice "Rocket" Richard did it some twenty years later. The date was March 14, 1938, and the accompanying article was a somewhat disjointed treatise that tried to explain hockey itself, through the eyes of the New York Rangers, to the magazine's readership. And, there on the cover, looking more than a little bit out of place, was a hawk-eyed (and hawk-nosed) Davey Kerr in a painting specially commissioned by *Time* by the artist S. J. Woolf.

"The guys ribbed me a lot about that magazine," Kerr said years later, "Cec Dillon in particular. Cec was pictured inside and said he should have been on the cover because he was better looking than me. He admitted that I was better looking than [racehorses] Seabiscuit, War Admiral, and Man o' War, whose photos were on the same page the hockey article began."

Kerr was a fine choice for a hockey cover boy. Being a goalie had something to do with it, of course, given the unique role that position has in the game. But Kerr was also one of the most erudite players of his time, earning his high school diploma in Iroquois Falls, Ontario, and attending McGill University in Montreal. While at McGill, he played for the famed Montreal Amateur Athletic Association team that won the Allan Cup, Canada's number-one amateur trophy at the time. In the summer, Davey was a stockbroker in Toronto. He kept fit by taking part in traditionally unhockey-like pursuits such as tennis and handball. The conditioning paid off. Kerr missed only one game during the course of seven seasons on Broadway.

The pinnacle of Kerr's career was the 1939–40 season. He played every minute of that championship season, won the Vezina Trophy as the League's top goalie, recorded an NHL-leading eight shutouts, and racked up a miserly 1.54 goals-against average. In the playoffs, he won eight games, lost four, posted three more shutouts, and a 1.56 goals-against. "Because we had so many stars that year, Kerr was often overlooked," recalled teammate Ott Heller, "but he was a great, great player. We relied on him terribly, especially in the playoffs. He was our leader." Sadly enough, Davey also led the Rangers as the first member of the 1940 team to die, passing away at sixty-eight years of age on May 12, 1978.

In front of Kerr was perhaps the best four-man defensive unit the Rangers have ever iced. Tough-as-nails Art Coulter and Lester's younger son, Muzz, were paired—two young belters who were much in the crowd-pleasing style of their predecessors, Ching Johnson and Taffy Abel. The other defensive tandem was Gerhardt "Ott" Heller, a stolid defender of German stock, and the ever fun-loving Walter "Babe" Pratt. "We never missed a game," Heller said years later. "It was just the four of us, not another defenseman played for us that entire season."

Goaltender David Alexander Kerr, below, played 427 games as a Ranger, including every game for the Stanley Cup-winning 1939–40 squad. He also gained renown as the first hockey player to make the cover of *Time* magazine, above right, on March 14, 1938. The Rangers of 1939–40 were saluted with a specially commissioned montage, opposite, that featured individual portraits, a subtle "V for Victory" design, and the then-slender Stanley Cup, far different from the Cup we know today.

New York Rangers Professional Hockey Club

Fun-loving defenseman Walter "Babe" Pratt squeezed every ounce of enjoyment he could out of New York City. "What a great place, New York," Pratt would say at every opportunity. "I loved it there." Rangers fans also loved Babe for just over seven seasons.

Walter "Babe" Pratt

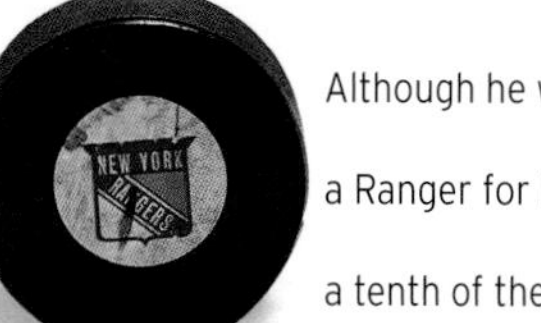

Although he was only a Ranger for less than a tenth of the team's long history, Walter "Babe" Pratt is a great part of the Rangers' legend and lore. Actually, he was the most prominent player, an imposing defenseman, to link the first era with the second era. On the ice and off, the Babe was a character. The nickname, for more than a few reasons, came from Babe Ruth. Pratt had been a terrific baseball player. The athletes were of similar stature and shared some facial resemblance as well. More importantly, the two "Babes" simply loved a good time. Ruth himself liked hockey, lived in Manhattan, and because of the nickname, would make a beeline for Pratt whenever he visited the Rangers dressing room.

A wide-smiling, fun-loving guy, Pratt arrived in New York midway through the 1935–36 season, taking the train up from Philadelphia where he had played twenty-eight games with the Ramblers of the Canadian-American League. Arriving at Penn Station, Pratt hopped a bus for the short ride up 8th Avenue to the Rangers' Madison Square Garden headquarters. "Afterwards, I walked over to look at Times Square," he said, "and, let me say, I liked what I saw. Where had this place been all my life? I looked out at all those beautiful bright lights of Broadway, and said to myself, 'Babe, you are personally going to look behind every single one of them.'" No doubt he did.

Pratt's arrival on the New York scene was serendipitous for the Rangers, coming just as the career of Ching Johnson was winding to a conclusion. Although his talent was great (the legendary Rangers' scout Al Ritchie called him "the finest prospect I have ever seen"), Pratt would become known more for his humor than for his hockey. Not even the taciturn Lester was immune.

"Behind his back, we called Lester 'Mr. First' because he and [his brother] Frank always said they were the first to do this and the first to do that," said Pratt. "We did the same thing later in Boston with Frank. But the truth is, they were the first to do all those things." Although their time together in the East was relatively short, Pratt knew Lester Patrick better than most. Simply said, the two big men had a lot in common. Many years later, after both had retired in western Canada, Pratt used to refer to (and sometimes even introduce) Patrick as "the man who invented ice, the hat trick, and sliced bread." After Lester's passing on June 1, 1960, Pratt was in great demand as an after-dinner speaker, kind of the Joe Garagiola of hockey. By then he was referring to Lester as "the guy who invented the Zamboni . . . and everything else."

Pratt was particularly adept at skewering Tommy Lockhart, the avuncular curmudgeon who ran the Garden's amateur hockey operation and also served as the Rangers' business manager. A blue ribbon needler himself, Lockhart used to say he carried "my own money in my right pocket and the Rangers' money in my left." Observed Pratt, "Tommy was born right-handed, but he's been strictly a lefty since I've known him."

ANG

Left wing Alex Shibicky scores one of his last National Hockey League goals against Boston's Paul Bibeault at Madison Square Garden on January 6, 1946. A great Ranger for 324 games over eight seasons, Shibicky would score ten goals in this, his final NHL campaign. The Bruins defenseman is Jack Church (18). The Rangers won, 4-2.

PLAYER'S CONTRACT
AS PRESCRIBED FOR THE
National Hockey League

The MADISON SQUARE GARDEN CORP. (NEW YORK RANGERS PRO HOCKEY CLUB) of NEW YORK N. Y. WITH ALEX SHIBICKY WINNIPEG MANITOBA

Regular Contract:—
Approved

PLAYER'S CONTRACT
AS PRESCRIBED FOR THE
National Hockey League

The NEW YORK RANGERS PROFESSIONAL HOCKEY CLUB INC. of NEW YORK N. Y. WITH NEIL COLVILLE EDMONTON ALBERTA

I hereby certify that I have, at this date, received, examined and noted of record the within Contract, and that it is in regular form.

President National Hockey League.

Regular Contract:—
Approved Oct 28 1936

PLAYER'S CONTRACT
AS PRESCRIBED FOR THE
National Hockey League

The NEW YORK RANGERS PROFESSIONAL HOCKEY CLUB, INC. NEW YORK N. Y. WITH ARTHUR COULTER PHILADELPHIA PENN.

President National Hockey League.

Regular Contract:—
Approved Oct 15 1936

Successor to the "A Line" was the Rangers' second great line, known as the "Bread Line," above. It featured Neil Colville at center between right wing Mac Colville (left) and left wing Alex Shibicky (right). The line was the youngest in the NHL at the time, and it was also known as the "Stream-Line."

Coulter was the team captain, and he was sometimes described as "mean." Teammate Lynn Patrick disagreed. "Art might have been mean in games, yeah maybe he was," said Lynn. "He wasn't mean in practices, but boy could he hit. Art was what we called 'a punisher.'" Patrick continued, "When he hit you in practice, you just knew it was him. Art's checks felt different. And it wasn't a good different, I can tell you that." Coulter's nickname was "The Trapper," not only because he was very adept at blocking shots, but because of his great prowess as an outdoorsman. "Art became a superb ice general," Boucher said. "He lent strength to our smaller players, always on the spot if opposing players tried to intimidate them. He was a great team man, a great captain. I relied on him tremendously."

Ever outspoken and opinionated, Coulter thought the Rangers were good enough to win at least four straight Cups. They didn't, of course, because of a number of factors. One, World War II came along and changed the entire landscape of professional sports. Two, on account of the circus, the Rangers were at a terrible disadvantage regarding home games in the playoffs. And, three, at least according to Coulter, was Lester Patrick himself. "He worked us too damn hard when the playoffs rolled around. He made a great team a good team." Because of the circus problem, Lester used to take the Rangers to Atlantic City for grueling workouts before the playoffs. "That alone cost us at least three Stanley Cups. We won one, but we should have had four."

Up front, the 1939–40 team was probably the most balanced squad in Rangers history. Lester Patrick's youth movement was in full swing, and no one mirrored the trend more brightly than a pair of stellar brothers, Neil Colville, a center, and Mac Colville, a right wing. The left wing was Alex Shibicky, and the trio was known as "The Bread Line." When it first formed, for the 1936–37 season, The Bread Line was the youngest regular trio in the NHL: Mac Colville was twenty while Neil and Alex were both twenty-two. The line's nickname had two origins. First, as the sportswriters were regularly pointing out, it was the team's "bread and butter." Second, it was a catchy name that people knew. Real bread lines were commonplace during the depression and one of the more popular ones formed at St. Malachy's Roman Catholic Church, just up the block from the Garden, on the north side of 49th Street between Broadway and 8th Avenue.

"The Prairie Boys" is what Boucher called the trio. The Colvilles hailed from Edmonton, Alberta, and Shibicky was out of Winnipeg, Manitoba. They were also the first of what would become known as Rangers "purebreds"—players who started, matured, and eventually starred in the same system. "Lester was always preaching 'the system,'" said Boucher, "and the Colvilles and Shibicky proved him right." The trio started with the New York Crescents of the Eastern League, matured with the Ramblers, and starred with the Rangers. Later, when the New York Rovers came on the scene, Lester's system was known as the "Three R System"—Rovers, Ramblers, Rangers. Boucher's second line also had a nickname, the "Powerhouse Line." Lynn Patrick was at left wing and Bryan Hextall was on the right side. The center was a tempestuous pepper pot by the name of Philipe Henri "Phil" Watson.

Captain of the 1939–40 Rangers was Art "The Trapper" Coulter, a solid and stolid defenseman, who strongly felt that his teams—had they not been overworked at playoff time—would have won not one, but four Stanley Cups.

7
A
16
NORTHLAND PROFESSIONAL

For a number of years, starting in the late 1940s, the Rangers held their training camp in Lake Placid, New York. The "Three R System" instituted by Lester Patrick was in full bloom as General Manager and Coach Frank Boucher (right) instructed a group of six board-straddling hopefuls in the fine art of puck control.

The "Three R" chain began with the amateur New York Rovers, continued with the professional Philadelphia Ramblers, and, ideally at least, ended with the "big team," the Rangers. For a while, there was even a fourth "R" at the beginning of the chain, the Lake Placid Roamers.

RANGE

Lynn Patrick's arrival on the NHL scene was not a traditional one, hardly a given in the mind of Lester Patrick himself. That Lester would find a great hockey player in his very own family was hardly surprising, given the family's athletic prowess. That he would find two was astounding. So much so that Lester grappled mightily with that unlikelihood. Muzz's NHL talents were a foregone conclusion in Lester's mind. That was hardly the case with his older son.

Lynn Patrick spent most of his formative years in the mild climate of Victoria, British Columbia. Although not the equal of brother Muzz, he was a tremendous performer in many sports—basketball, rugby, and football among them. The elder Patrick sibling would even play football professionally in Montreal and in Winnipeg before heading to New York for the 1934–35 hockey season. Between the ages of seventeen and twenty-two, Lynn had hardly been on skates at all, and certainly not competitively. Lester, quite simply, didn't think Lynn was NHL material, and he was vocal about it. Equally vocal, and on the other side of the fence, were Bill Cook and Frank Boucher. They saw great potential in the red-haired left wing and urged Lester to sign him. Somewhat reluctantly, he did. It turned out to be one of the best signings the Silver Fox ever made.

To be sure, Lynn Patrick was a finesse player, highly skilled but hardly out of the mold of his rambunctious brother Muzz. Lynn could almost dance on his skates, much in the manner of Bun Cook, his teammate for two seasons. Much to Lester's dismay, the Garden crowd usually rode Lynn pretty hard, calling him "Twinkletoes" and "Sonja," the latter a reference to the world-famous figure skater Sonja Henie. Lynn persevered mightily, however, winning the Stanley Cup in 1940, leading the NHL in goal scoring with thirty-two, and making the NHL's first All-Star Team in 1941–42.

Late in his life, Lester Patrick reflected on the many triumphs he had enjoyed in professional hockey. "High on my list of thrills," Lester reminisced, "was witnessing Lynn's determination to succeed. Nothing has given me the flush of satisfaction that came with the realization that my bungling but persistent redheaded son had made the grade to hockey stardom."

The third line on Boucher's juggernaut featured Wilfred "Dutch" Hiller on left wing with Alf "The Embalmer" Pike in the middle and Clint "Snuffy" Smith on the right side. This trio was almost interchangeable. In addition to all three players having nicknames, all three also shot left-handed. Kilby MacDonald, yet another lefty, could substitute for any of them at any time.

Hiller was the fastest skater in the league at the time. "The others were good skaters, too," recalled Boucher, "but nobody could keep up with Dutch." Smith, whose nickname came from the then-popular "Snuffy Smith" comic strip, was just a little guy (5' 7", 165), but he was almost impossible to hit and one of the best in the league at winning face-offs. Pike's nickname was legitimate: He was a licensed mortician in the off-season, and obviously the brunt of much locker-room humor.

Coming into the championship season, the Rangers and the Boston Bruins were clearly the NHL's elite teams. The Beantowners were led by the "Kraut

Opposite: Left wing Lynn Patrick (right) joined his center Phil Watson and right wing Bryan Hextall (left) on the famed "Powerhouse Line." In 1941–42, when the Rangers finished first overall, Hextall finished first in the NHL scoring race, Patrick was second, and Watson third. Hextall and Patrick would also make the first All-Star Team.

Lynn Patrick, left, eldest son of the boss, Lester Patrick, would play 455 games for his father and score 335 points. Later in his career, Lynn would coach the Rangers, leading the 1950 team to within a single goal of the Stanley Cup.

Defenseman Art Coulter, a veteran at thirty years of age and in his ninth NHL season, was a great force on the 1940 team. He never missed a game in the regular season or in the playoffs. "You couldn't have asked for a better captain," recalled teammate Muzz Patrick. "He wasn't a 'holler guy,' but he led by example."

Line," hockey's most famous line at the time. Left wing Woody Dumart, center Milt Schmidt, and right wing Bobby Bauer would eventually all make the Hockey Hall of Fame. Later, during World War II, many found the line's nickname offensive, so it was changed to the "Kitchener Kids," as all three players hailed from the Kitchener-Waterloo area of Ontario. Boucher was so respectful of Boston's prowess that he called the Bruins "the second best team I had ever seen."

Despite their obvious talent and their incredible balance, the Rangers of 1939–40 hardly got off to an imposing start. The team won only one of its first eight games, the last two of which were ties. However, the two deadlocks, road games against Montreal and Boston, began a "lightning in a bottle" streak that stands to the present as the longest unbeaten streak in team history—nineteen straight games without a loss, stretching from before Thanksgiving (November 23) to after New Year's (January 13). The streak included fourteen victories and five ties.

When the streak finally ended with a 2-1 road loss to the Chicago Blackhawks, the Rangers promptly ran off five more consecutive wins for a record of 19-1-5 for that period. "It was almost like we couldn't lose," Boucher said years later. "Even the loss to the Blackhawks, we outplayed Chicago that whole game."

The 1940 playoffs began, fittingly enough, with the two best teams, the Rangers and Bruins—only a train ride apart—drawing each other in the first round. It was too early for the circus, so the Rangers got their fair share of home games in the first round, and dispatched the Bruins four games to two. Goalie Kerr, winner of the Vezina Trophy in the regular season, was the hero, posting back-to-back 1-0 shutouts in games four and five, the first and only time in team history that a goalie posted successive shutouts in the playoffs.

So, it was on to the finals, the heavily favored Rangers versus the Toronto Maple Leafs, whom the New Yorkers had outdistanced by eleven points during the regular season. Heading into the series, captain Coulter knew it had been seven years since the Rangers last won the Cup, and that only Ott Heller remained from the 1933 squad. "So, I sent each of the players a telegram—yes, each one—just to remind everybody that it could be done."

The first two games were at the Garden, back to back on April 2–3. The Rangers, with Kerr still holding the hot hand, won them both: 2-1 on Alf Pike's overtime goal and 6-2. As the teams dressed following the conclusion of game two, workers were already dismantling the boards and melting the ice. The rest of the series would be played at Maple Leaf Gardens in Toronto. "I hated the sound of the ice cracking," Pratt recalled. "You could hear it from our dressing room. They had a machine with like a 'cattle catcher' on the front to scrape up the ice. I hated that machine. There is nothing sadder than a hockey rink without ice."

The Leafs, with the great Turk Broda in goal, quickly rebounded and won game three on April 6 by a score of 2-1 and game four on April 9 in a 3-0 shutout.

A turning point came in game five, a tight-checking April 11 contest that went to overtime. The unlikely hero was defenseman Muzz Patrick, whose goal at 11:43 of the extra session gave the

For half a century, starting in 1950, the Rangers have been boosted, bolstered, cheered, and exhorted by as rabid a bunch of hockey fans as has ever existed. The Rangers Fan Club, whose membership once was fifteen hundred strong, has done just about everything from holding annual dinner dances (this one was at the Hotel Martinique) to assisting at charity functions to making road trips and holding regular meetings with player guests. Win, lose, or tie, the Rangers have always been number one with the members of the Rangers Fan Club. The club's banner was a familiar sight for decades at Madison Square Gardens number three and number four. The 2000–2001 season marks the Golden Anniversary of the Rangers Fan Club, fifty consecutive years of cheering for the Rangers.

In the 1940 Stanley Cup finals, the Rangers faced the Toronto Maple Leafs. With their goalie Turk Broda flat on his stomach, four Leafs struggle to clear the puck during a Ranger power play. Ranger center Phil Watson (standing, left) appears to swing his hockey stick as if it were a golf club.

Despite having only two "genuine" home games at Madison Square Garden, the Rangers managed to oust the Leafs in six games, coming back from a 2-0 deficit in game six. The Rangers were the "stingiest" team in the NHL that season, allowing only seventy-seven goals in the forty-eight-game regular season and ten more in the playoffs.

Rangers a 2-1 victory. It was Patrick's third goal of the playoffs, one more than he had scored during the entire forty-eight-game regular season.

Patrick's goal gave the Rangers momentum and set the stage for game six, two nights later, Saturday, April 13. Fans from New York, as they had years earlier, journeyed to Toronto by train even though few of them had game tickets. The New York Central Railroad made a promotion out of it called "Hockey Week-End Excursion"—Grand Central Station in New York to Union Station, Toronto, round-trip fare: $31.15.

The Leafs took a 2-0 lead after two periods of game six, but the Rangers battled back to tie it on third-period goals by Neil Colville and Alf Pike. So, it was on to overtime, and even more than half a century later, it stuck in Dutch Hiller's mind. "I can remember it as though it was yesterday."

As Hiller remembers it, barely two minutes into overtime, he muscled a Maple Leaf out of the play behind the Toronto net and zipped a pass to Watson near the Toronto blue line. "It was kind of a fast play, bang-bang, just like that," Watson recalled. Watson slipped the puck to Hextall, the ever-dangerous left-handed-shooting right wing. "Bryan came burning in like an elephant," Watson continued. Hextall's winning shot was a hard backhander, high to the right on Broda, who moved to stop the puck but missed. Suddenly the Rangers were hollering and hugging. The Cup was theirs for a third time.

Smiles all around as Coach Frank Boucher congratulates Bryan Hextall on scoring the Stanley Cup–winning goal at 2:07 of sudden death overtime on April 13, 1940. Despite having only two games at home due to the ongoing "circus problem," the Rangers prevailed in six games.

"Was it the biggest goal of my career?" Hextall mused years later. "Of course it was. You betcha. I'll never forget it."

General Kilpatrick made a rare dressing room appearance to celebrate and to invite the Rangers—and their friends—to a party that followed in the Tudor Room of the Royal York Hotel, the tallest building in Canada at the time and the largest hotel in the British Empire. And what a party it was. Waiters in tuxedos. Players in suits and ties. Champagne replaced the usual beverage of choice, beer.

"It was the first time I ever tasted champagne," recalled Herb Goren, who covered every game of the 1939–40 season for the *New York Sun* and later served the Rangers as team publicist for more than a decade. Goren also recalled someone attempting to steal the Stanley Cup itself that evening. "Suddenly, I looked up and the Cup was gone. The guy got the Cup down the elevator and almost out the door before the assistant maitre d'hotel, a guy named George Bourjot, collared the culprit."

Recalled Snuffy Smith, "The next day, General Kilpatrick and Lester took a plane back to New York. The rest of us and the sportswriters took the train. We saved a few beers from the night before and had another party." In the custom of the day, six Rangers didn't even go back to New York, returning instead by train to their homes in western Canada. The official team picture of the Cup-winning team wouldn't be taken until training camp the next season.

Surviving members of the 1940 team recall incredible closeness and bonding on the squad. "We were a family," Smith said. "Anytime we went anywhere, we went as a body. We stuck up for each other and knew where everybody was all the time." Said Coulter, "There were no strangers, no wildcats on that team." Said Shibicky, "What that team had was something special, a togetherness."

Just how good were the 1939–40 Rangers, "the best team" Frank Boucher had ever seen? Kilby MacDonald, the spare forward, the guy who played the least, was the NHL's top rookie that season, winning the Calder Memorial Trophy.

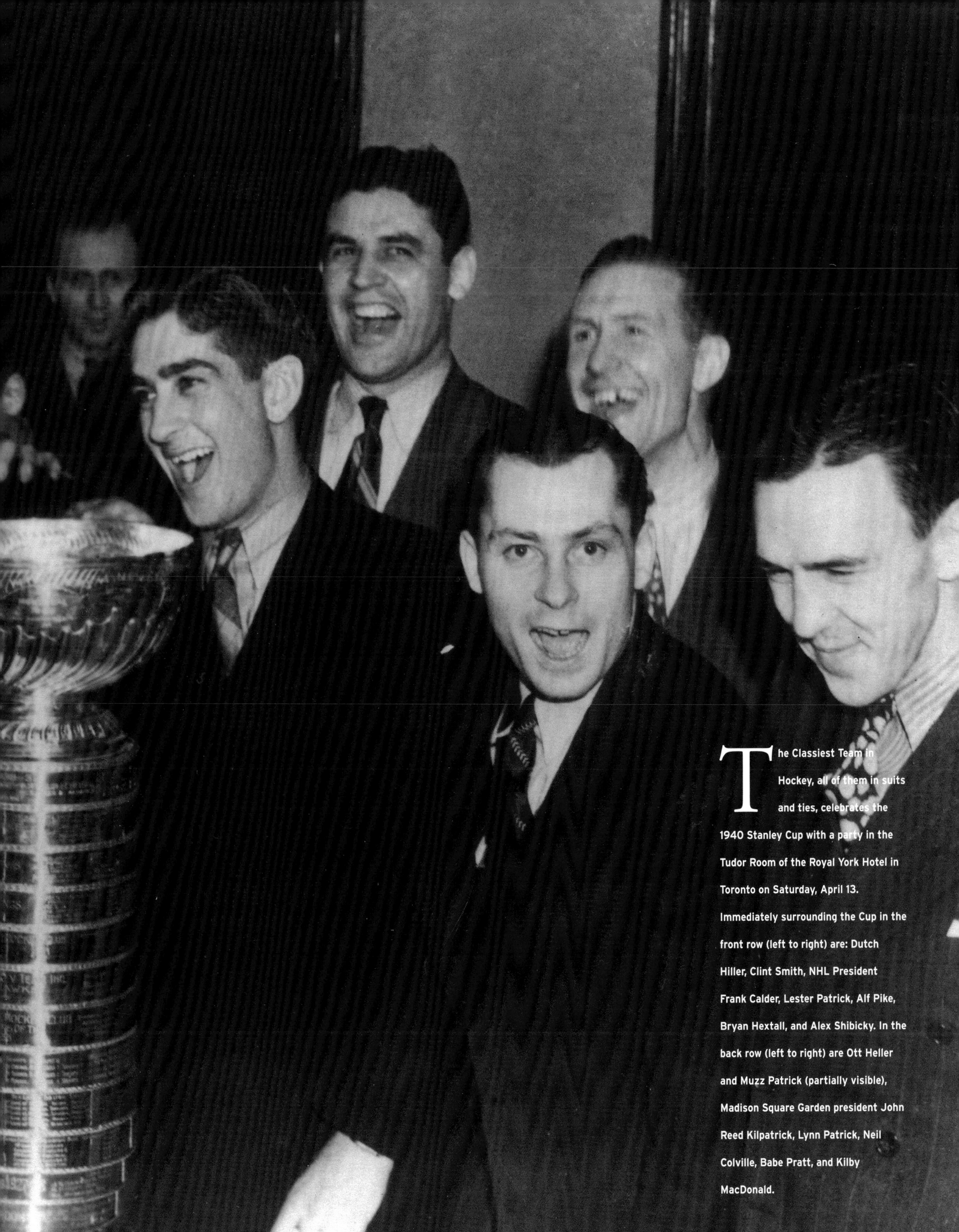

The Classiest Team in Hockey, all of them in suits and ties, celebrates the 1940 Stanley Cup with a party in the Tudor Room of the Royal York Hotel in Toronto on Saturday, April 13. Immediately surrounding the Cup in the front row (left to right) are: Dutch Hiller, Clint Smith, NHL President Frank Calder, Lester Patrick, Alf Pike, Bryan Hextall, and Alex Shibicky. In the back row (left to right) are Ott Heller and Muzz Patrick (partially visible), Madison Square Garden president John Reed Kilpatrick, Lynn Patrick, Neil Colville, Babe Pratt, and Kilby MacDonald.

HOCKEY
Season 1957-58

NEW YORK RANGERS

Side Loge		$5.00
Side Arena		5.00
Side Promenade		4.00
End Loge		4.00
End Promenade		3.50
End Arena	*Rows A thru G*	3.50
End Arena	*Rows H thru T*	2.50
Mezzanine	*Rows A and B*	2.50
Mezzanine	*Rows C thru F*	2.25
End Balcony		1.50
Side Balcony (Admission)		95c

All prices include Federal and City Admissions Tax.

GAME TIME:

Sundays	
Wednesdays	7:00 P.M.
Saturday Afternoons, Nov. 2 & Nov. 30	7:30 P.M.
	3:00 P.M.
Saturday Afternoons, Jan. 4 & Feb. 1	2:00 P.M.

Assure yourself of same choice seats for all games by subscribing. Call or write for details.

MAIL ORDERS PROMPTLY FILLED
Add 25c per order for handling and mailing

MADISON SQUARE GARDEN
307 W. 49th St., N. Y. C. 19
For Information Call COlumbus 5-6811

MSG: The Old and the New

Madison Square Garden is "the world's most famous arena," and there have been four of them dating all the way back to May 31, 1879. Only the second Garden, however, was actually on Madison Square. But to the more than eight hundred players who have worn the red, white, and blue livery of the New York Rangers and their millions of fans over the years, there have really been only two Gardens: the ones with ice in them.

They are Garden number three, on 8th Avenue between 49th and 50th Streets, and Garden number four at Pennsylvania Station, spanning 31st to 33rd Streets and 7th to 8th Avenues. For the last thirty years or so, to hockey fans at least, Garden number three has been known as the "old" Garden and Garden number four as the "new" Garden.

Garden number three was a comfy place, kind of like an old pair of slippers, and full of nooks and crannies. The majority of patrons entered from 8th Avenue directly under a marquee recognized around the world that said in capital letters on three sides: MADISON SQ GARDEN. That the "Q" facing 49th Street was permanently askew, forever listing to the left, only added to the charm, as did the marquee's seemingly endless abbreviations, "Rgrs," "Tonite," "Thru," "Tomw," and "V/S" among them.

On the corner of 50th Street was Davega's, later Gerry Cosby & Co.; next was a bygone New York City institution, Nedick's, whose name came from its orange drink (not to be confused with juice!) and whose succulent hot dogs were far better than the ones served inside the Garden. As late as the early 1960s, for 15¢, you could get a "breakfast special" that consisted of a small orange

Sixty-two NHL greats slowly circled the ice for one last Broadway curtain call, above, as Madison Square Garden number three hosted its final hockey game on February 11, 1968. Opposite: Madison Square Garden had an Art Deco-style marquee not unlike the nearby Broadway theaters.

Water barrel, which preceded the Zamboni

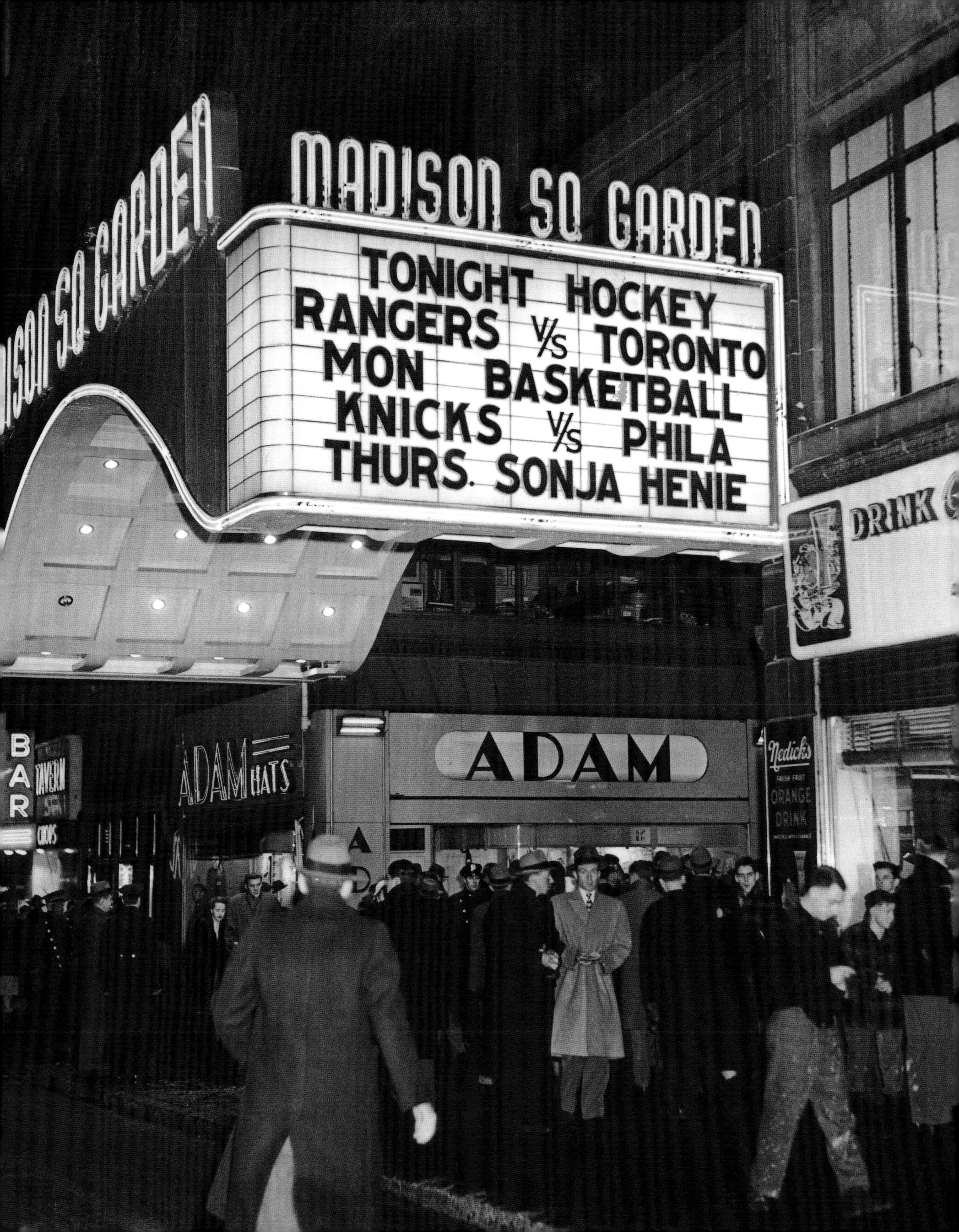

MADISON SQ GARDEN
TONIGHT HOCKEY
RANGERS V/S TORONTO
MON BASKETBALL
KNICKS V/S PHILA
THURS. SONJA HENIE
ADAM
ADAM HATS
BAR
TAVERN
Nedick's
FRESH FRUIT
ORANGE
DRINK
DRINK

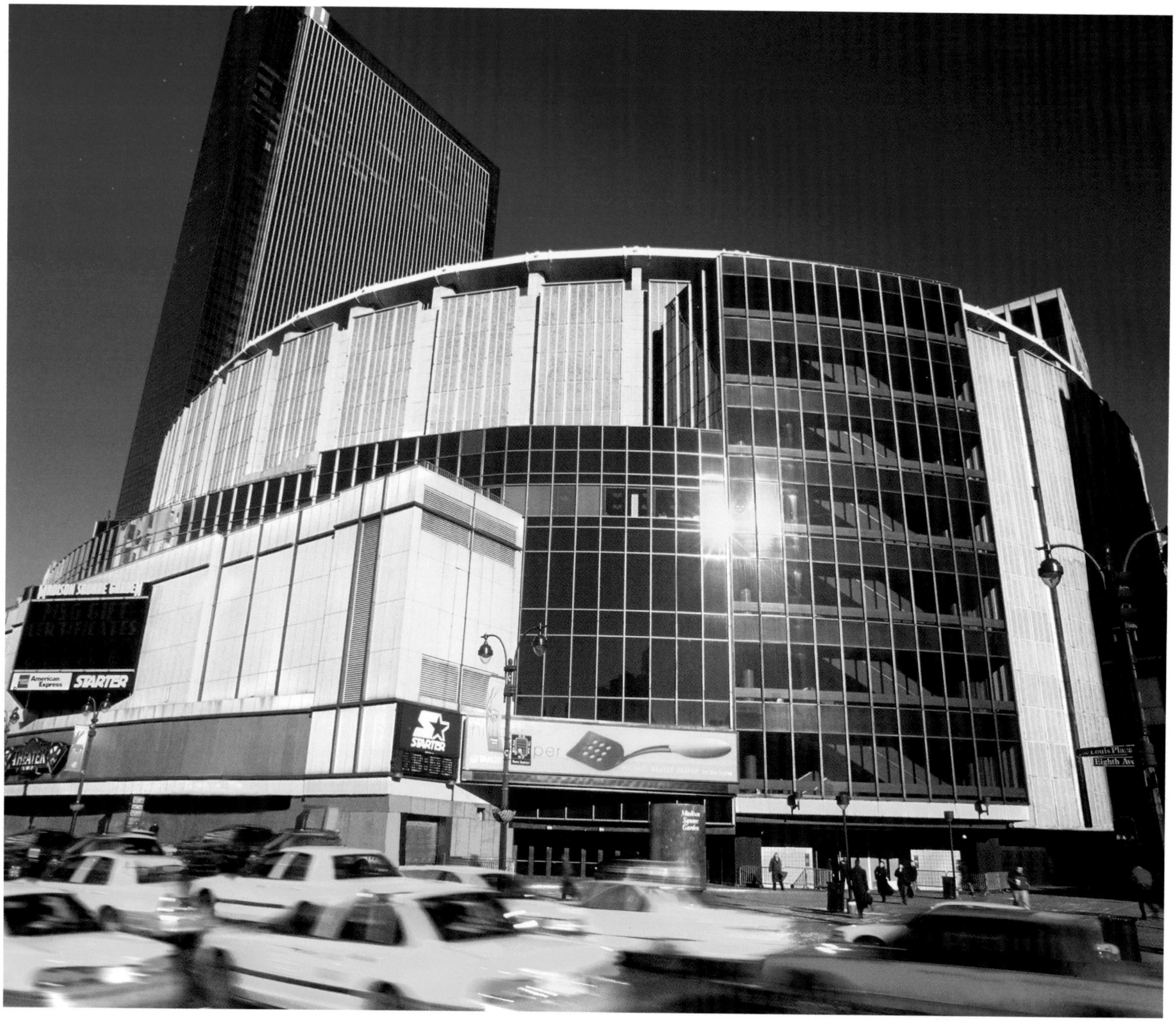

Madison Square Garden spans 7th to 8th Avenues and 31st to 33rd Streets in vibrant midtown Manhattan. In addition to being the home of the New York Rangers, it also hosts the New York Knicks and New York Liberty basketball teams, boxing, the circus, and big-time musical acts like Bruce Springsteen, Pavarotti, and Tony Bennett.

drink, a doughnut (plain or sugared), and a cup of coffee. And no extra charge for take-out, napkin included.

To the left, toward 49th Street were Adam Hats, Regal Shoes, and United Cigar, names that fans of a certain age remember with great fondness.

"It was a wonderful place to play, it really was," recalled Charlie Rayner of the "old" Garden. "People were like family. We'd wave or nod at them, usually in the same seats. The icemen, the ushers, the concession guys, we all knew each other," he continued. "They say 'old soldiers never die,' well old ushers don't die either. They just keep on ushering. I mean, once an usher said hello to me in the current Garden, and I hadn't played a game in thirty-five years."

The final sports event in Madison Square Garden number three was a 3-3 tie between the Rangers and the Detroit Red Wings, a Sunday afternoon game on February 11, 1968. The honor of scoring the last goal in that glorious old barn went to center Jean Ratelle, who slipped the puck past Detroit goalie Roger Crozier. But the real stars of the afternoon show were the greatest collection of hockey talent ever to skate as one group—sixty-two of them, in fact. Every living member of an NHL All-Star Team was invited to attend, and most of them showed. They all wore the jerseys of their most famous team.

There were dramatic introductions, particularly of the Rangers' first great line—Frank Boucher between the Cook brothers, Bill and Bun—the A Line. Jacques Plante and his mask did a curtain call to great cheers, and Hall of Famer Aurel Joliat, at sixty-seven years of age, amazed most everyone by doing "figure eights" at center ice. The great Maurice "Rocket" Richard scored a ceremonial goal, and Bill Cook did the same, another ceremonial tally, the last ever, even in make-believe. For one last time, the Garden organ played "Auld Lang Syne," and the All-Stars slowly skated around, waving their sticks to an adoring crowd that stood and clapped, and clapped some more, the bellowing cheers engulfing the stars of yesteryear, almost all of whom had tears in their eyes. That night, the current Garden opened with a gala entertainment special that starred Bing Crosby and Bob Hope.

A week later, Sunday night, February 18, 1968, the Rangers opened their second home at Pennsylvania Plaza against the brand-new Philadelphia Flyers, who were paying their first-ever visit to New York. Ratelle took the first face-off against Forbes Kennedy of the Flyers. Philadelphia right wing Wayne Hicks scored the first goal in the new building, and center Phil Goyette got the Rangers' first goal in their new home. The Rangers won, 3-1, an auspicious beginning for a team that was quickly jelling into one of the most powerful sextets in club history, a club with a new home, sixteen blocks south of its original one, and ready to stock itself with as many memories as the old one.

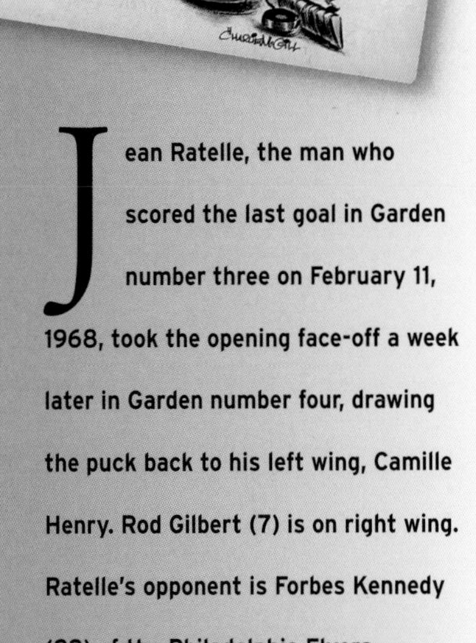

Jean Ratelle, the man who scored the last goal in Garden number three on February 11, 1968, took the opening face-off a week later in Garden number four, drawing the puck back to his left wing, Camille Henry. Rod Gilbert (7) is on right wing. Ratelle's opponent is Forbes Kennedy (22) of the Philadelphia Flyers.

World War II meant lean times for the Rangers. So decimated was the team that it finished in last place five out of seven seasons. But a thrilling turnabout was to come.

1947

Nov. 16—Don Raleigh set an NHL record with three assists in a span of one minute and twenty-one seconds during a 4-2 Rangers win against the visiting Montreal Canadiens.

1948

Dec. 19—Emile Francis played his first game as a Ranger, and led the team to a 3-2 win over Montreal. New York called up Francis from New Haven following an injury to their goalie Chuck Rayner.

1952

Oct. 9—Lorne "Gump" Worsley made his NHL debut in goal for the Rangers, replacing the injured Chuck Rayner, but New York lost to the Red Wings 5-3 in their season opener.

Dec. 17—Goalie Chuck Rayner recorded his twenty-fifth (and final) career shutout as New York won 5-0 against the visiting Boston Bruins.

1954

Jan. 12—Rangers announced that Murray "Muzz" Patrick would take over permanently as coach of the team, beginning the following night against Detroit. Patrick was brought in to succeed Frank Boucher, who remained as general manager.

1957

Jan. 5—CBS became the first U.S. network to televise an NHL game as the host Rangers beat Chicago 4-1 in an afternoon game at Madison Square Garden.

1959

Nov. 1—Montreal's goalie Jacques Plante returned to the ice wearing a mask after being hit in the face with a shot by the Rangers' Andy Bathgate in New York. It marked the beginning of a new era in hockey, as Plante led the Canadiens to a 3-1 win over the Rangers.

"Gump" Worsley

Jacques Plante

Routed Then Rebuilt

Unlike the breakup of the original Rangers, which was basically accomplished through attrition—a trade here, a graceful retirement there—the end of "the best team ever seen" was sudden, stunning, and numbing. World War II changed the landscape of professional sports in North America, and nowhere (at least so it seemed to New York hockey fans) was the numbness felt more than in New York City.

The logistical issues of keeping the National Hockey League running during wartime were staggering. The overwhelming majority of players were Canadian, yet four of the franchises were in the United States. Money was tight due to the lingering effects of the depression. Rationing of vital materials, including gas and rubber, meant fewer fans would be able to drive to games. For a time, it appeared the NHL would shut down completely, and the Rangers' Canadian citizens prepared to continue their hockey careers—after thirty days of compulsory basic training—on military teams in Canada. As it turned out, the league never missed a game, but by the same token, it would never again be the same.

However, before the war clouds opened in full, there remained one more lightning bolt in the aging Blueshirts. The 1941–42 team finished atop the NHL, in first place, and annexed the Prince of Wales Trophy as the regular season's best team. Effectively, this was the last hurrah for a great team.

From November 25, 1941, to February 5, 1942, the Rangers posted twenty victories against only four losses and a single tie. Included in this streak was an 11-2 pasting of the Detroit Red Wings at the Garden on January 25, 1942, a team record for most goals in a game that stood until 1971. The remarkable streak—and the first-place finish—would be the last Rangers bright spot, from a team standpoint at least, for the next eight years. World War II beckoned.

The Patrick brothers, Muzz and Lynn, were among the first to depart. Though born in Canada, the siblings were naturalized American citizens, so they headed for the United States Army: Lynn to Camp Custer in Michigan and Muzz to Hampton Roads, Virginia. Captain Art Coulter joined the United States Coast Guard and played for the Coast Guard Cutters team out of Baltimore. Neil and Mac Colville, Alex Shibicky, Kilby MacDonald, and Alf Pike all enlisted in the Canadian armed forces. Add to those mighty defections pepper pot Phil Watson. Thinking that wartime border restrictions would not allow Watson into the United States that season, the Rangers arranged a loan of Watson to the Montreal Canadiens in exchange for four players for the 1943–44 season. And a disastrous loan it was. Watson helped the Canadiens to the Stanley Cup, and the Rangers finished dead last. The total effect of the wartime changes rendered the Rangers a shell of the team that had won it all in 1940.

Muzz Patrick

Murray "Muzz" Patrick, below, was a menacing presence on defense for the Rangers for 166 games over five seasons. His rough play and thumping body checks were reminiscent of earlier defensive stalwarts such as Ching Johnson and Taffy Abel. Muzz was teamed with Art Coulter on defense, one of the Rangers' toughest pairings ever.

Over seventy-five years, three quarters of a century, who was the greatest athlete ever to play for the Rangers? No contest: Murray "Muzz" Patrick. Hands down. That his athletic skills did not necessarily translate into being a successful coach or a successful general manager was beside the point. Muzz Patrick was the greatest athlete the Rangers have ever had.

As the second son of Lester Patrick, the Rangers' first general manager, coach, and paterfamilias, Muzz Patrick was bred to be a hockey player. But starting as a schoolboy in his native Victoria, British Columbia, he excelled in all sports—boxing, track and field, bicycle racing, wrestling, football, baseball, rugby, and basketball. As a boxer at nineteen years of age, he became the Canadian amateur heavyweight champion by knocking out Tommy Osborne in the second round in 1935. In basketball, at seventeen years old and still in high school, Muzz was voted the best forward in Canada when his team, the Victoria Blue Ribbons, won the national championship in 1933.

The Blue Ribbons traveled east to play some games in the Montreal Forum in the early 1930s, providing Muzz with his first exposure to that great hockey shrine. He would go on to play hockey there, of course, but also to box professionally and compete in six-day bicycle races, making him undoubtedly the only man to compete in four different sports in the Forum. Similarly, in New York, Muzz is thought to be the only man ever to play three pro sports—hockey, boxing, and six-day bicycle racing—in Madison Square Garden.

Muzz Patrick was a physical specimen like no other. "I was a nut on physical fitness and couldn't stand to be idle for a week," he recalled. "If the sports overlapped, I would pass up basketball to scout a fighter I was scheduled to meet. It wasn't uncommon for me to ride a bike race on a Friday night, play hockey Saturday, and box on Sunday. I wanted to keep doing things, and I enjoyed them all.

"Why did I do it? More than anything else I think it was to please other people. Making others happy was a thrill for me," he said. "When I was fighting in New York, I'd run around the Central Park reservoir on my own because [brother] Lynn expected me to. Sometimes I'd beat a fighter to show

Lynn because he said I couldn't do it, and other times I'd win because he'd shown he had faith in me, too."

Given his genes, it was hockey that finally captured Muzz Patrick's full-time attention. A bruising six-foot-two, 200-pound defenseman, he joined the Rangers during the 1938–39 season, and scored the winning goal in overtime to give the Rangers a 2-1 victory over the Toronto Maple Leafs in game five of the 1940 Stanley Cup finals. Two days later, the Rangers would win their third Stanley Cup. Muzz was a great favorite of the fans in New York and gained great renown with a celebrated one-punch victory over Boston defenseman Eddie Shore in 1939.

Later, in the 1939 playoffs, Muzz delivered a crushing check that injured the ankle of Boston right winger Mel Hill, prompting stories in the Boston papers about Patrick's "dirty play." Rangers publicist Jersey Jones asked Muzz what all the fuss was about, and he replied, "Oh, they're just making a mountain out of a Mel Hill." Gregarious and fun-loving by nature, Muzz drove a tour bus at the 1939 World's Fair at New York's Flushing Meadow. He even claimed to have gotten the Fair's organizers to include a hockey puck in the time capsule that was buried there, a claim some have disputed. We'll find out in 2039, when the capsule is scheduled to be unearthed.

World War II interrupted Patrick's hockey career, and he was the first NHL player to enlist for military service in the United States Army. His athleticism continued to show when he led his battalion on the rifle range, scoring ninety-eight out of a possible one hundred. Muzz rose to the rank of captain and served as an officer in North Africa, in the battle for Anzio in Italy, and during the invasion of southern France.

The war pretty much ended Patrick's playing career. He was ineffective in a half-season of play in 1945–46 and retired. Muzz returned to the Rangers, first as coach in 1954 and a year later as general manager, following in his father's footsteps. After his death on July 23, 1998, Muzz's widow, Jessie, had his ashes scattered on the Strait of Juan de Fuca in his native Victoria, a fitting tribute for the greatest athlete the Rangers had ever known.

Muzz Patrick (left) and brother Lynn (right) join dad Lester on Lester Patrick Night at Madison Square Garden, December 4, 1947. The Patrick clan beam as they read a special proclamation from the city of New York. Lester had served the team since its very inception in 1926–27. Lynn, and later, Muzz, would both succeed him as coach of the Rangers.

Allan Stanley's elbow pads

There was one constant, Frank Boucher, who was forty years old by the time the war broke out and, in his own words, "not likely to frighten many Germans."

By the mid-1940s, Boucher had been on the New York scene for the better part of two decades and was the most recognizable—not to mention most affable—hockey face in town. He was also a regular luncheon guest at the era's most fashionable sporting haunt, Jack Dempsey's restaurant, smack on Broadway, between 50th and 51st Streets, just a wrist shot from the Rangers' headquarters at the Garden. Such was his stature that Frank was often seated with Dempsey himself, right at the window table of honor, hard by the Broadway sidewalk.

Ever the pixie with devilishly dancing eyes, Frank would occasionally connive with Dempsey and have Harry Westerby, the Rangers' first trainer, sit alone with Dempsey at lunch. "People would come over, the regulars you know, and say, 'Who's that sitting with the Champ?' 'It's a secret,' I would say." That would leave the regulars puzzled, scratching their heads to figure out just whom Dempsey was chatting with, since his table normally attracted only recognizable celebrities like Boucher himself. Dempsey, himself a great practical joker, loved the ruse. No doubt he also loved the companionship and the conversation, as Westerby had been a featherweight boxer in Toronto, knew the fight game well, and was quite an adept yarn spinner.

The lunches were often extended ones, Boucher sometimes lingering over a piece of Dempsey's cheesecake and a glass of Hungarian wine called Tokay. Frank could needle Dempsey better than most of his patrons, and would often say the cheesecake was "good, but not as good as Lindy's," up the block. Boucher's luncheon of choice, at Dempsey's at least, was "smoked meat on rye." New Yorkers knew that better as corned beef or pastrami. Boucher's boss, Lester Patrick, was only an occasional visitor to Dempsey's since he preferred Lindy's. Ever the conservative, Lester also opted for simpler luncheon fare, a broiled half chicken being a particular favorite. And no practical jokes.

Lester may have thought he was the brunt of a practical joke at one particular game on January 23, 1944. Boucher's brother Carroll had died in Ottawa, and Frank headed home for the funeral, leaving Lester to coach the Rangers, who were scheduled to play the Red Wings in Detroit. The result was a 15-0 win for the Red Wings, the most lopsided defeat in Rangers history. The unfortunate victim of the barrage was goalie Ken McAuley, who played all fifty games that season, allowed 310 goals, and finished with a whopping goals-against average of 6.24. "He deserved the croix de guerre," said Boucher.

So decimated were the Rangers that the team finished in last place five times in seven seasons, next to last once, and only sneaked into the playoffs a single time, in 1948. In 1943–44, the team was so undermanned that Boucher himself attempted a comeback that lasted fifteen games and produced four goals, ten assists, and more than a few aching muscles. "It was clear, painfully clear, that I just couldn't do it any more," Boucher said. It was the exact same scenario for the players who tried to come back after the war: the two Patricks, Pike, the two Colvilles, and Shibicky. They just couldn't do it anymore.

By the late 1940s, new blood was taking over the Rangers. The team had two great goalkeepers in Sugar Jim Henry and Chuck "Bonnie Prince Charlie" Rayner, best friends off the ice who were

Jack Dempsey's restaurant, opposite, sat on the west side of Broadway between 50th and 51st Streets, just around the corner from the Rangers headquarters at the third Madison Square Garden. Dempsey's opened in 1935 and stayed in business until 1974, six years after the Rangers had moved to Madison Square Garden number four.

Dempsey himself was not a hockey fan, but he loved the company of Frank Boucher and the Rangers' first trainer, an ex-boxer named Harry Westerby. Boucher and Westerby often lunched with the champ himself, at the table of honor near the front door and in full view of the passersby on Broadway.

BALLROOM
AVALON
SPAGHETTI
ROMEOS
PIZZERIA
Jack
DEMPSEY'S
BAR
GRUEN
JACK DEMPSEYS
WATCH
Hector's
Hector's
CAFETERIA
ROULETTE
RECORDS
CINERAMA
LOEWS CINERAMA

Goaltender Claude Earl "Chuck" Rayner, who starred for the Rangers from 1945 to 1953, is visited by his brother Scotty in the Rangers' dressing room at Maple Leaf Gardens in Toronto.

Jimmy Powers, sports editor of the *New York Daily News* said of Rayner, "He is to the Blueshirts what DiMag [Joe DiMaggio] is to the Yanks." Headline writers of the era sometimes called the Rangers the "Rayngers."

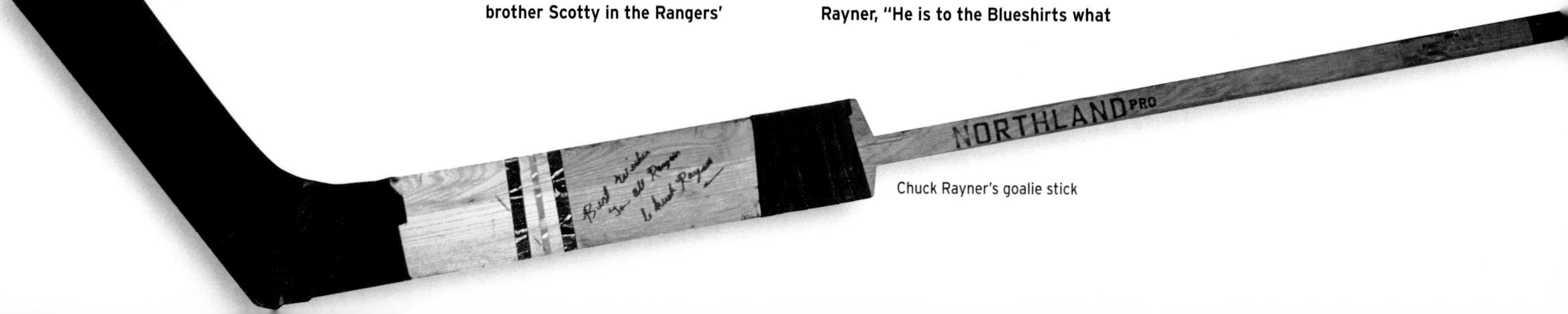

Chuck Rayner's goalie stick

so even in talent that Boucher kept them both at the start of the 1945–46 season. Boucher would play them in alternate games, and on a few occasions, would change them from shift to shift as he switched defensemen. In essence, this was the start of the two-goalie system that really didn't become regular practice until the 1960s.

When Don Raleigh, a willowy center who learned his hockey in Winnipeg, joined the Rangers for fifteen games during the 1943–44 season, he was just seventeen years of age and the youngest player in team history—a distinction he still holds. Standing just over five feet, ten inches, Raleigh weighed just 150 pounds, earning him the nickname "Bones." He was the first Ranger to score four goals in one game, tallying all four of the Rangers' goals in a 7-4 Garden defeat at the hands of Chicago on February 25, 1948.

Above: Goalie Rayner (left) gets a face full of ice for his efforts, but he makes the save in a game against the Toronto Maple Leafs. Don "Bones" Raleigh, below, was only seventeen and the youngest player in Rangers history when he played in 1943. A willowy center, Bones scored two overtime goals in the 1950 Stanley Cup finals against the Detroit Red Wings.

Lynn Patrick was the Rangers coach by then, only the third in team history. Midway through the 1948–49 season, Boucher decided to concentrate strictly on his general manager's chores and handed the coaching reins to Patrick, who had prepped for the job the last two and a half seasons by coaching the New Haven Ramblers of the American Hockey League. The Rangers had made the playoffs only once in seven years, yet in just over a year under Patrick, they suddenly found themselves in the Stanley Cup finals for the first time in a decade.

Were it not for the 1950 Rangers and their improbable run to the finals, the Rangers as a team would really have been without any meaningful success for more than a quarter of a century. Despite finishing fourth in the regular season (and twenty-one points behind the first-place Red Wings), the Rangers surprised the Montreal Canadiens, four games to one, in the first round of the postseason, setting up the final-round matchup with Detroit.

As was the norm at the time, the circus once again ruled. There would be no games at Madison Square Garden. Observed Bob Cooke, the hockey-friendly sports editor of the *New York Herald-Tribune*: "The Greatest Show on Earth (the Rangers) is leaving rather than entering our town." Coach Lynn Patrick's team would get two so-called "home" games, games two and three, but they would be played at Maple Leaf Gardens in Toronto. The balance of the series (four more games if it went the distance) would be played at the Olympia in Detroit. It went the distance.

The Rangers battled the Red Wings on even terms through six games, with Raleigh dramatically delivering his back-to-back overtime winners in games four and five. They would be the last playoff goals of Raleigh's career. Bones would stay with the Rangers until 1955 but the team would never again qualify for the postseason in his time.

Goalie Rayner, the leader of the 1950 squad and winner of the Hart Trophy as the NHL's MVP during the regular season, remembered that Bones had yet another great opportunity to win game seven in overtime, "but the puck just rolled over his stick." The Wings eventually prevailed in double overtime on a rare goal by utility forward Pete Babando. "To this day, I still wake up thinking how close we came to the Cup that year," Rayner recalled. "What a shame that was. Just one goal, and there never would have been a fifty-four-year drought."

The Rangers of 1950 are a happy bunch, having beaten the Montreal Canadiens to advance to the Stanley Cup finals and a matchup with the heavily favored Detroit Red Wings.

(Front row, left to right): Jack McLeod, Jack Gordon, Nick Mickoski, Ed Slowinski, coach Lynn Patrick, Buddy O'Connor, Wally Stanowski, Pat Egan, Frankie Eddolls, an unidentified stickboy, Chuck Rayner, and Allan Stanley. (Back row, left to right): Alex Kaleta, an unidentified stickboy, Don Raleigh, Pentti Lund, Tony Leswick, Edgar Laprade, trainer Frank Paice, Dunc Fisher, Jack Lancien, and Gus Kyle.

RANGERS

RANGERS

Despite the overwhelming lack of team success from approximately 1943 to 1970, the Rangers were hardly without individual stars during their "doldrum years." Herbert "Buddy" O'Connor, who won the team's first MVP honors in 1948, Nick Mickoski, Wally Hergesheimer, Alex "Killer" Kaleta, "Eager" Edgar Laprade, Ab DeMarco, Hy Buller, and Pentti Lund, the NHL's first Finnish-born player, were particular Garden favorites during the decade following WWII. Fans started saluting their heroes with banners—some of them crude bedsheets, others more professionally done—that hung over the facades of the end arena and the end and side balconies.

The adulatory signs were simple in content, usually shouting nothing more than the player's name: KRAFTCHECK . . . MICKOSKI . . . KULLMAN . . . HERGESHEIMER. By the 1950s, the signs became more complex: "Storey Is a Bum," hardly a paean to Red Storey, the most colorful referee of the time; "Looie [sic] Get Moore," an exhortation for tough defenseman "Leapin'" Lou Fontinato to rattle the cage of Dickie Moore, the despised Canadiens' winger (he did); and "Tout Le Monde Détestent Montreal," translated: "The Whole World Hates Montreal."

"Once a Ranger, always a Ranger" was still very much a part of the team's tradition in the 1950s. So it was hardly surprising when former star center Phil Watson was named coach in the summer of 1955. Watson became the team's eighth coach, each and every one of whom had also played for the team. He was tough, too tough probably—whipping, cajoling, and lambasting his charges, even publicly. His style was particularly irritating to his players, especially given the relatively benign natures of his seven predecessors. Never one to miss a good jab, goalie Lorne "Gump" Worsley said of Watson, "As a coach, he was a good waiter."

Worsley and Watson truly disliked each other. "Hate would be a better word," Worsley would say later. The two delighted in needling each other in the press. "Worsley has a beer belly," Watson would charge. "Shows what he knows, I only drink VO," Worsley would fire back, referring to his favorite brand of whiskey. This was great fodder for the sportswriters, but the acerbic goalie-coach relationship only served to underline the fact that after three solid playoff seasons the Rangers had become a team in disarray. That disarray reached its zenith on February 15, 1959.

The Rangers were particularly bad that night, dropping a lopsided 5-1 decision to the Montreal Canadiens. No sooner had the lethargic Blueshirts reached the refuge of their dressing room than Watson ordered them back onto the ice for a grueling postgame practice. This was hockey torture, pure punishment. There were no pucks, just wind sprints, stops and starts, up and down, over and back. Hundreds of fans remained for the "free show." No one had ever seen a practice before, particularly one of this magnitude. Even some of the victorious Canadiens, freshly showered and smiling, watched in amazement before heading off to their hotel and a good night's sleep.

Recalled Harry Howell, winner of the Norris Trophy in 1967 and the team's all-time leader with 1,160 games played: "That practice killed us physically and psychologically. We were dead after that." Indeed they were. The team won only five of its final twenty games, and missed the playoffs on the final night of the season.

One of the most famous fights in Rangers history matched Ranger defenseman Lou Fontinato, opposite, against Detroit's peerless Gordie Howe on February 1, 1959, at the Garden. Not even officials Art Skov (left) and Frank Udvari looked as a bloodied Fontinato, his nose badly askew, left the ice for repairs. Although he was clearly the loser, Fontinato always claimed that he more than held his own in the battle. Louie may have lost the fight, but the Rangers won the game, 5-4. Below: Lester Patrick, already ten years into retirement, greets an old favorite and new Ranger coach Phil Watson prior to the 1955–56 season.

Harry Howell also recalled the Rangers' inadequate practice facility of the time, a tiny "puddle" of a rink called Iceland on the fifth floor of the Garden that served principally as a figure skating venue. "We called it the 'Tin Box,' and there was no way you could properly train a hockey team on that surface. It had aluminum boards, and the players, particularly Andy Bathgate, would love to boom slap shots into them just for the loud noises. Watson hated the noise, so we would just do it more," Howell said. "Hey, we were only practicing, right?"

Another way to get under Watson's skin was to talk about money. That would get his Gallic blood roiling. "I was always underpaid in New York," he fumed years later. "Mon Dieu, the publicity guy, 'Scoop,' was making more than me, and I had to share an office with him!" "Scoop," Watson's pet name for anyone in the newspaper game, was really Herb Goren, a keen hockey and baseball writer of his time and an innovative Rangers publicist from 1951 to 1964. It was Goren (the "Old Scout" to his readers in the *New York Sun*) who brought great PR to the Rangers, keeping the team in the news when its on-ice exploits did not shout for coverage.

The always-acrobatic Lorne "Gump" Worsley makes a sliding save to rob Toronto's Dave Keon of a goal at Maple Leaf Gardens during the 1961–62 season. Worsley needed no help from Rangers' player-coach Doug Harvey (2).

Brush-cut Worsley, who appeared on a trading card from the 1950s, below, was probably the most popular Ranger of his era. He was a three-time winner of the Frank Boucher Trophy presented by the Rangers Fan Club to the most popular Ranger on and off the ice.

Goren, in his first year as team publicist in 1951–52, had thousands of orchids delivered to the Garden for a "date night" promotion. The orchids arrived the night before the game, and logically enough, Goren had them stored in the huge fifth floor refrigerators of the Garden's concessions department. Unfortunately, the refrigerators were far better designed for chilling beer than for pampering delicate flora. The orchids didn't survive. The promotion did, and the wilted flowers were distributed. "They looked more like poppies, sick poppies at that, than they did like orchids," recalled historian Stan Fischler. "If ever anything could give orchids a bad name, that was it."

Watson finally departed the New York scene on November 12, 1959, ending an association with the Rangers that stretched all the way back to 1935–36. Not surprisingly, Murray "Muzz" Patrick, having succeeded Boucher in the GM's office, picked an "anti-Watson" as the team's ninth coach. He was Alfred George "Alf" Pike, a Ranger from 1939–40 through 1946–47. The mild-mannered Pike was a disaster, winning just 36 of 123 games over a season and a half and posting the worst winning percentage (.378) of any Rangers coach who worked more than 100 games.

Pike had inherited a pretty good group of players, but many said the coach simply lacked passion. In the words of one, "He couldn't fire up a furnace." Goalie Worsley was at his prime, night after night "going in the barrel," as he liked to describe his netminding position, and usually facing a barrage of enemy rubber. Worsley was also the team's resident wit and number-one quipster. Asked which NHL team gave him the most trouble, Gump replied without missing a beat, "The Rangers."

Pike had a very capable arsenal with Howell, Fontinato, and Bill Gadsby on defense, and a top line that featured superstar Andy Bathgate at right wing with Larry Popein at center and Dean Prentice on left wing. Forwards Red Sullivan, Andy Hebenton, and Camille Henry were popular and talented.

Hebenton never missed a game, playing in 560 consecutive games over eight seasons and adding 22 more in the playoffs. The 582-game streak stands as the Rangers' all-time record, surpassing by 19 the oft-chronicled streak of original Ranger Murray Murdoch. "I was a plugger," recalled

Long-time defensive partners Lou Fontinato (left) and Harry Howell (center) team with Worsley to repel an enemy attack. Fontinato and Howell were members of the so-called "Guelph Gang," along with Andy Bathgate, Dean Prentice, Aldo Guidolin, and Ron Murphy, who arrived to lead the Rangers in the mid-1950s. They had all played junior hockey for the Guelph Biltmore Mad Hatters of the Ontario Hockey Association.

In January of 1967, right wing Rod Gilbert became the second Ranger (Andy Bathgate was the first) to appear on the cover of *Sports Illustrated.* It was Bathgate who Gilbert also succeeded as the team's all-time leading goal scorer with goal number 273 early in the 1973–74 season.

Hebenton, who won the Lady Byng Trophy in 1957. "I just came to work every day and did my job, and was fortunate to spend so much of my career with the Rangers." Continuing his career, first with the Boston Bruins and later with the Victoria Cougars and the Portland Buckaroos of the Western League, Hebenton eventually played 1,062 consecutive games as a pro without a miss. It was the death of his father that finally snapped the streak on October 18, 1967.

By 1960, it was obvious that things were not improving, so General Manager Patrick decided on three bombshell trades that were especially painful for the fans. Defenseman Louie Fontinato, the people's choice, was the first to depart, even up, for the great Doug Harvey of Montreal on June 13, 1961. Harvey became the Rangers' player-coach, promptly won the Norris Trophy (the first player ever to do so back to back with different teams), and propelled the Rangers into the 1962 playoffs. Less than two years later, Fontinato would suffer a career-ending broken neck in a game against the Rangers at the Montreal Forum on March 9, 1963.

Goalie Worsley was the next to depart, packaged with teammates Dave Balon, Leon Rochefort, and then–minor leaguer Len Ronson, and shipped to Montreal in return for the great Jacques Plante, Don Marshall, and Phil Goyette on June 4, 1963. Worsley would win four Stanley Cups and two Vezina Trophies for the Canadiens, while Plante never really found his mark in New York.

On February 22, 1964, it was Andy Bathgate's turn. Patrick dealt his popular captain and ace right wing to the Toronto Maple Leafs with Don McKenney in exchange for five players: Dick Duff, Bob Nevin, Rod Seiling, Arnie Brown, and then–minor leaguer Bill Collins. Bathgate was an immediate success in Toronto, winning the Stanley Cup just two months after the deal.

In retrospect, however, the Bathgate trade was a long-term winner for the Rangers. Historically, it was even more important, marking the passing of the torch from old to new, bridging the gap from the Rangers of the 1940s and 1950s, and planting the seeds for a team that would soon come of age in the 1970s.

One of the seeds could trace his roots to the dates of April 1 and April 2, 1962. Down two games to none in a semifinal playoff series with the Toronto Maple Leafs, the Rangers reached into their future and summoned a twenty-one-year-old right wing from their Guelph junior team to fill in for the injured Ken Schinkel. He wore number 14, twice the number he would become famous for. His name was Rod Gilbert. If he was nervous—and "believe me I was," Gilbert recalled—it hardly showed. He played with a pair of veterans, Dave Balon at center and Johnny Wilson on the left side, and posted an assist in his first game, a 5-4 Rangers win.

Two nights later, Gilbert was afire—two goals in the first period and an assist in the third as the Rangers evened the series at two games apiece. The Garden was raucous in support of the new "cover boy." More important, the evening launched a Hall of Fame career and records that still stand today, as Gilbert began a lifelong love affair with New York City.

Andy Hebenton (left) who played 1,062 straight professional hockey games without a miss, was honored during the 1962-63 season for playing his five hundredth straight game as a Ranger. Making the presentation is Johnny Wilson, then recently retired but who had once played 580 straight NHL games. The two were teammates on the Rangers from 1960 to 1962.

Including twenty-two playoff games, Hebenton played 582 straight games for the Rangers, nineteen more than Murray Murdoch, the team's first "Iron Man."

Andy Bathgate, the Rangers' first superstar in more than a decade, was "Mr. Hockey" in New York for 719 games from 1952-53 to 1963-64. The handsome right wing liked to emulate Bryan Hextall, the star right wing from an earlier era.

In turn, Bathgate himself was emulated by his successor, another star right winger, Rod Gilbert. Bathgate won the Hart Trophy as NHL MVP in 1959, and joined Hextall in the Hockey Hall of Fame in 1978. Gilbert would follow with election to the Hall of Fame in 1982.

Andy Bathgate

There was a certain elegance that permeated Andy Bathgate's career. Al Laney, the eloquent sportswriter for the old *New York Herald Tribune*, may have said it best: "All of the superstars are at once individuals and great team players," Laney wrote. "And what they have in common is an uncommon skill and flair. They alone try the new, the unexpected. Andy Bathgate has this ability to an unusual degree."

Quite simply, Andy Bathgate *was* the New York Rangers during his heyday, from the mid-1950s to the early 1960s. A strapping right wing, Bathgate was the Rangers' first superstar since before World War II, a hero to Rangers fans in an era that produced some highs, some lows, but no overwhelming success.

Bathgate had taken part in a neck-and-neck scoring duel with Chicago's great Bobby Hull that culminated in a classic Garden game on the final night of the 1961–62 season. His dramatic 1962 penalty shot against the Detroit Red Wings had clinched a playoff berth and shaken Madison Square Garden with cheers. He was the first New York Ranger to appear on a *Sports Illustrated* cover. And he sported an incredible fighting ability that, though rarely used, became etched in fans' collective memory. When he was traded to the Toronto Maple Leafs on February 22, 1964, it was an unbelievable blow to those same adoring fans.

But it was the Bathgate penalty shot that has remained the most searing memory. The erudite Kenneth Rudeen, writing in *Sports Illustrated*, captured the scene:

"To the fascinated crowd filling New York's Madison Square Garden, it was like watching the clash of the cobra and the mongoose. The broad expanse of white

ice was empty except for the two opposing players. The crowd hushed. The referee blew his whistle. Gracefully, lazily, the New York Rangers ace shooter, Andy Bathgate, laid his stick alongside the puck at the first blue line and moved goalward at half throttle. Detroit's goalie, Hank Bassen, cruised out of his cage, cautious and hesitant. Bathgate feinted to the south. Bassen responded. Then, quick as a mongoose and smooth as the ice itself, Bathgate wheeled north, flicked a backhand, and the puck was in the net. The Garden's grimy old steelwork rang with a million decibel shout of jubilation, for in this one rare penalty shot New York Rangers fans not only saw a victory assured but a whole season redeemed."

Overlooked in the drama of the moment was the fact that referee Eddie Powers had awarded the penalty shot to the wrong man. According to league rules, Dean Prentice, Bathgate's left winger, should have taken the shot. Forgotten completely was the fact that Gordie Howe, Detroit's nonpareil right wing, had scored his five hundredth NHL goal earlier in the game.

Bathgate's active career covered more than twenty seasons, nine of them in New York, where, after a painfully slow start, he became one of the greatest Rangers of all time. There were the Cooks and Boucher before him, Rod Gilbert, Brad Park, Eddie Giacomin, Mike Richter, Brian Leetch, Adam Graves, Wayne Gretzky, and Mark Messier after him, but from the mid-1950s to 1964, there was only one superstar of New York hockey, number 9, Andy Bathgate.

With a little help from his center Dave Creighton (center), Andy Bathgate (right) controls the puck behind the goal at Maple Leaf Gardens in Toronto. The Maple Leaf goalie is Ed Chadwick. Bathgate's trade to Toronto on February 22, 1964, was a shocker, but the Maple Leafs won the Stanley Cup that season, the only Cup of Bathgate's career.

With astounding feats, star-quality players, and record-breaking triumphs, the Rangers of the mid-1960s through the mid-1970s had it all—except a Stanley Cup Trophy.

1965

May 18—The Rangers obtained minor league goaltender Eddie Giacomin in trade from Providence of the AHL in exchange for Marcel Paille, Aldo Guidolin, Sandy McGregor, and Jim Mikol.

1968

Feb. 11—In the final hockey game played at the old Madison Square Garden in New York, the Rangers tied 3-3 with Detroit. Jean Ratelle scored the final goal in the old Garden.

1970

Feb. 1—Terry Sawchuk recorded his 447th (and final) victory, and 103rd career shutout when New York defeated Pittsburgh, 6-0. Sawchuk's 447 wins and 103 career shutouts became the most in NHL history.

Apr. 5—The Rangers routed the Detroit Red Wings, 9-5, at Madison Square Garden and made the playoffs on the final night of the season as the Montreal Canadiens lost to the Blackhawks in Chicago, 10-2. It was the first season to be decided on total goals rather than points.

1972

Mar. 5—Brad Park became the third defenseman in NHL history to score twenty goals in a season when he picked up a goal in a 6-1 New York win over the Vancouver Canucks, at Madison Square Garden. Park joined Flash Hollett and Bobby Orr as the NHL's twenty-goal defensemen.

Gilbert, Hadfield, and Ratelle

Mar. 8—Rod Gilbert scored his fortieth goal of the season, to make the Rangers trio of Gilbert, Vic Hadfield, and Jean Ratelle, above, the first line in NHL history with three forty-goal scorers. It came in a 3-3 New York tie against the visiting Chicago Blackhawks.

We Did It All Except Win

By October 1964, the decision had been made. The Rangers needed a makeover, a knockdown, a total redo. No more cosmetic surgery or patch jobs; this was to be the real thing. To orchestrate this Herculean task, the team turned to Emile Francis, a flinty, combative, diminutive ex-goalkeeper who had bounced around hockey's high minors for many years, played a handful of games for the Rangers, and even backed up Chuck Rayner in the 1950 finals, although he never dressed for a game.

There was only one problem: Francis wasn't sure he wanted the job of general manager. This was for a number of reasons, not the least of which was his loyalty to Muzz Patrick, who had brought him to New York as his assistant just a year earlier. Said Francis: "I told [team president Bill] Jennings that I wasn't comfortable with the circumstances, and he said, 'Why don't you talk to Muzz about it?' So I did."

Muzz nearly exploded when Francis told him of the offer, but not because he was about to be fired. "Are you crazy?" Muzz ranted. "If you don't take that job, I'll break your neck. Why do you think I brought you here? They'll find something else for me. I've got a long-term contract."

With that personal issue resolved, Francis now had the leverage to address three other things that were bothering him. Recalled Francis, "I said 'OK, I'll take the job, but only if I get a guarantee that we will fix three things immediately.'" First and foremost, Francis wanted the "circus problem" corrected. Second, he wanted a real practice facility for the team. And third, he wanted to spend "a lot of money" on scouting and building a farm system.

"The circus thing was absolutely critical," Francis recalls. "I insisted that if we made the playoffs we would play all the home games we were entitled to at the Garden. Otherwise, it wasn't fair to the players, to the management, and most importantly to the fans. They agreed. The practice rink was a joke. There was no way a big league team could practice properly in that facility. They agreed again. The farm system overhaul was really a no-brainer. That was just money. So, I took the job."

Francis certainly knew firsthand just how big a job he had accepted. But that point was hammered home quite forcefully at the end of his first season, 1964–65. It was customary at the time for big league teams to ship their used uniforms to their junior teams to use in practice. So, the Rangers sent their 1965 uniforms to their junior A development club, the Kitchener Rangers in Kitchener, Ontario. There was only one problem: almost all the kids (hockey players in their late teens) in Kitchener were too big for the Rangers' uniforms.

Emile Francis was always a commanding and crafty presence behind the Rangers' bench. "Not winning a Stanley Cup in New York is probably my biggest disappointment," he recalled. "The fans were so great, I really felt for them. We were right there, but it didn't happen. Hey, it's a slippery game."

"That told me one thing: we just had to get bigger," Francis said. "I mean, I knew that already, but the uniform thing kind of emphasized the obvious."

In addition to size, Francis wanted youth and depth as he began to rebuild the Rangers. "That and a great goalkeeper. I believed in building a hockey club from the goal out, so I had to get a good goalie." A couple of scouting trips to the American Hockey League convinced Francis that Eddie Giacomin of the Providence Reds was his man, his goalie of the future.

Francis had seen Giacomin play maybe a dozen times, and his American League scout, Johnny Gagnon, who lived in Warwick, Rhode Island, saw all of the Reds' home games. There was only one problem: Giacomin wasn't invisible. Other teams, particularly the Detroit Red Wings, were also courting the Reds and their owner, Lou Pieri.

Francis finally put together a package of four players worth approximately $100,000, and Pieri accepted the deal. "Believe it or not, the deal really went through because of an eight-by-ten, black-and-white publicity picture," Francis recalled. "Pieri believed that good-looking, helmetless players sold tickets. I brought four pictures to his office early one morning and slid them across his desk, one by one." Goalie Marcel Paille, right wing Sandy McGregor, and defenseman Aldo Guidolin were in the deal all along. "At the end of our chat, I slid a picture of Jim Mikol [a left winger] in front of Pieri. Mikol was a pretty good-looking guy. Pieri smiled, and I had a goalkeeper." The date was May 18, 1965.

At 5' 6" and 145 pounds, Emile Francis was too small to be a boxer, but he certainly was a fighter. He stuck to his word, stuck by his players, and quickly built the team into a contender.

Francis worked extremely hard with Giacomin in practice, especially when the twenty-six-year-old netminder struggled in his first season, 1965–66, the team's fortieth anniversary. "He had a couple of flaws, like not keeping his stick on the ice and not hugging the posts tight," Francis remembered, "but they were easily corrected. And he used his leg pads too much, giving rebounds. He had to learn to use his catching hand more. He was a great student though, very coachable."

Still, the Rangers were hardly remade just because they had a new goalie. On a couple of occasions in the old Garden, the fans threw garbage at their maskless netminder. Giacomin would stuff the trash in the back of the net and shoulder on. Francis liked that, telling Giacomin, "You're my goalie, and that's it! Throw the garbage back at them if you want."

Giacomin was an extremely strong skater, particularly in his early years. He often dashed to the corners to retrieve loose pucks, and occasionally even skated up to the blue line. The fans loved it. "Goalie a-Go-Go" and "Go-Go Eddie" were two nicknames the press pinned on him. Giacomin was also the focus of much of the Rangers' publicity efforts. He was the first—and the most prominent—of the "new look" Rangers, a look that was about to begin a quick climb up in the standings of the National Hockey League.

Giacomin had a series of backups in the early years, including Cesare Maniago, Don Simmons, and Terry Sawchuk. But by 1970, Francis had decided on a permanent backup, and he found him in his own organization: red-haired Gilles Villemure. Giacomin and Villemure virtually shared the Rangers net for the next five seasons, sharing the Vezina Trophy in 1970–71 and setting off a wild Garden celebration following the final game of the season, a 6-0 whitewash by Giacomin over the Detroit Red Wings on April 4, 1971.

When Terry Sawchuk reveled in a 6-0 whitewash of the Pittsburgh Penguins on February 1, 1970, some of his teammates teased that it might have been the old goaltender's last shutout. They were right. Less than four months later, Sawchuk was dead, the victim of what the police called "horseplay" during a scuffle with teammate and roommate Ron Stewart in the yard of their rented house.

The complete details were never fully explained. Whether the fight was fueled by alcohol, or whether it was over a woman or money, was immaterial. Sawchuk was gravely injured, probably when the two-hundred-pound Stewart landed heavily on his abdomen during the fray.

As Sawchuk recovered from a May 1 operation, he repeatedly exonerated Stewart for the accident. Initially the whole affair remained a secret. Sawchuk wanted to keep the news from his estranged wife and seven children back in Michigan. By the third week in May, too many people knew of the accident, and word got to the press, making for a big story in New York and Canada.

Suddenly, on May 27, Sawchuk took yet another turn for the worse and more surgery was performed. On Sunday, May 31, a blood clot to the lungs took the life of the great Sawchuk. He was forty.

Stewart faced criminal charges, and the Rangers hired an attorney to represent him. A grand jury eventually found no reason to bring charges and the case was closed.

"The whole Sawchuk affair was one of the toughest things I had ever faced in my whole life," recalled Emile Francis. "Terry was one of the greatest, maybe even the greatest. It was a tragedy that far transcended hockey."

SHER-WOOD
Cooper

Goaltender Ed Giacomin, still maskless during the 1966–67 season, makes a sliding save on Toronto Maple Leafs left wing John Brenneman (24), above. One of the most popular players in Rangers' history, Giacomin, also opposite, played 532 games as a Ranger, winning 266 of them and posting a team record forty-nine career shutouts. His number, 1, was eventually retired and hangs from the ceiling of Madison Square Garden.

Ed Giacomin's chest protector, circa 1970

Defenseman Brad Park (2), a great leader (and eventually captain) of the Rangers from 1968 to 1975, chases a loose puck along with Dennis Hull (10) of the Chicago Blackhawks. Goalie Ed Giacomin is behind them, along with defenseman Dale Rolfe (5) and Chicago's Jim Pappin (8). The referee is Art Skov.

Park would make the NHL's first All-Star Team three times and the second team twice. He was elected to the Hockey Hall of Fame in 1988.

Brad Park's skates, circa 1975

With his goalkeeping solidified, Francis set about building the defense. He had two solid, long-term youngsters in Rod Seiling and Arnie Brown from the Bathgate trade, plus homegrown Jim Neilson. The great Harry Howell was nearing the end of a career that would span a record 1,160 games in New York. Wayne Hillman was very capable for three-plus seasons, coming over from the Chicago Blackhawks in a painful trade for fan favorite Camille Henry. Francis also snared the great Tim Horton from the Toronto Maple Leafs for fifteen games in 1970 and a full season in 1970–71.

The team's defense would change forever with the 1968 arrival of the Rangers' top pick in the amateur draft, Brad Park, who was coming off a stellar junior career with the Toronto Marlboros. Park quickly became a star whose only real fault was a matter of timing. He happened to come along at the same time as Boston's wunderkind defenseman Bobby Orr. "Believe me, Brad Park could do just about everything Bobby Orr could do," Francis said, "but, come on, there's only one Bobby Orr, right?" In fact, for ten games in the 1975–76 season, Orr and Park, two of the greatest offensive defensemen in hockey history, played together as point men on the Boston power play. "That was a sight I will never forget," recalled longtime Bruins executive Nate Greenberg. "That was magic."

Park was the first Rangers defenseman to score a hat trick and the first defenseman to score twenty goals, notching twenty-four in 1971–72. He would go on to score ninety-five goals as a Ranger, but it is the very first one that he remembers best. It was on February 23, 1969, the final goal of a 9-0 rout at the Garden against the Boston Bruins. "I took a slap shot, leaped into the air, and fell flat on my face," Park remembered. "I never saw the puck go in. It was simple: I forgot to land." How much did Park mean to the Rangers of the early 1970s? *Sport* magazine put it this way in 1973: "When Brad Park gets hurt, every Ranger feels the pain."

The real strength of the Rangers as they began to approach championship caliber was the balance of the team's forward lines. Center Jean Ratelle and right wing Rod Gilbert were the team's top offensive threats, among the best in the league at the time. They were playing with little left winger Camille Henry. Francis recalled a particular game in Toronto when the Maple Leafs' Eddie Shack flattened all three of the Rangers on the same rush. "The three of them were all laying on the ice, and Shack had taken control of the game. That night, on the plane home, I decided to put Vic Hadfield with Ratelle and Gilbert. It was one of the best decisions I ever made."

The three of them, Hadfield-Ratelle-Gilbert, were as diverse as their numbers (11-19-7): Gilbert was the suave Manhattan sophisticate; Ratelle, the modest homebody; and Hadfield, the merry and carefree prankster. On the ice, they blended perfectly. Ratelle was the quarterback of the line, making elegant plays and passes to both of his linemates. The Gallic Gilbert was a pure goal scorer. Hadfield was initially a digger, a cornerman, but like Gilbert, he also had a great slap shot. Despite two badly injured thumbs, Hadfield became the first Ranger to score fifty goals in a season, scoring twice

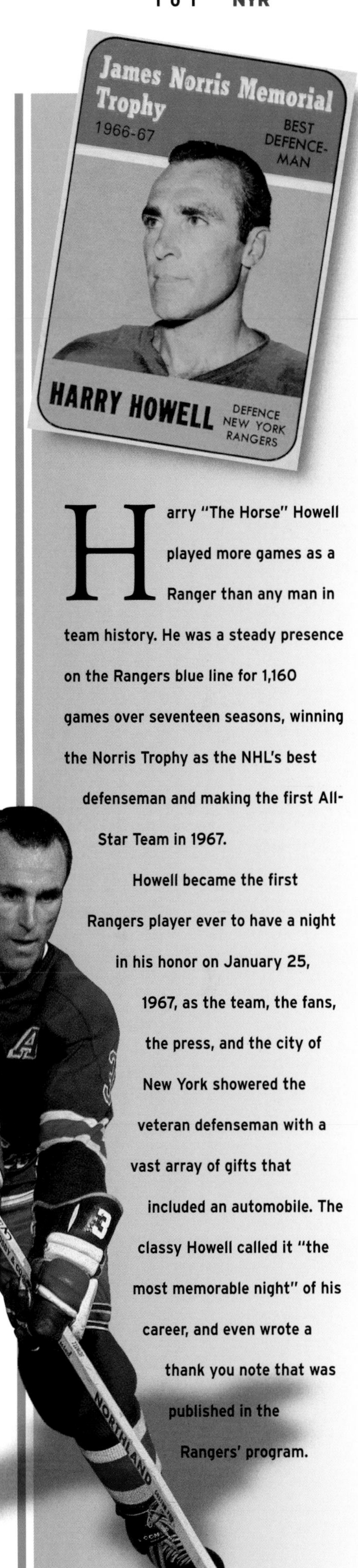

Harry "The Horse" Howell played more games as a Ranger than any man in team history. He was a steady presence on the Rangers blue line for 1,160 games over seventeen seasons, winning the Norris Trophy as the NHL's best defenseman and making the first All-Star Team in 1967.

Howell became the first Rangers player ever to have a night in his honor on January 25, 1967, as the team, the fans, the press, and the city of New York showered the veteran defenseman with a vast array of gifts that included an automobile. The classy Howell called it "the most memorable night" of his career, and even wrote a thank you note that was published in the Rangers' program.

NORTHLAND

Vic Hadfield, above, who played more games at left wing (839) than anyone else in Rangers history, controls the puck despite the efforts of Montreal Canadiens Dick Duff (left) and Jimmy Roberts (center). Hadfield became the first Ranger ever to register fifty goals in one season, a mark that has since been eclipsed by Adam Graves.

Rangers defenseman Arnie Brown, opposite, had the unenviable task of trying to contain Boston's superstar defenseman Bobby Orr behind the net at Boston Garden. Orr's heroics, particularly in game six of the 1972 Stanley Cup finals, deprived the Rangers of a great chance to win it all.

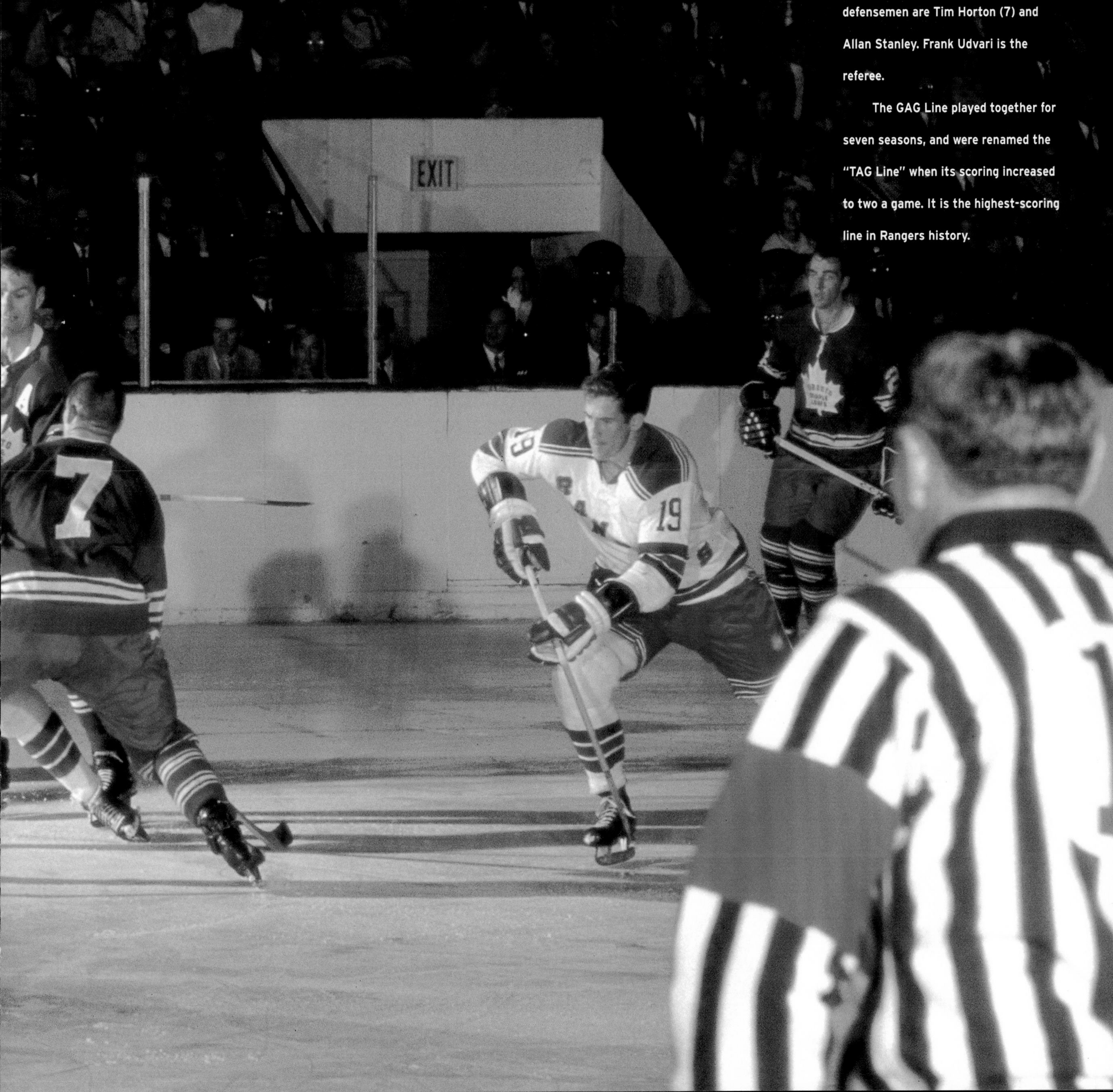

defensemen are Tim Horton (7) and Allan Stanley. Frank Udvari is the referee.

The GAG Line played together for seven seasons, and were renamed the "TAG Line" when its scoring increased to two a game. It is the highest-scoring line in Rangers history.

against Montreal's Denis DeJordy in the final game of the 1971–72 season. Twenty-two years later, in 1994, Hadfield was among the first to congratulate Adam Graves when he became the second Ranger to hit the fifty-goal plateau.

Hadfield, Ratelle, and Gilbert were called the "GAG Line," the acronym for "goal a game." The moniker owed its birth to Arthur Friedman, the team's longtime and highly innovative statistician, who habitually tabbed Rangers and visiting players alike with catchy nicknames. "Milton Gross [columnist for the *New York Post*] had written a piece on the line for the next day's paper. He called me at about 1 P.M. and said 'I need a nickname for the line by two,'" recalled Friedman. "I thought about it for awhile, and called him back with 'GAG Line' because they were scoring in every game." When the line continued to score at a phenomenal pace, Friedman changed its name to the "TAG Line" for "two a game." It was Friedman, too, who named the team's second line the "Bulldog Line" after Francis remarked one night that Dave Balon, Walter Tkaczuk, and Billy Fairbairn played like "bulldogs out there." In November 1971, when Balon was traded to Vancouver, Steve Vickers replaced him at left wing on the Bulldog Line. Known for their ferocious checking and penalty killing, two of the "bulldogs" (Tkaczuk and Fairbairn) once kept control of the puck for one minute and fifty seconds of a two-minute penalty in a game against the Los Angeles Kings.

"It was really depth and versatility that made those teams so great," Francis recalled. "We had scoring with the Ratelle line, checking with the Tkaczuk line, and a third line called the 'Holding Line' that did a little of everything." That line had Peter Stemkowski at center with Ted Irvine on left wing and Bruce MacGregor on right wing. It was Stemkowski who pounded the puck past goalie Tony Esposito to end a triple overtime playoff classic at the Garden against the Chicago Blackhawks on April 29, 1971, a game that ranks as one of the most dramatic in team history.

Despite the depth, despite the talent, and despite the versatility, the Rangers still came up short in the playoffs year after year. From 1967 to 1971, the Blueshirts were ousted in the opening round four times and the second round once. The following season the team was at its best, downing the Montreal Canadiens four games to two in round one, and flattening the

Jean Ratelle's 1972 Team Canada gloves

Jean Ratelle, the highest-scoring center in Rangers history, scored 817 points in 862 games. Ratelle won the NHL's Lady Byng Trophy for clean, effective play in 1971–72. He also scored the last goal in Madison Square Garden number three on February 11, 1968.

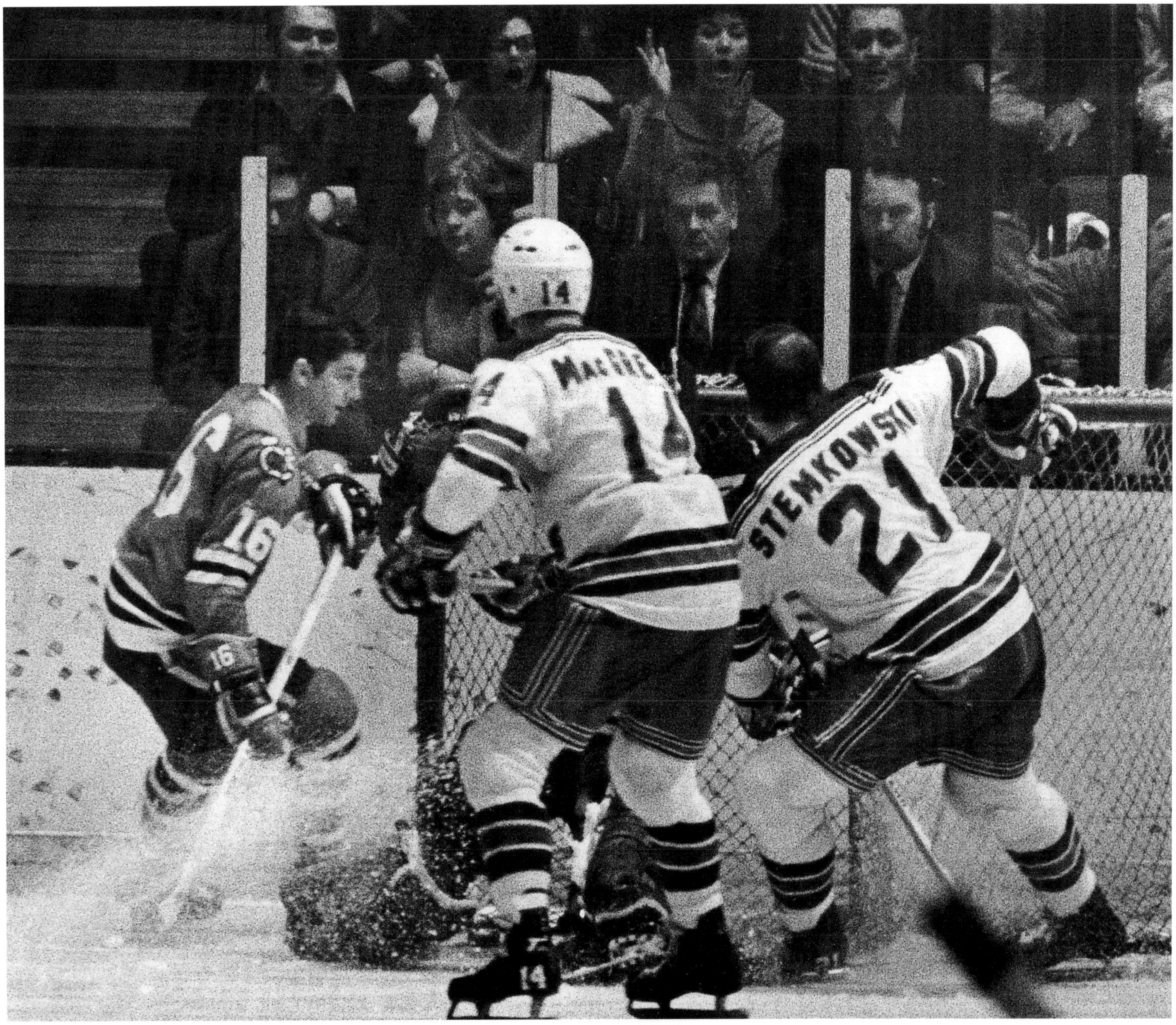

Peter Stemkowski (21) jams the puck past Chicago Blackhawks goaltender Tony Esposito for one of the most important goals in Rangers history on April 29, 1971. The goal came at 1:29 of the third overtime period, the longest overtime victory by a Rangers team on home ice. It capped a 3-2 triumph that deadlocked the series with the Blackhawks at three games apiece, and was assisted by right wing Bruce MacGregor (14). Stemkowski proudly displayed the game-ending puck in the Rangers' dressing room, right.

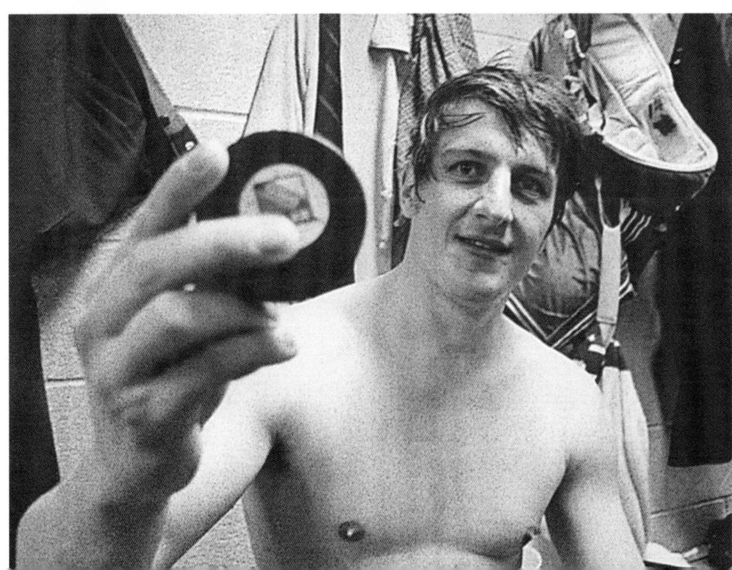

Blackhawks four games to none in the second round. It was on to Boston for the finals—the Bruins of Esposito, Orr, and Cheevers versus the Rangers of Gilbert, Park, and Giacomin.

Cruising along with forty-six goals and 109 points a month before the end of the season, Ratelle broke his ankle with seventeen regular season games still left to go. The team pushed Ratelle's recovery hard and he managed to return for the six final games. It was all for naught, however, as Orr almost single-handedly took control and won the series, four games to two. "With Jean we might have beaten them, but without him, Orr just proved to be too much," Francis recalled. "It was a shame. We were right there."

Two years later, in 1973–74, the Rangers faced the Philadelphia Flyers in the second round of the playoffs. Flyers tough guy Dave Schultz simply hammered the stuffing out of defenseman Dale Rolfe early in game seven and no one came to Rolfe's aid, which shocked Francis to no end. The Flyers won the game and the series. "That's when I really knew the end had come for that group," Francis remembered. "We did it all except win it all."

Less than a month after the Flyers debacle, Hadfield was exiled to Pittsburgh in exchange for defenseman Nick Beverley. The start of the 1975–76 season saw Giacomin and Villemure off within days of each other—Giacomin on Halloween night to Detroit on waivers, and Villemure to Chicago in exchange for defenseman Doug Jarrett. Giacomin returned dramatically as a Red Wing three days later in as emotional a game that was ever played at the Garden. He won the game, 6-4, but the story was the fans and their reaction. The fans cheered Eddie's every move, and rooted openly against the home team. "I don't think I had ever seen anything like that," Francis recalled. "That's how much Eddie meant to the fans. Hey, it wasn't easy for me either. Trading Eddie Giacomin was one of the toughest things I'd ever had to do in my career."

Yet the Giacomin trade was merely a popgun compared to the howitzer Francis had up his sleeve. He fired it on November 7, 1975, during the team's fiftieth anniversary season. "The Trade," as it became known, was a tremendous shocker, a broadside that shook the team to its roots. And that's what it was intended to do, provide a collective wake-up call (a bomb would be more like it) to a team that, in Francis's words, "had run out of chances to win." All of hockey was shocked by the move that brought superstar center Phil Esposito and defenseman Carol Vadnais to New York from Boston in exchange for stars Brad Park and Jean Ratelle and minor league defenseman Joe Zanussi. Zanussi called himself "the fifth wheel" in one of the biggest trades in hockey history.

No one was more shocked by the trade than Esposito himself, who was with the Bruins in Vancouver at the time. "At first I thought it was a joke," Esposito recalled. "I mean, we were always playing gags on each

A teary Ed Giacomin, clad in the jersey of the Detroit Red Wings after eleven seasons in Rangers togs, buries his face to hide his emotions prior to the Rangers-Red Wings game of November 2, 1975, opposite. The fans cheered Eddie throughout the warm-up and drowned out the national anthem with cheers of "ED-DEE . . . ED-DEE . . . ED-DEE." There were banners galore saluting Giacomin's popularity.

Every so often, Giacomin would give small waves of acknowledgement to the fans. It was his night from beginning to end, in effect a Red Wings home game at Madison Square Garden. The Red Wings responded with a 6-4 victory.

When Phil Esposito became a Ranger on November 7, 1975, he was the second-highest scorer in National Hockey League history. The blockbuster trade was made less than a month into the team's fiftieth anniversary season.

With Rod Gilbert still wearing number 7 on the Rangers, Esposito wore number 5 for a handful of games, then number 12 before finally switching to number 77, starting a trend toward the higher, twin digit numbers that are now more than commonplace.

other. But when I realized it was true, I felt like I had been shot." No doubt, Park and Ratelle felt the same way. Park's part in the deal was very strange, as he had been so bitterly critical of the Bruins in his stinging autobiography *Play the Man*, which had been published a few years earlier.

In Boston, it was like the impossible had happened. The great Esposito had been traded—and to the Rangers, no less! "Nobody liked it, nobody," recalled Nate Greenberg of the Bruins. "Harry [Sinden] even received some death threats. That's how intense it was." None of the death threats came from Esposito's longtime linemate and pal Wayne Cashman, but the volcanic Cashman proved to be as eruptive off the ice as he was on, hurtling a television set out the window of the Westin Bayshore Hotel when he heard about Esposito's trade. The set crashed into a parking lot. Cashman also ordered one hundred sandwiches from room service, just to stick the Bruins with the tab.

Esposito, ever the consummate hockey player (a "dog of war" they called him in Boston) flew immediately to Oakland, where the Rangers were to play the California Seals that night. He looked awfully uncomfortable in sweater number 5, but promptly scored two goals and an assist in a 7-5 Rangers loss.

Vadnais, as unflappable as his ever-present cigar, considered his options for a few days since he had a "no trade" clause in his Boston contract, which Francis didn't find out about until fifteen minutes before the trade was to be announced. Francis and Boston GM Harry Sinden went ahead with the deal anyway, and Vadnais got $100,000 from the Bruins to waive the "no trade" provision. Vadnais eventually got number 5, and Esposito took number 12 for a couple of games—and still looked uncomfortable. He eventually started the twin digit craze by donning number 77. Esposito was also named the Rangers' sixteenth team captain, succeeding Park and bypassing the team's all-time leading scorer, Rod Gilbert.

Two months later (sixty-one days to be exact), Francis would be replaced as only the fourth general manager in Rangers history, a position he had held for eleven and a half seasons. In the words of folk great Bob Dylan, "the times, they were a-changin'." The team that almost did but didn't was no longer.

Esposito was immediately named the Rangers' sixteenth captain, replacing Brad Park, one of the men for whom he was traded. Esposito was a terrific leader, vocal in the dressing room, and one of the NHL's best at taking face-offs.

Esposito's first regular linemates with his new team were right wing Ken Hodge (left) and left wing Pat Hickey (right). The three sported newly designed uniforms, commissioned by general manager John Ferguson for the 1976–77 season.

Bernie Geoffrion, 1966–67

Brian Leetch, 1997–98

Brad Park, 1974–75

Mike Richter, 1993–94

Phil Esposito, 1976–77

Jean Ratelle, circa 1975

Buddy O'Connor, circa 1947

Jersey emblem, 1976–77

Stanley Cup finals patch, 1993–94

Terry Sawchuk, 1969–70

Fiftieth anniversary patch, 1975–76

Twenty-fifth anniversary patch, 1950–51

The 75th Anniversary Team

selected by John Davidson

Not many teams in any sport can boast the level of tradition, popularity, and quality that the New York Rangers have maintained for three-quarters of a century. Seventy-five years of players, some eight hundred in all, have set skate to Madison Square Garden ice, making a formidable field from which to choose "the greatest."

So when I was asked to select the 75th Anniversary Team, it was not without reservation that I accepted the challenge. Believe me, this was a dominating task, one that I agonized over.

I have come up with six names, six of the greatest names in the history of the New York Rangers, players who brought great fame and great honor to one of the proudest franchises in all of sports. Like most everything in sports, this team will probably raise a few eyebrows and even spawn a few heated debates. But, hey, a little controversy never hurt anyone.

Selecting the goaltender, Mike Richter, was probably the toughest choice since the Rangers have a long tradition of exceptionally strong goalkeeping. John Vanbiesbrouck, Eddie Giacomin, Gump Worsley, Chuck Rayner, and Davey Kerr all deserve to be mentioned. But in the end, I took Richter, the guy who was the last line of defense on the team that won the Stanley Cup in 1994.

Choosing the defensemen—Brian Leetch and Brad Park—was a little easier. The two are very much alike, free-skating defensemen, "quarterbacks" on the power play, and both with a wicked slap shot. And they both served as captain of the Rangers. Others who got close attention were Harry Howell, Art Coulter, and the team's first two star defenders, Ching Johnson and Taffy Abel.

At left wing, I picked Vic Hadfield, but Adam Graves could easily have been there, along with Steve Vickers, Lynn Patrick, and Bun Cook.

I chose Mark Messier as the center, despite his relative lack of longevity with the Rangers. Mark was the heart and soul of the 1994 team, and I hope fans of other great Rangers centers like Wayne Gretzky, Jean Ratelle, Neil Colville, and Frank Boucher will understand my selection.

Rod Gilbert, the Rangers' all-time leading scorer, is my right wing choice, but Andy Bathgate, Alex Shibicky, and the Rangers' first captain, Bill Cook, all received consideration.

Once again, let me say that this was not an easy job. But I was honored to do it. Being a part of something momentous like a seventy-fifth anniversary celebration gives me a special feeling, a feeling of history, really.

LXXV
75
1926
2001
NEW YORK
RANGERS

Mike Richter's mask, 2000

Eddie Giacomin's mask, circa 1971

Gilles Gratton's mask, circa 1976

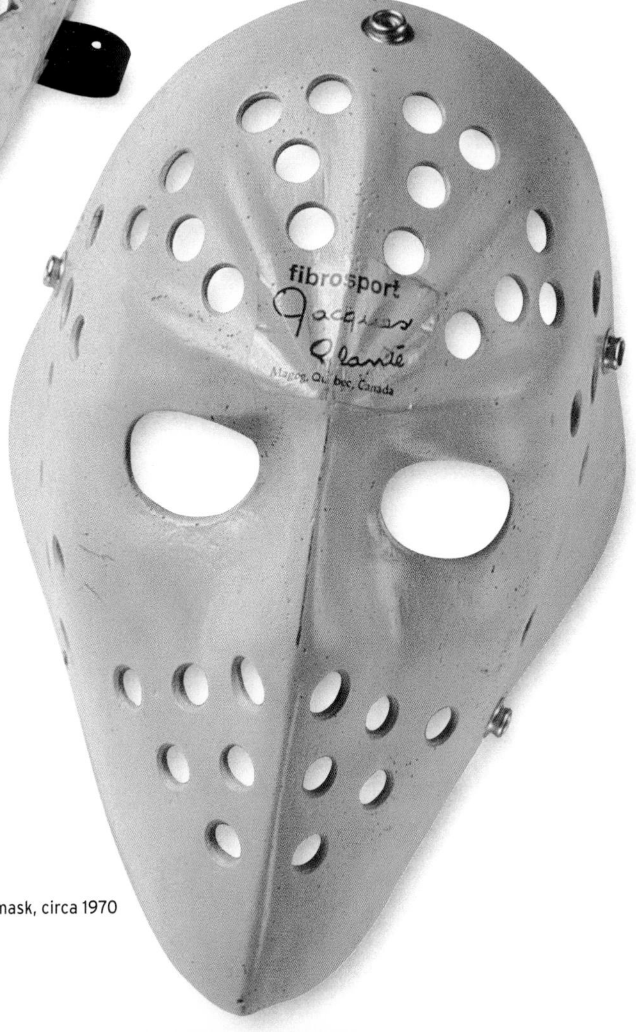

Jacques Plante's mask, circa 1970

Goaltender mask, circa 1972

Goaltender mask, circa 1970

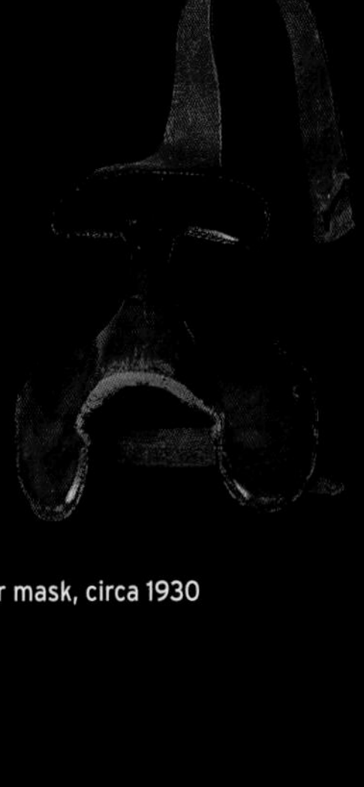

Goaltender mask, circa 1930

The 1980s were filled with highs and lows for the New York Rangers: No major victories were racked up, but some individuals who would be key to later successes came on board.

1978

June 5— Rangers signed free agents Ulf Nilsson and Anders Hedberg. The two Swedish stars had been playing with Winnipeg in the WHA.

1979

Oct. 21—Phil Esposito scored a power play goal for his fifteen-hundredth NHL point, in a 6-3 Rangers win over Pittsburgh. Esposito became just the second player in NHL history to reach that milestone.

1983

Nov. 5—Rangers and Nordiques set an NHL record for the fastest two goals at the start of a period by two teams (fourteen seconds). Andre Savard scored for Quebec eight seconds into the third and Pierre Larouche replied for the Rangers at fourteen seconds into the period. New York tied 4-4 in Quebec City.

1986

July 14—Phil Esposito was named vice president and general manager of the Rangers, replacing Craig Patrick.

1989

Mar. 15—Rangers honored former goaltender Ed Giacomin by retiring his jersey, number 1. Giacomin joined Rod Gilbert (number 7) as the only two Ranger players to have had their numbers retired.

Mar. 29—Brian Leetch set an NHL record for most goals by a rookie defenseman, when he scored his twenty-third of the season (breaking the mark of twenty-two set by Barry Beck in 1977-78), in a 4-3 New York loss at Detroit.

July 17—Rangers hired Neil Smith as their new general manager, replacing Phil Esposito, who had been fired two months earlier.

Oct. 6—Roger Neilson became the first man in history to coach five different NHL teams, when he led New York to a 4-1 win over the Jets, in Winnipeg, in his first game as head coach of the Rangers.

A Mixed Bag

Could they have been much more different, much more unalike? Probably yes, but not by a lot. For thirteen seasons, from 1976 through 1989, the New York Rangers were run by four people about as diverse from each other as any four people could be: John Bowie Ferguson, Frederick Alexander Shero, Craig Patrick, and Philip Anthony Esposito. Ferguson was the first to arrive, on January 7, 1976, replacing Emile Francis in the general manager's chair and needing a major adjustment to his feelings about New York if he was going to succeed.

"For years I had hated the Rangers," Ferguson confessed in his autobiography, *Thunder and Lightning*. "I had a lot of fights with them and had hounded Rod Gilbert as a player. Basically, I was Public Enemy Number One at Madison Square Garden. But I had been out of hockey long enough to realize that I could get as used to the Broadway Blueshirts as I had been accustomed to the *bleu, blanc, et rouge* of the Montreal Canadiens. Besides, Madison Square Garden checks don't bounce."

Ferguson, happy-go-lucky but extremely strong-willed, arrived raring to go, with a positive can-do attitude that was somewhat infectious. Francis had only the previous August offered Ferguson the coaching part of the job, but "Fergy" held out for the manager's portfolio, too, and he got it. Francis stayed on for a time as a vice president, but that was really just a holding pattern until he landed another general manager's job. Ever the consummate professional, Francis showed up for work every day, even though he had little meaningful to do, and he even started going to lunch, something he rarely did during the course of his regular twelve- to fourteen-hour days. He was clearly the odd man out in the executive turmoil that was roiling Madison Square Garden.

One event that preceded Francis's demotion was a brush with the team's top executive. Alan N. Cohen, who became president and chief executive officer of the Madison Square Garden Corporation in 1974, quickly gained fame in the media and infamy among fandom when he stated publicly that he would rather make a profit than win the Stanley Cup. That remark, which made the "Quotation of the Day" in the *New York Times* and earned Cohen the nickname "Bottom Line," particularly irked the feisty Francis. The two inevitably clashed and, much as Connie Smythe had lost out to Tex Rickard fifty years earlier, Francis would do the same.

Ferguson's first task was an unpleasant one. He had to fire Ron Stewart as coach. He did it on his very first day on the job, delivering the news at the team's practice facility in Long Beach, New York. "Stewie is a good guy, I hate doing this,"

Rookie right wing Rick Middleton, above, was one happy New York Ranger after scoring four goals in a 10-0 Garden rout of the California Seals on November 17, 1974. Middleton would eventually be traded, even up, for another right wing, Ken Hodge, right, of the Boston Bruins on May 26, 1976.

The Middleton-for-Hodge swap became one of the most lopsided trades in Rangers history, prompting then–general manager John Ferguson to lament years later, "Why, oh why, did I ever trade Rick Middleton?" Hodge continued the craze of twin digit uniform numbers, donning number 88.

Ferguson moaned in the limousine taking him to Long Beach. "But that's the business. You gotta do what you gotta do." He did it, and put himself behind the bench. It didn't help. Ferguson went 14-22-5 in forty-one games. Stewart was 15-20-4 in thirty-nine games.

Not surprisingly, one of Ferguson's first moves to improve the Rangers was to get some "toughness," the quality he'd been best known for as a player in Montreal. The new GM was visibly shocked by the Rangers high-priced contracts and the laissez-faire coaching style of Stewart. "We've got some guys getting paid like they are the second coming of Jean Beliveau," he said. "One guy has twenty-five bonus clauses in his contract. Can you believe that?"

The move for "toughness" sent Ferguson in pursuit of Nick Fotiu, who had played for the New England Whalers of the World Hockey Association (WHA) but was now toiling with the Cape Cod Codders of the North American Hockey League. Many thought that Ferguson signed Fotiu, a native New Yorker, because Nick reminded him of himself. This was true. Born on Staten Island, Fotiu first skated on the local municipal rink and didn't play organized hockey until he was fifteen. Like Ferguson, Fotiu was a left wing with a pair of ham-sized fists that almost always found their mark.

Fotiu arrived at Rangers rookie camp in Pointe-Claire, Quebec, in 1976. He and Fergy had an instant rapport, often engaging in a stinging repartee that kept everyone else in stitches. "How many Stanley Cups have you won?" Ferguson would tease Fotiu. "You're the captain of Team Staten Island! Even your pranks are bush league, WHA stuff." Fotiu would shoot back, "Beliveau's got the strongest shoulders in the world, carrying you around all those years."

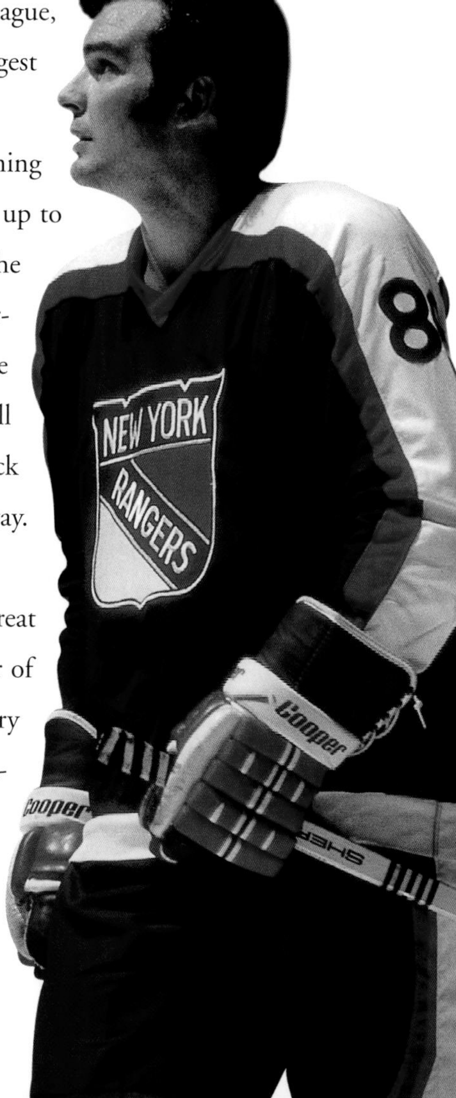

Fotiu became an instant hero with the Garden faithful, signing autographs during pregame skates, and heaving pucks all the way up to the blue seats, where he had grown up watching and idolizing the Rangers years earlier. Garden security types, not to mention the corporate lawyers, were aghast at the puck throwing, envisioning the enormous lawsuits that might ensue if an overzealous fan were to fall from the balcony while scrambling for one of Fotiu's pucks. Nick kept throwing them anyway, and Ferguson just looked the other way. The two left wingers were very much alike indeed.

Ferguson and his inherited captain, Phil Esposito, had a great time together, Ferguson having been the assistant general manager of Team Canada 1972, which Esposito had carried to a dramatic victory over the Soviet Union in hockey's first Summit Series. With considerable prompting ("Yapping was more like it," Ferguson said) from Esposito, the general manager reluctantly traded crafty right winger "Slick" Rick Middleton to the Boston Bruins for Esposito's

New York City-born Nick Fotiu (left), who was raised a staunch Rangers fan on Staten Island, became the first home-grown New Yorker to play for the team, starting in the 1976–77 season and continuing until 1984–85.

A deceptively quick skater with a surprisingly forceful wrist shot, Fotiu was a combative left wing who rarely backed down from the rough stuff. Never one to forget his roots, Fotiu quickly became one of the most popular players in Rangers history. Members of the Rangers Fan Club twice voted him the team's most popular player.

Center Walt Tkaczuk hurtles through a pair of St. Louis defenders for a clear route to the rolling puck. Tkaczuk was one of the greatest defensive players in Rangers history, and played on the "Bulldog Line" with left wing Dave Balon and right wing Billy Fairbairn. Steve Vickers eventually followed Balon as the left wing on the line.

Walt Tkaczuk's 1970 All-Star stick

longtime linemate Ken Hodge. Many thought Middleton was taking too big a bite out of the Big Apple's nightlife, prompting Walt MacPeek, a staunch Middleton supporter with the *Star-Ledger* out of Newark, to observe, "I guess they don't have nightlife in Boston."

The Hodge-for-Middleton swap would turn out to be the worst trade in Rangers history. Middleton went on to score 442 goals in twelve seasons with the Bruins, 419 more than Hodge would manage in one-plus seasons with the Rangers.

Despite spending just over two seasons in Manhattan, Ferguson had overhauled the team's uniforms and the club's Garden dressing room. Designer Edd Griles, an NHL employee, did both makeovers. The dressing room was a winner, the uniforms were a flop. At the time, the Rangers were the only NHL team without their official crest on their chests. On Ferguson's instructions, Griles designed the new threads to make the Rangers look bigger. Griles cut the uniforms more fully in the shoulder, widened the stripe from shoulder to wrist, and gently flared the stripes on the pants from hip to knee. He also displayed the team emblem prominently on the chest. The players, particularly Rod Gilbert, hated the new uniforms, finding them too heavy. The fans hated them as well. When he succeeded Ferguson as general manager, Fred Shero quickly changed back to the old uniforms.

Ferguson also brought his old Montreal buddy, Jean-Guy Talbot, to town to coach the Rangers. Both men were "players' coaches," not that far removed from their own playing days and still young enough to have a great time, both at home and on the road. The parties were frequent, particularly in Montreal, and Chinese food at midnight was regular fare. "Sleep fast!" Ferguson would regularly tell fellow revelers when faced with an early morning flight. Talbot's chief claim to fame would be that he became the first NHL coach to wear a sweatsuit during games. "Hey, coaches sweat, too," he reasoned.

Ferguson also presided over the unceremonious dismissal of Rod Gilbert, on Thanksgiving Day, nineteen games into the 1977–78 season. Gilbert had played 1,065 games for the only team he had ever known, scoring a team record 406 goals, 615 assists, and 1,021 points. He was retained as a Garden executive, and later became coach of the New Haven Nighthawks for one year before returning to the Rangers in a variety of positions in which he continues to function today.

Executive politics at the Garden continued to percolate. The impresario David "Sonny" Werblin was running the operation by 1978–79, and Ferguson was soon on his way out, succeeded by the enigmatic Fred Shero, who had coached the Philadelphia Flyers to back-to-back Stanley Cups in 1974 and 1975. Shero insisted on the GM's duties, just as Ferguson had two years earlier, as a precursor to taking the coaching reins. Oddly enough, it would be Shero, ever the traditionalist in many ways, who radically changed so many of the team's conventional practices.

Walt Tkaczuk was one of the most durable Rangers, rarely missing a game during his thirteen years in New York. An eye injury ended his career prematurely, fifty-five games short of one thousand with the Rangers. He also served the team as an assistant coach.

The Rangers of 1979 celebrate their playoff victory over the New York Islanders by mobbing goalie John Davidson in front of the Rangers' net. The six-game series captivated New York hockey fans like few others had. Columnist Mike Lupica of the *Daily News* called it the "Miracle of Madison Square Garden," and said, "Sports fans in New York are going to feel differently about hockey for a long time because of the show the Rangers and Islanders gave us. Maybe it is better to call it a gift."

Said Phil Esposito, who was really having his last great moment in the game, "For two weeks, I haven't been able to walk down the street without somebody stopping me, wanting to talk about this. What we did here will always be remembered in New York." The victory propelled the Rangers into the finals against the Montreal Canadiens.

17
JOHNSTONE

One of Shero's first acts as general manager and coach was to eliminate the team's oft-ridiculed pregame meals. "Why don't they eat what they want to eat when they want to eat it?" reasoned Shero. "Most of that stuff [the traditional lunches] gets thrown out anyway." The players were ecstatic. "No more ball bearings," was the triumphant refrain, referring to the ubiquitous green peas that invariably accompanied the noon-hour steaks.

Single rooms on the road, previously rarer than hen's teeth and usually limited to heavy snorers or heavy spenders, were easier to obtain, much to the dismay of the Garden's accounting department. One of the chief accountants, a man named Steve Jones, told Fred that Garden policy required the players to stay in double rooms on the road. Replied Fred: "Mr. Jones, these are hockey players; they are going to do what they are going to do. They don't need company." The accountants eventually tried to deduct the difference between a single room and a double room from the players' paychecks. Freddie kiboshed that as well, saying, "It's a big company, they'll never miss it."

The move toward more chartered flights, initiated back in the Francis years, gained further momentum under Shero, who had a distinct distaste for commercial flights. More often than not, or at least so it seemed, Shero would end up three-across in coach class, next to a colicky newborn or a jet-lagged traveler almost sure to fall asleep on his shoulder. Waiting in line for customs and immigration always proved nettlesome to Shero. "Canada has always had twenty million people, and it always will have twenty million people," he once said. "It's easier to get into jail than it is to get into Canada."

For all of his well-earned reputation (he had won at every level he had ever coached), Shero brought with him an off-ice management style that bordered on anomie and basically flabbergasted his superiors as well as his players. The team's traditions, many of them stretching back decades, were starting to crumble, curiously enough at the hands of a man who himself was intrinsically "old school."

Much to the dismay of his Garden superiors, Shero was rarely on the ice with his players (pictures of him on skates at all are extremely rare). There was one training camp, in 1979 in Richmond, Virginia, when he never touched the ice at all, leaving those chores entirely to his assistant, Mike Nykoluk. Nykoluk covered for his boss very well, telling the press that Fred preferred watching training camp from the upper reaches of the cavernous Richmond Coliseum, or that he was back at the Holiday Inn resting a sore back.

One of Shero's favorite pastimes was to wander around, looking at building facades and examining architecture. This got him in trouble prior to one afternoon game in Boston in 1979 when he went outside the Boston Garden for some "quiet time." The Boston Garden was several stories above North Station, and when the exit door slammed shut, Freddie found himself stranded on a fire escape with no way back in. Bang as he did on the door, it was nearly ten minutes before he attracted someone's attention to open the door. By then, the game was about four

The broad shoulders of John Davidson have served the Rangers for nearly a quarter of a century, first as a charismatic goaltender and then as an equally charismatic television analyst. Davidson was acquired from the St. Louis Blues in 1975, and replaced Eddie Giacomin as the Rangers' netminder. Davidson, right, was at his best as the team roared through the 1979 playoffs, but a knee injury hampered him in the finals, which the club lost to the Montreal Canadiens, four games to one.

The Rangers of general manager Fred Shero began wearing "New York" on the road sweaters instead of "Rangers," and no one personified the team's new emphasis on urbanity better than center Ron Duguay, opposite. Duguay became a heartthrob to female fans and enjoyed the New York City scene like few players had before him.

14
10
YORK
KOHO
221

Swedish-born right wing Anders Hedberg, hurtling past Bobby Clarke of the Philadelphia Flyers, brought great talent and great energy to the Rangers from 1978 to 1985, coming over from the Winnipeg Jets of the World Hockey Association along with teammate and linemate Ulf Nilsson.

In 1985–86, Hedberg would become an assistant to general manager Craig Patrick, the first Scandinavian-born player to be named to a front office position in the National Hockey League.

minutes old, and Nykoluk was handling the coaching. Freddie was nonplussed as he took his position behind the bench, looking for all the world like nothing at all had happened.

Freddie was nicknamed "The Fog," quite aptly, during the Philadelphia days. It wasn't just his tinted glasses, nor his oblique roundabout replies to reporters' queries. It was also the way he walked (gently) and the way he talked (gently again), often in parables. "Surround them with sound," he once explained with a wink. "They may not understand what you're saying, but at least you've got their attention. Something might sink in."

Improbably, the Rangers streaked to the Stanley Cup finals and a matchup with the mighty Montreal Canadiens in Shero's very first season, 1978–79. Esposito, the captain, was nearing the end but was determined to go out a winner. The Swedish stars Anders Hedberg and Ulf Nilsson performed mightily with three-year contracts of $1 million apiece. Don Murdoch, Ron Duguay, Ron Greschner, Pat Hickey, and Dave and Don Maloney were key performers, but it was the heroics of goalie John Davidson that carried the team that far. By the finals, Davidson was nursing a sore knee.

When the Rangers unexpectedly won game one of the finals in Montreal, Esposito pleaded with Shero to get the club out of town, to take them up to the Laurentians, away from the bright lights, before the second game two nights later. "I mean, I was virtually on my knees with him," Esposito recalled, "but it didn't work." Freddie, for whatever reason, refused. A certain segment of the team partied hard that night, and it showed. "We took a 2-0 lead in the second game," Esposito remembered, "and never won another face-off." Montreal took the series handily, four games to one.

Things came unraveled quickly by the next season. Shero was losing his edge. He showed up at the Garden for a November game against Minnesota, but there was one small problem: The New York Knickerbockers were getting ready to play a basketball game against the Detroit Pistons. The hockey game was the next night. Then, near the end of the 1979–80 season, the Rangers acquired right winger Cam Connor from the Edmonton Oilers in exchange for Don Murdoch. Freddie, in an alliterative mix-up if ever there was one, thought he had obtained defenseman Colin Campbell instead of Connor, and had Connor briefly working with the defensemen in his first practice with the club. It was a huge gaffe, contributing in no small part to Shero's eventual dismissal twenty games into the 1980–81 season.

The Rangers turned to Craig Patrick as their next general manager on November 21, 1980. The son of Lynn Patrick and the nephew of Muzz Patrick, Craig certainly had the name and the pedigree to be a great success in New York. He had experienced major junior hockey (Montreal Junior Canadiens), college hockey (University of Denver), the WHA (Minnesota Fighting Saints), minor pro hockey (four different teams in the American and Central Leagues), and the NHL (California, St. Louis, Kansas City, and Washington). Plus he had considerable experience at the international level.

At forty, Patrick lacked only hands-on NHL managerial savvy and firsthand knowledge of the League's doings at the ownership level. The plan was for him to learn

Ron Greschner's sixteen-year career with the Rangers was marked by frequent injuries, but he managed to play 982 games for New York, the third highest total in team history. Among defenseman, only Brian Leetch has scored more goals and more assists than the man who wore number 4.

Greschner (left) was one of the smoothest-skating defenseman in team history, and his 1,226 penalty minutes are more than logged by any Ranger ever.

the former on the job and the latter at the elbow of William Jennings, the team's president and governor for some two decades. But Jennings died on August 17, 1981.

Patrick was somewhat uncomfortable with the New York area's swarming group of hockey reporters, and the constant intrusions and inspections that, quite simply, went with the territory. He was a quiet man and very friendly to those who knew him well, yet the relentless media branded him "Vague Craig" or "Stand Patrick." Craig genuinely cared for his players, agonizing long and hard before trading one of them or even deciding to send them on a stint in the minors. His style had a calming effect on a team that had become somewhat disenchanted and certainly ineffective under Shero, with all of his mystery and all of his mystique.

The Rangers of the early 1980s were a very popular bunch, and made regular appearances in the New York City gossip columns. Captain Phil Esposito (back row center) and mates, the "Ranger Rockers," even cut a record, "The Hockey Sock Rock," which never made a dent on the hit music charts. Espo's fellow "Rockers" were left wing Pat Hickey (16) and defenseman Dave Maloney (26), plus goalie John Davidson (30) and center Ron Duguay (10).

Patrick quickly brought in his former Olympic boss Herb Brooks to coach in 1981–82. Brooks changed a lot of things, introduced a European style of play, and made the playoffs his first three seasons. But the Patrick-Brooks combination was probably doomed to failure: The two men were nearly a decade apart in age; they had completely different personalities; and the two had to flip-flop the boss-employee relationship that Brooks had enjoyed at the Olympics but Patrick now held in New York. Brooks was also more comfortable and artful with the press, a distinct advantage for him. Patrick was eventually forced to fire Herb and take the coaching duties himself in January 1985, losing twice as many games as he would win before hiring Ted Sator to coach the next season.

* * *

Following his retirement midway through the 1980–81 season, Phil Esposito became a broadcaster for the Madison Square Garden Network. There was little doubt that the future Hall of Famer's heart belonged closer to the ice than the broadcast booth, and Phil used his position quite frankly, criticizing Patrick, Sator, and individual players and strategies whenever he felt it necessary. By the summer of 1986, Esposito would be running the entire operation himself, taking over for Patrick, whose teams had achieved no great success despite making the playoffs for six straight years. Esposito wanted to win so badly he could taste it, and brought the actual Stanley Cup to the team's hotel in Armonk, New York, during his first training camp as general manager in 1986. "Guys," he said, "this is what it's all about. Take a look. Work hard, and this could be ours." Many players, especially the younger ones, were in awe, touching the Cup with reverence and snapping photos.

Impulsive by nature, Esposito was every bit the straight shooter behind the desk that he was on the ice. He moved quickly to put his distinctive stamp on the Rangers, engineering a dizzying series of trades, two of which brought aging superstars Marcel Dionne and Guy Lafleur to New York. Both were well past their prime, but they still had flashes of brilliance that thrilled Garden fans. Esposito's call to arms was "Enough Waiting," and he set about changing things with flamboyance and brio. He was fun to be around, the players loved the scene, but there was really no great improvement over the regimes of Patrick, Shero, and Ferguson that had preceded him. Esposito's departure, on May 24, 1989, brought to an end what was basically a mediocre stretch of team history, but nonetheless a period that would set the stage for a coming era of great stability . . . and great triumph.

Explosive-scoring right wing Don "Murder" Murdoch celebrates after scoring the game-winning overtime goal against the Buffalo Sabres on April 13, 1978. Murdoch was a first-round draft choice of General Manager John Ferguson in 1976. He made team history in only his fourth National Hockey League game by scoring five goals in a 10-4 victory over the Minnesota North Stars on October 12, 1976.

Murdoch's feat was only the second time in NHL history that a rookie had scored five times in one game. Rookie Howie Meeker had done it for the Toronto Maple Leafs in 1947. And no one else has done it since.

14
14

Right wing Bruce MacGregor (14) and center Pete Stemkowski (21), although usually overshadowed by the GAG Line and the Bulldog Line, were terrific Rangers contributors in the early 1970s. Their linemate was usually left wing Ted Irvine, and the trio had quite a knack for coming up with the important goal at the important time.

Although he never played for the team he grew up idolizing, New York City–born and raised Joey Mullen, below, would win three Stanley Cups—one with the Calgary Flames and two more with the Pittsburgh Penguins. Joey and younger brother Brian became the highest-scoring United States–born brother combination in the history of the National Hockey League, combining for 1,685 points.

The Mullen Brothers
by Dave Anderson

On that Sunday in 1966, the Rangers would be playing at the old Madison Square Garden in a few hours. To ease the wait, Emile Francis, the Rangers' general manager, took a walk in the neighborhood known as Hell's Kitchen. After crossing 9th Avenue and continuing along West 49th Street past the old tenements there, he noticed youngsters zooming around in what appeared to be a big hole.

"I thought, 'I didn't know there was an artificial-ice rink there,'" he had often recalled, "but then I realized it was cement. They were playing roller hockey."

The next time Francis met with Bill Jennings, then the Rangers' president, he mentioned that the Rangers had a responsibility to provide those roller-hockey kids with an opportunity to play ice hockey.

"If we get lucky," Francis added, "we might get a player for the Rangers in ten years."

Francis organized the Metropolitan Junior Hockey Association ("the Met") and, a decade later, it produced Nick Fotiu, a Rangers left wing from Staten Island. But little did Francis realize that two youngsters living on the top floor of a five-story tenement across West 49th Street from that cement rink, Joey Mullen and Brian Mullen, would also skate in the National Hockey League.

That tenement deserves historic landmark status. Kids from the streets of New York City aren't supposed to do what the Mullen brothers did as NHL right wings—score a combined total of 762 goals, plus another 72 in the Stanley Cup playoffs. Joey Mullen also would star for three Stanley Cup championship teams: one in Calgary (1989) and two in Pittsburgh (1991 and 1992).

With a total of 1,063 regular-season points (502 goals) over seventeen seasons with St. Louis, Calgary, Pittsburgh, and Boston, Joey was the first United States–born player to accumulate 1,000 points in the NHL. He was a first-team All-Star in the 1988–89 season and a two-time winner of the Lady Byng Trophy. He is also a member of the U.S. Hockey Hall of Fame.

Brian scored 260 goals over eleven seasons with Winnipeg, the Rangers, San Jose, and the New York Islanders before a stroke and heart surgery in 1993 ended his career. He and Joey were opponents in the 1989 All-Star game at Edmonton. He is now the director of off-ice programs in the NHL office, only a few blocks from that West 49th Street tenement and cement rink.

"But if it wasn't for Mr. Francis," Brian Mullen said when the two brothers were honored with the Lester Patrick Award in 1995 for outstanding service to hockey in the United States, "me and Joey wouldn't be here."

The Mullen brothers also would not have been there if their parents, Tom and Marion, had not moved from the East Side to Hell's Kitchen in order to be close to the old Garden where Tom worked on the maintenance crew. He helped make the ice for Rangers games, then he helped resurface it between periods in the pre-Zamboni era.

Quite naturally, the four Mullen brothers grew up sneaking into the old Garden to watch Rangers games when they weren't playing roller hockey. The two oldest, Tommy and Kenny, played ice hockey in the Met right away. Joey had to wait.

"Roller skating takes a different style from ice skating; you don't glide well," Joey said, referring to the old clip-on roller skates he wore strapped over his shoes long before modern in-line skates were fashionable. "You can do almost anything on roller skates that you can do on ice except one thing—on roller skates you can't stop."

As soon as Joey began playing ice hockey in the Met for the Westsiders, he was a star. In only forty games one season, he scored 110 goals and added seventy-nine assists. He went on to Boston College and would have been a member of the 1980 U.S. Olympic team that upset the Soviets at Lake Placid, but he chose to sign with St. Louis for a $50,000 bonus.

Why the Blues instead of the Rangers? Because by then Emile Francis was the St. Louis general manager. And why was he later traded to Calgary? Because by then Francis was no longer with the Blues.

Brian roller-skated early, but at age seven he was on ice skates. After several seasons with the Westsiders (and as a Rangers stickboy in the current Garden), he helped the University of Wisconsin win the 1981 NCAA championship. Strangely, the Rangers didn't draft him but as the Winnipeg general manager, an ex-Ranger manager and coach, John Ferguson, did.

Brian would be acquired by the Rangers in 1987; he scored a total of one hundred goals in four seasons with them. Joey never joined the team that had played in the old Garden when he was a youngster growing up a block away in Hell's Kitchen. But in 1989, playing for the Calgary Flames, he became the first native New Yorker to have his name engraved on the Stanley Cup.

As for that tenement, when its main beam rusted through in the middle of a cold night in 1980, the rear wall collapsed into the backyard. The five-story building had opened like a dollhouse. After the Mullens had moved to Bergenfield, New Jersey, that tenement stayed empty and boarded for more than a decade before a new five-story apartment house appeared at 418 West 49th Street.

But across the street, outside the High School of Graphic Communications, is the same cement playground where youngsters were playing roller hockey when Emile Francis just happened to walk by.

Native New Yorker Brian Mullen, below, grew up within a city block of the third Madison Square Garden and learned his hockey on roller skates. He first made it to the Rangers dressing room as a stickboy in the mid-1970s. Acquired by the Rangers from the Winnipeg Jets on June 8, 1987, Mullen would play 307 games and score an even one hundred goals for his favorite team. The highlight would be a hat trick against the Washington Capitals on October 19, 1988.

Acquired from the Colorado Rockies in exchange for five players on November 2, 1979, lumbering defenseman Barry Beck (left) spent seven injury-plagued seasons on Broadway. Beck was a team leader, and served as captain of the Rangers from 1981 to 1986.

United States–born goalie John Vanbiesbrouck (right) was a popular Ranger for nine seasons, winning the Vezina Trophy as the NHL's top goalie in 1986, and often gaining cheers of "Bee-ZER . . . Bee-ZER . . . Bee-ZER" from the Madison Square Garden faithful. When Vanbiesbrouck played his first NHL game on December 5, 1981, he was just eighteen years old, the youngest goalie in Rangers history—except for emergency goalie Harry Lumley, who was seventeen when he played one game for the Blueshirts in 1943–44.

Few players in Rangers history have succeeded in their first year with the team quite the way Mike Rogers did. The speedy center arrived in a trade with the Hartford Whalers on October 2, 1981, and with a team-leading 103 points, became only the fourth man in Rangers history to surpass 100 points in a single season.

Rogers' first season in New York included a sixteen-game point-scoring streak that included ten goals and eighteen assists and was the longest consecutive-game scoring streak in team history at the time. Brian Leetch would surpass the streak with seventeen games a decade later.

After a long wait, everything came together for the Rangers. The 1994 Stanley Cup win, the Messier-Gretzky partnership, and Leetch's continuing excellence gave fans the glory they were waiting for.

1989

Oct. 19—Rookie goalie Mike Richter made a save on Kevin Dineen's penalty shot in his first career regular season start. He went on to win his first NHL game as the Rangers beat the visiting Hartford Whalers, 7-3.

Unemployed Darryl

Now is time for Strawberry to turn life around / Lupica, Page A100

SPORTS FINAL

Newsday SPORTS

THURSDAY, MAY 26, 1994

Heroic Messier scores 3 goals in third period to save Rangers from elimination

On The Mark

GAME 6 COVERAGE BEGINS ON PAGE A110

1990

Jan. 14—The Rangers beat the Flyers 4-3 in overtime to win their thousandth home game. The victory gave them a record of 1,000-715-373 at Madison Square Garden.

1991

Oct. 4—The Rangers obtained Mark Messier from Edmonton, in exchange for Bernie Nicholls, Steven Rice, and Louie DeBrusk.

1994

May 25—Mark Messier's absolute "guarantee" of a victory was secured when he scored three goals in the third period of game six of the Eastern Conference finals to lead the Rangers to a 4-2 win over the New Jersey Devils.

May 27—Stephane Matteau scored the winning goal at 24:24 of overtime to lead the Rangers to a 2-1 win over the Devils in game seven of the Eastern Conference finals. The Rangers advanced to the Stanley Cup finals vs. Vancouver.

1999

Mar. 29—Wayne Gretzky scored his 1,072nd all-time goal, surpassing Gordie Howe as the leading scorer in pro hockey history (twenty NHL seasons and one season in the WHA) as the Rangers won 3-1 against the visiting New York Islanders.

Laurels, Legends, Legacy

After nearly a decade and a half of widely fluctuating management styles, the Rangers wanted—and needed—stability. They found it in the person of Neil Smith, who ushered in one of the most successful periods in team history. One of the outstanding young minds in the game at the time, Smith had never himself played in the National Hockey League, honing his skills instead in the scouting departments of the New York Islanders and the Detroit Red Wings. There were far bigger names than Smith on the general manager's job horizon at the time, a couple of fellows named Herb Brooks and Scotty Bowman among them. But the Rangers took Smith, and it was a brilliant selection, even more so when the move is viewed in hindsight.

In less than five seasons, Smith accomplished every hockey executive's goal: he won the Stanley Cup, erasing the so-called "curse of the Rangers," a forbidding albatross that had hung around the team's neck for fifty-four seasons and haunted the club.

As the Rangers rolled into the 1994 Stanley Cup playoffs, the team was as compelling a bunch of hockey players as ever starred in New York. The Rangers were mesmerizing, although "Mess-merizing" might be a better word. That's how much captain Mark Messier meant. But the others were equally fantastic: Brian Leetch and Sergei Zubov on the power play were a sight to behold. Mike Richter continued to dazzle. Wings Steve Larmer and Adam Graves seemed to be everywhere. Right wing Joey Kocur and defensemen Jeff Beukeboom and Jay Wells provided toughness, while Alexei Kovalev added finesse. Defenseman Kevin Lowe provided leadership—always with great perspective off the ice. Sergei Nemchinov, Glenn Anderson, Craig MacTavish, Greg "Gibby" Gilbert, and Brian Noonan brought drive. Esa Tikkanen brought his own special style of gritty play, plus a language known as "Tikkanese"—a combination of Finnish, English, and profanity—that was understood only by Tikkanen himself.

That charmed team was a juggernaut of a freight train that was not about to be derailed. And all of New York, fans and media alike, got on for the ride. The city was awash with Rangers Fever. It was exhilarating.

The Rangers had finished a whopping twenty-seven points ahead of the Vancouver Canucks in the regular season, and great optimism surrounded the Blueshirts as they went into the playoffs. The Rangers easily trounced the arch-rival Islanders with a sweep, then went on to deny the Washington Capitals any further postseason glory.

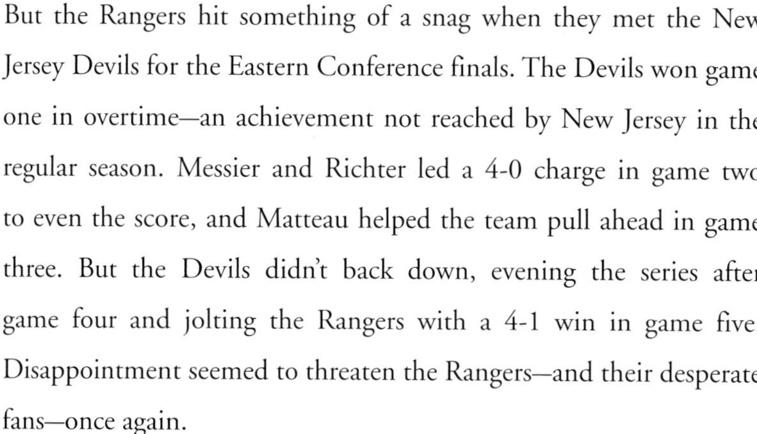

But the Rangers hit something of a snag when they met the New Jersey Devils for the Eastern Conference finals. The Devils won game one in overtime—an achievement not reached by New Jersey in the regular season. Messier and Richter led a 4-0 charge in game two to even the score, and Matteau helped the team pull ahead in game three. But the Devils didn't back down, evening the series after game four and jolting the Rangers with a 4-1 win in game five. Disappointment seemed to threaten the Rangers—and their desperate fans—once again.

The team turned to Messier, and he did not falter. With a prophetic confidence not seen since Joe Namath guaranteed victory for the Jets, Messier declared that the Rangers would beat New Jersey. Newspapers all over featured Messier's claim—which looked to be nothing but false hope when the Devils took a fast 2-0 lead in game six. But Messier would not give up. After an assist and a tying goal, Messier completed a natural hat trick that sent the Rangers to a climactic game seven.

Brian Leetch's sharply angled wrist shot beyond the reach of Vancouver goaltender Kirk McLean opened the scoring in game seven of the finals at 11:02 of the first period. The assists went to Mark Messier and Sergei Zubov.

It was the Rangers' first trip to the Stanley Cup finals since 1979. Game one was scheduled for May 31 at the Garden, giving the Rangers only four days to settle down from the high of beating the Devils. The Canucks, by contrast, had not played in a week's time and came to town well rested and led by Pavel "The Russian Rocket" Bure, the superstar right winger who was coming off back-to-back sixty-goal seasons. Larmer, in the first period, and Kovalev, in the second, scored for the Rangers. They were answered by goals from Bret Hedican and Martin Gelinas of the Canucks, the latter's coming with just a minute left in regulation to set up yet another overtime match. Despite being outplayed in the overtime, the Canucks won it on a "one-timer" by Greg Adams that eluded Richter's glove hand. The real star of the contest was Canucks goalkeeper Kirk McLean. He set an NHL record by making fifty-two saves, the most ever by a goaltender in a Stanley Cup finals game that was decided in the first overtime.

True to their talent, the Rangers took control of game two early. Defenseman Doug Lidster, a former Canuck who had first joined the lineup for game six of the Devils series and was playing well, scored at 6:22 of the first period, but Sergio Momesso's second goal of the series tied it. Anderson put the Rangers ahead halfway through the second period, and Leetch's empty netter sealed victory number one at 19:55 of the third. It was on to Vancouver, three thousand miles to the west in British Columbia, for games three and four. The Rangers would take them both handily, 5-1 on June 4, and 4-2 on June 7. The Cup was tantalizingly close, almost too close for comfort, as it turned out.

The Garden was thumping for game five as the rollicking fans anticipated a Cup presentation, something the Rangers had never managed on home ice. It wasn't to be, as the Canucks scored the first three goals of the game—and the last three goals as well—in a decisive 6-3 victory that meant another three-thousand-mile trip for both teams. Despite the distance involved, the Rangers crisscrossed

As the puck rests in the back of the net, Stephane Matteau (left) begins to celebrate the Rangers win in game seven of the Eastern Conference finals by a score of 2-1 over the New Jersey Devils. This goal—the biggest of Matteau's career—came at the 4:24 mark of the second overtime period, and sent all of the Rangers into a back-slapping scene of celebration. It was Matteau's second goal in double overtime in the New Jersey series. He had won game three in similar fashion. Matteau's victim on both occasions was New Jersey goaltender Martin Brodeur.

Seconds after the Rangers become champions, there is bedlam and backslapping at the Rangers net as the team wildly celebrates its first Stanley Cup championship in fifty-four years. Somewhere in the scrum is goalie Mike Richter, who played every minute of the tense, seven-game series, and surrendered nineteen goals.

North America in the comfort of their own airplane, a modified 737. Actually, there were two charters, the first for the players, Smith, the coaching staff, the trainers, the doctors and dentists, and the front-office staff. Ever the perfectionist, Coach Mike Keenan even had a seating chart, which was not a requirement for private flights. The second plane carried wives, girlfriends, other team staff, Garden staffers, and even a few of the team's longtime season ticket holders. The planes left from Newark, New Jersey, but came back to JFK, in case the team won game six and carried the Cup home to New York. Unfortunately, it was more of the same in game six, on June 11. The Canucks won it, 4-1, and the series was tied at three; the teams would hopscotch the continent yet another time.

The Rangers would make no mistakes in game seven. Messier wouldn't let them dare. The captain was at his glowering best. But while he kept a steely hold on his emotions during the game, Messier lept in the air—giddily and repeatedly—when Craig MacTavish controlled the final faceoff with 1.6 seconds to play. The dragon had been slain. The "curse" had been lifted. The championship was New York's!

New York being New York, and the Rangers being the Rangers, there was one thing that was sure to follow and not to be ignored. That was the nonstop celebration that followed the end of the fifty-four-year drought. There was, of course, that quintessential New York tradition, a thunderously explosive parade up lower Broadway's Canyon of Heroes. A day earlier, on Thursday, by the time the Rangers assembled for their official team picture, some of the guys hadn't even been home yet. The parties were endless. The Rangers were the toast of New York. Messier was seen with Daisy Fuentes. Or was it Madonna? Who cared? It didn't matter. The Rangers celebrated for months. The Cup was theirs. There was *Late Night with David Letterman*, Page Six seemingly every day, Gracie Mansion with Mayor Rudy Giuliani, the White House visit with President Clinton, and, finally, a magnificent Madison Square Garden banner-raising ceremony on January 20, 1995. Even a Kentucky Derby–winning racehorse, Go For Gin, managed to eat from the Rangers' Stanley Cup at Belmont Park.

The run to the Stanley Cup had come with only one wart, but it was a public one that the press regularly explored. That was the icy relationship that existed between Neil Smith and his one-year coach, Mike Keenan. Even as Smith raised the Cup, his euphoria had to be somewhat muted by the contretemps. Nonetheless it hardly tainted Smith's personal tour de force, the greatest Rangers accomplishment in fifty-four years. Smith and Keenan seemingly celebrated the magnificent Cup triumph separately. Keenan, as he raised the Cup in triumph, might have already been thinking about the next stop on his coaching career, be it St. Louis, Detroit, or Vancouver.

To the players, the rift between Smith and Keenan wasn't really a big deal. Recalled Leetch: "That whole thing with Mike and the stories in

Moments after presenting the Stanley Cup to Mark Messier, National Hockey League Commissioner Gary Bettman presented the Conn Smythe Trophy for playoff MVP to peerless defenseman Brian Leetch. For the Rangers, it was their first Smythe Trophy, named after the man who mostly assembled the original Rangers in 1926 but was dismissed before the first season began.

Conn Smythe Trophy

The captain, Mark Messier, simply did it all on Broadway. He was a leader. He was a sniper. He played through injuries and he became the very soul of the team that would win the Prince of Wales Trophy, opposite, the Presidents' Trophy, and the Stanley Cup in 1994.

Messier was even a seer, a successful prognosticator. His now-famous "guarantee" of a victory in game six of the Conference championships against New Jersey on May 25 will be forever remembered in Rangers history. The final score was Rangers 4, Devils 2.

the finals about him going to Detroit really didn't mean a thing to us. It never got into the [dressing] room. Things [like that] happened all year. We were used to Mike. It was routine." Actually, everyone knew about Keenan's aloofness. It was legendary. The younger guys sometimes cowered. The veterans usually ignored him.

One thing that none of the players ignored was the way that Keenan had grabbed their attention before the season had even begun, on the very first day of training camp, in fact. He did it in a way that no other coach ever had. He did it with a specially prepared video of a New York–style parade with all the ticker tape flying and the fans celebrating. The message was a simple one: this can be yours, let's make it happen. They did. So, a parade began the season and a parade ended it.

In addition to the Stanley Cup, the Smith-built Rangers captured a pair of Presidents' Trophies as the league's best team in the regular season along with three division championships, doubling the number of banners that hung from the Garden ceiling.

Underscoring the enormity of Smith's accomplishments was the fact that only two of the key players (Mike Richter and Brian Leetch) were on board when Smith took office on July 17, 1989. Smith vowed to devote every working hour to building a winner. "As long as the coffee doesn't run out" was the way he put it at the time. The coffee didn't run out, and neither did Smith's energy. Smith was adroitly able to strike a most delicate balance between two seemingly impossible ends—the "win now" demands that loom with the New York territory and his "scouting pedigree" that called for a solid farm system and a future built on youth. The greatness of Neil Smith's teams really lay in their depth. The general manager traded a player here, a player there, but the moves were usually made with an eye on the future. But while Smith stressed the importance of younger players, a big part of his legacy came from the great fact that he managed to bring Messier and Wayne Gretzky, two of the biggest all-time stars in the hockey firmament, to New York.

Unlike any of the twenty-one men who preceded him as captain of the New York Rangers Hockey Club, Mark Messier willed his team to win. There have been, to be certain, many great captains in Rangers history, but no one—not Bill Cook, not Art Coulter, not Andy Bathgate, not Vic Hadfield, not Phil Esposito—took hold of a hockey club quite the way number 11 did. Writer Rick Carpiniello called Messier "hockey's dragon slayer," in the subtitle of his book on the center in 1999. He was all that and more.

Even after the triumphant Cup, Messier continued his unflinching leadership for three more seasons. On the road, it was not uncommon for him to marshal the Rangers for a team dinner at some expensive restaurant or golf club in order to promote team unity and bonhomie.

The Russian Rangers

by Stu Hackel

Alexei Kovalev, as smooth as the ice itself, became a familiar and delightful sight to Rangers fans. Dramatic rushes and flashy stickhandling became Alex's trademark. Kovalev seemed able to stop on a dime and suddenly change direction. He scored a goal and assisted on two others when the Rangers beat the New Jersey Devils in game six of the Conference finals.

Walk the streets of this city, not just Manhattan but all five boroughs, and the one truth you will discover is this: New York soaks up the many pools of Earth's distinct cultures and makes them its own. No one thing contributes more to the identity of the world's greatest city.

New York's hockey club is no different. The Rangers have added so many international flavors to the game's stew, it seems appropriate that the team adopted the great symbol of immigration—the Statue of Liberty, which stands just a few miles south of Madison Square Garden—as the crest of their "third jersey."

The NHL's first American star, Taffy Abel, was an original Ranger; the first Finnish-born NHLer, Pentti Lund, was a Ranger; the first Swede in the NHL, Ulf Sterner, was a Ranger; the first German invited for an NHL tryout, Erich Kuhnhackl, came to Rangers camp; the first NHL team to play a Soviet club team, the Central Army Hockey Club, was the Rangers; the first great offensive European stars in the NHL, Anders Hedberg and Ulf Nilsson, jumped to the Rangers in 1978.

To this impressive list, we must add that the first Russian born and trained players whose names are inscribed on the Stanley Cup—Sergei Nemchinov, Alexei Kovalev, Sergei Zubov, and Alexander Karpovstev—earned this distinction as members of 1994 New York Rangers.

These four weren't just along for the ride. All played significant roles in the triumph and made lasting impressions on Rangers history.

A smooth skater and playmaker, the daring Zubov led the club in scoring and teamed with Brian Leetch to form perhaps the best tandem of point men ever seen on a power play. The Rangers' man advantage play rated best in the NHL that year, thriving on their uncanny anticipation in cutting off clearing attempts at the blue line.

Kovalev, who galloped through defenders with flashy stickhandling on piston legs, peaked that spring when he finished sixth in league and third in club playoff scoring. The Legend of '94 always begins with Mark Messier's hat trick and "guaranteed" victory in game six of the Conference Championships, but few recall Alex igniting the comeback victory that night in New Jersey, blasting the Rangers' first goal and setting up two Messier scores.

As a new arrival from Russia, Karpovstev played a solid defensive game for much of 1993–94, until the rigors of the long season and the newness of Stanley Cup competition thrust veteran Doug Lidster into his spot as the playoffs waned. Three years later, "Potsie" evolved into the Rangers' steadiest defenseman, but he rarely stood in the spotlight, claiming no facility in English. It was a ruse. "He knew everything everyone said and spoke pretty well," reveals Matt Loughran, who was director of team operations. "In Russia, players never talked to the press. He just didn't want the distraction, so he begged off."

Nemchinov, an exceptional two-way player and a quiet leader in the room, became the first Russian Ranger in 1991. His arrival coincided with the startling events in his homeland, as the Soviet Union crumbled the very week the Nemchinovs began their new life. Jim Stout, the *Danbury Times* Rangers writer, visited their Connecticut hotel for "Sarge's" first interview. Stout brought a friend to translate—Peter Fedorov, a Latvian-born computer professional.

"It was a day I'll never forget," says Fedorov. "The TV was on and we were watching history unfold. Jim asked Sergei questions about hockey, which I translated, and Sergei asked us questions about what Dan Rather was reporting on TV."

People may move, governments may change, but Russians everywhere maintain a deep, undying pride and love of their national culture. So when the Russian Rangers saw an opportunity to put their culture on display for their teammates, they threw the most unique of the many parties which followed the Cup victory.

The entire organization—players, executives, staff, doctors, trainers, wives, and girlfriends—found their way to Brooklyn's Little Odessa, the heart of the Russian émigré community. Under the "el" tracks on bustling Brighton Beach Avenue, the Rangers family all walked through the gold-and-glass doorway of The National, New York's top nightclub for Russian cuisine and entertainment.

As hosts, the four Russian Rangers "wanted to thank the organization for the way they were accepted and made part of a great team and show off a slice of their culture," Loughran says.

It was quite a slice. As their cars arrived, the players were greeted by a throng of cheering fans who lined the street, eager to connect with their championship team. It seemed to Loughran as if "the whole Russian community was parading outside, kids, adults, there must have been a thousand people out there."

From early evening to early morning, the party inside never flagged. "There was a huge spread of Russian food," Loughran recalled, "caviar, dumplings, trays and trays of foods none of us had ever seen or tasted before. Lots of seafood, big lobsters. It was a lavish spread. And it just kept coming.

"They brought out a performing troupe, who put on a European-style cabaret. It was entirely in Russian. The men in the troupe all dressed in different types of uniforms and the women, well, they didn't wear much at all. They performed little skits, there was lots of singing, they had juggling acts, Cossack dancing. Some of our guys got up and tried to dance and they fell flat on their rears.

"And the vodka! We were just drinking vodka straight, like water, which is the way the Russians drink it. The guys could have had anything they wanted that night, but most of us stuck with vodka just to stay with the spirit of the evening.

"Except for the four Russians on the team, none of us had ever experienced anything like that. It was like stepping into another world, taking a little limo ride and, suddenly, you were in the middle of Moscow. It was surreal. There was nothing American about the evening. It transcended the North American celebration of the Stanley Cup. But we all loved it and it was a very, very special night for those four guys."

Fans were still outside when the Rangers departed the National—not terribly sober and not terribly long before the sun came up. The celebration continued later that morning with the parade up Broadway to City Hall, a parade that would be a little late getting under way.

The world's greatest city certainly understood.

A daring rusher and a crafty playmaker, defenseman Sergei Zubov, above, teamed with Brian Leetch to form one of the most potent Rangers power plays of all time.

RANGERS
MasterCard
HESPELER

Nearly seventy years after Lester Patrick took New York by storm in 1926, another legend—merely the game's greatest ever—arrived in New York and did the same. The name was Gretzky, first name Wayne, and like Patrick, he had mostly honed his professional skills on the rinks of western Canada and the United States. The comparison hardly ended there. Like Patrick, Gretzky had a nickname. He was "The Great One" when he arrived in New York, just two years removed from winning the Lester Patrick Trophy for outstanding service to hockey in the United States.

There was a glittering Garden welcome with all the bells and whistles on October 6, 1996, and even though the team didn't win in its first five games, Gretzky was on his way to a ninety-seven-point season. He led the team in scoring and his seventy assists were the most ever by a Rangers center. Reunited with old pal Messier, the twosome, number 99 and number 11, seemingly turned back the clock. It was a magical ride for Rangers fans young and old.

Gretzky's Rangers performance was far, far different from that of other aging superstars, notably Marcel Dionne and Guy Lafleur, who preceded him as Rangers during what was clearly in the twilight of their splendiferous careers. While Dionne and Lafleur showed only flashes of former greatness in their New York tenure, The Great One was still that—great. He gave the Rangers—and their fans—quite a show for three full seasons, rarely missing a game and providing untold inspiration to the team's younger players.

When he finally decided to retire, Gretzky did it on his own terms, quietly and with dignity. Rangers fans appreciated that. There was an emotional farewell to Edmonton on February 21, 1999, a teary final game in the Canadian capital of Ottawa on April 15, and finally, a fireworks-studded, spotlight-bathed farewell at the Garden on April 18. The clearly emotional "greatest player ever," with his wife and children at his side, slowly circled the Madison Square Garden rink one last time, and the Gretzky era was over. There will never be another like it. In historical terms, three years can hardly be considered an era. But to Rangers fans, young and old alike, 1996–99 can truly be named for Gretzky.

But despite the fanfare of Gretzky's ride with the Rangers, the team's record foundered: three straight years under .500 and without any playoffs, an oft-times impatient fan base, and a somewhat unforgiving media corps. Much as they had done under Roger Neilson half a decade earlier, the Rangers simply weren't responding under Colin Campbell, who took over for Keenan in the season following the Stanley Cup victory.

Before skating off to retirement, Wayne Gretzky put in three terrific seasons as a New York Ranger, and put a New York exclamation point on the greatest hockey career of all time. He did it "his way," with dignity and with grace, despite all of the deserved hoopla that surrounded the event. Garden fans cheered and cheered for their adopted hero, whose nickname—The Great One—said it all.

On April 18, 1999, Gretzky, left and opposite, skated the last game of his career taking a final lap around the rink to a standing ovation. The next day, the news hit the front page of newspapers across the United States and Canada.

NATO takes the blame for a terrible tragedy in Kosovo A32

THE Province

Serving B.C. for more than 100 years

It's all over

Superstar Wayne Gretzky will announce his NHL career is finished. Province columnist Tony Gallagher got the word at breakfast with the Great One yesterday. A3

99

■ No. 99 played his last game in Canada last night. Fans gave him a moving sendoff. Pages A72-70

The New York

A Growth Spurt Is Transforming TV for Children

Lost Horizons: The Billboard Prepares to Give Up Smoking

After 1,487 games, 894 goals & 1,963 assists

THE ICEMAN GOETH

Full coverage of Gretzky's last game starts on Pages 2 & 3

In one of the most memorable moments of the 1994 championship season, limber-legged goaltender Mike Richter stoned Vancouver's ace right wing, Pavel "The Russian Rocket" Bure, on a penalty shot at 6:31 of the second period of game four on June 7, 1994. It was only the fourth penalty shot against the Rangers in their entire playoff history, and the first ever whistled against them in a final-round game.

Richter's save was the turning point in the game. Said coach Mike Keenan, "It was the most important save of Michael's career. It gave us a chance to come back." The Rangers scored the next three goals and won, 4-2.

VAUGHN
VAUGHN
LEGACY

Left wing Adam Graves has provided grit, leadership, and moxie during the course of his career in New York, often sacrificing himself for the good of the team. Graves, opposite and below, has always played a physical game, one that is loudly appreciated by teammates and fans alike. Graves secured the team record for goals in a season when he scored fifty-two in 1993–94.

So just past the midway point of the 1997–98 campaign, Smith was forced into yet another coaching change. He turned to sage John Muckler, a four-time winner of the Stanley Cup who had coached Gretzky in the Great One's Edmonton days. At sixty-four years of age, Muckler was the oldest coach in team history. But he was not a miracle worker, and both he and Smith were relieved of their duties before the end of the 1999–2000 season.

Pat LaFontaine's 1,000th-point gloves

The responsibility of leading the players through the management transition fell to the only two players who were there before Neil Smith was: Mike Richter and Brian Leetch, best friends off the ice, adopted sons of New York City, cornerstones for the 1994 team, and cornerstones for the future. The Rangers wisely had signed both players to long-term contracts, basically assuring that the two superstars would end their illustrious careers in New York. In all probability, so too will Adam Graves, whose grit, intensity, and ability to play through injuries have meant so much to the team.

"We have been forced to grow a lot, all of us, over the last couple of years, and we have to continue to grow," said Graves. "That starts with having Brian here. He is one guy on one team who is irreplaceable."

It was Leetch, of course, who assumed the captain's responsibilities after Messier's numbing departure for the Vancouver Canucks—the same team Messier had helped flatten in the 1994 playoffs—in July 1997, and he's proven a very different type of leader. One who leads by example rather than through rousing speeches, Leetch has what every captain needs: the total respect of his teammates. "New York is a special place, it really is," said Leetch. "I have been privileged to spend my whole career here. The fans are special, the Garden is special. I have always said that as long as I can play at a high level, I would want to stay here."

After the announcement of Smith and Muckler's departures, even more of the spotlight that Leetch seemed to eschew became focused on him. But Leetch has met the scrutiny head on. "Now's the time for us to move forward," Leetch said. "We've got to concentrate on getting this team back on the right track." A huge step to gain that direction was taken in June 2000 with the naming of Hall of Fame executive and former Ranger Glen Sather as president and general manager.

The winning, Leetch, Richter, and Graves know all too well, had come in 1994. It would come again. John Davidson, himself a veteran of more than a few 1979 magic moments, put it this way: "If you are a winner in New York, you're a winner forever. Win in New York and you become part of the New York folklore, not just a part of sports history. Your victory never dies. This city, New York City, will never let you forget it."

BAUER
NYR
Supra

NEDVED
93
93
NEW YORK
RANGERS

Petr Nedved (left) is on the outside looking in during this classic "hockey scrum" with members of the Phoenix Coyotes as beleaguered linesman Derek Amell tries to break up the fight.

Nedved, in his second tour of duty with the Rangers, centered the Rangers' most exciting line during the 1999–2000 campaign with rookie Jan Hlavac on left wing and Radek Dvorak on right wing. The three natives of the Czech Republic were called, quite naturally, the "Czechmates."

Rangers NHL Award Winners

CALDER MEMORIAL TROPHY

Kilby MacDonald	1939–40
Grant Warwick	1941–42
Edgar Laprade	1945–46
Pentti Lund	1948–49
Lorne Worsley	1952–53
Camille Henry	1953–54
Steve Vickers	1972–73
Brian Leetch	1988–89

ART ROSS TROPHY

Bill Cook	1926–27
Bill Cook	1932–33
Bryan Hextall	1941–42

STANLEY CUP

The 1927–28 New York Rangers
The 1932–33 New York Rangers
The 1939–40 New York Rangers
The 1993–94 New York Rangers

VEZINA TROPHY

Dave Kerr	1939–40
Ed Giacomin and Gilles Villemure	1970–71
John Vanbiesbrouck	1985–86

LESTER B. PEARSON AWARD

Jean Ratelle	1971–72
Mark Messier	1991–92

JAMES NORRIS MEMORIAL TROPHY

Doug Harvey	1961–62
Harry Howell	1966–67
Brian Leetch	1991–92
Brian Leetch	1996–97

LADY BYNG MEMORIAL TROPHY

Frank Boucher	1927–28
Frank Boucher	1928–29
Frank Boucher	1929–30
Frank Boucher	1930–31
Frank Boucher	1932–33
Frank Boucher	1933–34
Frank Boucher	1934–35
Clint Smith	1938–39
Buddy O'Connor	1947–48
Edgar Laprade	1949–50
Andy Hebenton	1956–57
Camille Henry	1957–58
Jean Ratelle	1971–72
Wayne Gretzky	1998–99

LESTER PATRICK TROPHY

Terry Sawchuk	1971
Murray Murdoch	1974
Phil Esposito	1978
Fred Shero	1980
Emile Francis	1982
Bud Poile	1989
Rod Gilbert	1991
Frank Boucher	1993
Wayne Gretzky	1994
Brian Mullen	1995
Pat LaFontaine	1997

CONN SMYTHE TROPHY

Brian Leetch	1993–94

BILL MASTERTON MEMORIAL TROPHY

Jean Ratelle	1970–71
Rod Gilbert	1975–76
Anders Hedberg	1984–85

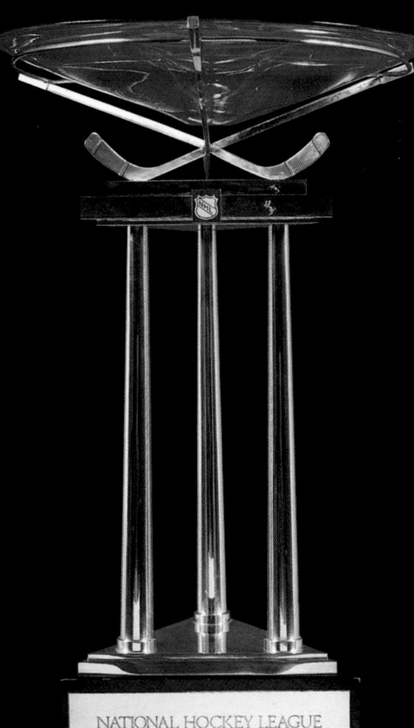

PRESIDENTS' TROPHY

The 1991–92 New York Rangers
The 1993–94 New York Rangers

KING CLANCY MEMORIAL TROPHY

Adam Graves	1993–94

HART MEMORIAL TROPHY

Buddy O'Connor	1947–48
Chuck Rayner	1949–50
Andy Bathgate	1958–59
Mark Messier	1991–92

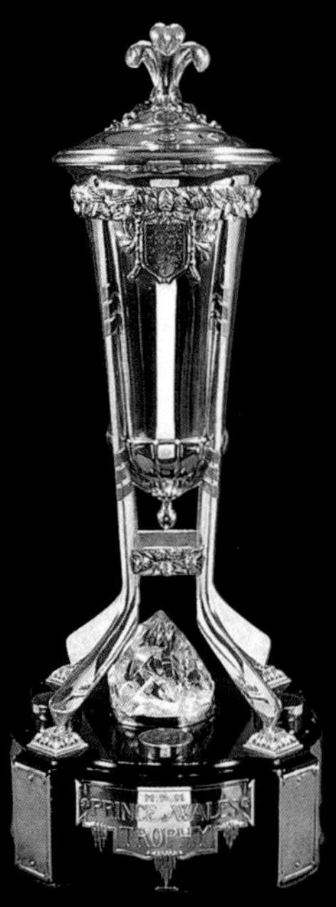

PRINCE OF WALES TROPHY

The 1931–32 New York Rangers
The 1941–42 New York Rangers
The 1993–94 New York Rangers

New York Rangers Records

New York Rangers Stanley Cup Champions

1927–28 Lester Patrick (manager and coach), Taffy Abel, Frank Boucher, Leo Bourgault, Bill Boyd, Lorne Chabot, Art Chapman, Bill Cook, Bun Cook, Patsy Gallighen, Alex Gray, Ching Johnson, Joe Miller, Murray Murdoch, Paul Thompson.

1932–33 Lester Patrick (manager and coach), Andy Aitkenhead, Jimmy Arnott, Ossie Asmundsen, Doug Brennan, Bill Cook, Bun Cook, Cecil Dillon, Ott Heller, Ching Johnson, Butch Keeling, Murray Murdoch, Gordon Pettinger, Babe Siebert, Earl Seibert, Art Somers, Wilfie Starr, Carl Voss.

1939–40 Frank Boucher (coach), Lester Patrick (manager), Mac Colville, Neil Colville, Art Coulter, Ott Heller, Bryan Hextall, Dutch Hiller, Dave Kerr, Kilby MacDonald, Lynn Patrick, Muzz Patrick, Alf Pike, Babe Pratt, Alex Shibicky, Clint Smith, Phil Watson.

1993–94 Mike Keenan (head coach), Neil Smith (president and general manager), Glenn Anderson, Jeff Beukeboom, Greg Gilbert, Adam Graves, Mike Hartman, Glenn Healy, Mike Hudson, Alexander Karpovtsev, Joe Kocur, Alexei Kovalev, Nick Kypreos, Steve Larmer, Brian Leetch, Doug Lidster, Kevin Lowe, Craig MacTavish, Stephane Matteau, Mark Messier, Sergei Nemchinov, Brian Noonan, Eddie Olczyk, Mike Richter, Esa Tikkanen, Jay Wells, Sergei Zubov.

Rangers Management

Rangers Presidents

John S. Hammond	(1926 through 1931-32)
William F. Carey	(1932-33)
John Reed Kilpatrick	(1933-34)
John S. Hammond	(1934-35)
John Reed Kilpatrick	(1935-36 through 1959-60)
John J. Bergen	(1960-61 through 1961-62)
William M. Jennings	(1962-63 through 1980-81)
John H. Krumpe	(1981-82 to Dec. 31, 1986)
Richard H. Evans	(Jan. 1, 1987 to June 28, 1990)
John C. Diller	(June 29, 1990 to April 22, 1991)
Neil Smith	(June 19, 1992 to March 28, 2000)

Rangers General Managers

Lester Patrick	(1926-27 through 1945-46)
Frank Boucher	(1946-47 through 1954-55)
Muzz Patrick	(1955-56 through 1963-64)
Emile Francis	(1964-65 to Jan. 6, 1976)
John Ferguson	(Jan. 7, 1976 to June 2, 1978)
Fred Shero	(June 2, 1978 to Nov. 21, 1980)
Craig Patrick	(Nov. 21, 1980 to July 14, 1986)
Phil Esposito	(July 14, 1986 to May 24, 1989)
Neil Smith	(July 17, 1989 to March 28, 2000)

Rangers Coaches & Records

	GC	W	L	T	RT
Lester Patrick (1926-27 through 1938-39)	604	281	216	107	–
Frank Boucher (1939-40 to 12/21/48)	486	166	243	77	–
Lynn Patrick (12/21/48 through 1949-50)	107	40	51	16	–
Neil Colville (1950-51 to 12/6/51)	93	26	41	26	–
Bill Cook (12/6/51 through 1952-53)	117	34	59	24	–
Frank Boucher (1953-54 to 1/6/54)	39	13	20	6	–
Muzz Patrick (1/6/54 through 1954-55)	105	35	47	23	–
Phil Watson (1955-56 to 11/12/59)	294	118	124	52	–
Alf Pike (11/18/59 through 1960-61)	123	36	66	21	–
Doug Harvey (5/30/61 through 1961-62)	70	26	32	12	–
Muzz Patrick (9/7/62 to 12/28/62)	34	11	19	4	–
Red Sullivan (12/28/62 to 12/5/65)	196	58	103	35	–
Emile Francis (12/5/65 to 6/4/68)	193	81	82	30	–
Bernie Geoffrion (6/4/68 to 1/17/69)	43	22	18	3	–
Emile Francis (1/17/69 to 6/4/73)	344	202	88	54	–
Larry Popein (6/4/73 to 1/11/74)	41	18	14	9	–
Emile Francis (1/11/74 to 5/19/75)	117	59	39	19	–
Ron Stewart (5/19/75 to 1/7/76)	39	15	20	4	–
John Ferguson (1/7/76 to 8/22/77)	121	43	59	19	–
Jean-Guy Talbot (8/22/77 to 6/2/78)	80	30	37	13	–
Fred Shero (6/2/78 to 11/22/80)	180	82	74	24	–
Craig Patrick (11/22/80 to 6/4/81)	60	26	23	11	–
Herb Brooks (6/4/81 to 1/21/85)	285	131	113	41	–
Craig Patrick (1/21/85 to 6/19/85)	35	11	22	2	–
Ted Sator (6/19/85 to 11/21/86)	99	41	48	10	–
***Phil Esposito** (1986-87)	43	24	19	0	–
***Tom Webster** (1986-87)	16	5	7	4	–
***Wayne Cashman/Ed Giacomin** (1986-87)	2	0	2	0	–
Michel Bergeron (6/18/87 to 4/1/89)	158	73	67	18	–
Phil Esposito (4/1/89 to 5/24/89)	2	0	2	0	–
Roger Neilson (8/15/89 to 1/4/93)	280	141	104	35	–
Ron Smith (1/4/93 to 4/16/93)	44	15	22	7	–
Mike Keenan (4/17/93 to 7/24/94)	84	52	24	8	–
Colin Campbell (8/10/94 to 2/18/98)	269	118	108	43	–
John Muckler (2/19/98 to 3/28/2000)	185	70	91	24	3
John Tortorella (1999-2000)	4	0	3	1	–

** (Due to illness to Tom Webster, head coaching situation changed several times during season.)*

Rangers Captains

Bill Cook	(1926-27 through 1936-37)
Art Coulter	(1937-38 through 1941-42)
Ott Heller	(1942-43 through 1944-45)
Neil Colville	(1945-46 to Dec. 21, 1948)
Buddy O'Connor	(1949-50)
Frank Eddolls	(1950-51 to Dec. 6, 1951)
Allan Stanley	(Dec. 20, 1951 to Nov. 3, 1953)
Don Raleigh	(Nov. 4, 1953 through 1954-55)
Harry Howell	(1955-56 through 1956-57)
George Sullivan	(1957-58 through 1960-61)
Andy Bathgate	(1961-62 to Feb. 22, 1964)
Camille Henry	(Feb. 23, 1964 to Feb. 4, 1965)
Bob Nevin	(Feb. 5, 1965 through 1970-71)
Vic Hadfield	(1971-72 through 1973-74)
Brad Park	(1974-75 to Nov. 7, 1975)
Phil Esposito	(Nov. 12, 1975 to Oct. 10, 1978)
Dave Maloney	(Oct. 11, 1978 to Dec. 6, 1980)
Walt Tkaczuk	(Dec. 7, 1980 to Feb. 3, 1981)
Barry Beck	(Feb. 4, 1981 to May 9, 1986)
Ron Greschner	(Oct. 9, 1986 to Dec. 3, 1987)
Kelly Kisio	(Dec. 24, 1987 to May 30, 1991)
Mark Messier	(Oct. 7, 1991 to May 25, 1997)
Brian Leetch	(Oct. 3, 1997 to present)

Rangers Hall of Famers

Howie Morenz	(1945)	Tim Horton	(1977)
Lester Patrick	(1947)	Andy Bathgate	(1978)
Bill Cook	(1952)	Jacques Plante	(1978)
Frank Boucher	(1958)	Harry Howell	(1979)
Ching Johnson	(1958)	Lynn Patrick	(1980)
Earl Seibert	(1963)	Gump Worsley	(1980)
Doug Bentley	(1964)	Allan Stanley	(1981)
Babe Siebert	(1964)	Rod Gilbert	(1982)
Max Bentley	(1966)	Phil Esposito	(1984)
Babe Pratt	(1966)	Jean Ratelle	(1985)
Neil Colville	(1967)	Ed Giacomin	(1987)
Bryan Hextall	(1969)	Guy Lafleur	(1988)
Bill Gadsby	(1970)	Buddy O'Connor	(1988)
Terry Sawchuk	(1971)	Brad Park	(1988)
Bernard Geoffrion	(1972)	Clint Smith	(1991)
Doug Harvey	(1973)	Marcel Dionne	(1992)
Chuck Rayner	(1973)	Edgar Laprade	(1993)
Art Coulter	(1974)	Fred "Bun" Cook	(1995)
Johnny Bower	(1976)	Wayne Gretzky	(1999)

Builders

John Kilpatrick	(1960)
William Jennings	(1975)
Emile Francis	(1982)

Rangers in the U.S. Hockey Hall of Fame

Taffy Abel
Victor Des Jardins
Robert E. Dill
Robbie Ftorek
William M. Jennings
Myles Lane
John W. McCartan
Bill Moe

Rangers Coaching Records

Games Coached

Emile Francis	654
Lester Patrick	604
Frank Boucher	525
Phil Watson	294
Herb Brooks	285
Roger Neilson	280
Colin Campbell	269
Red Sullivan	196

Wins

Emile Francis	342
Lester Patrick	281
Frank Boucher	179
Roger Neilson	141
Herb Brooks	131
Phil Watson	118
Colin Campbell	118

Losses

Frank Boucher	243
Lester Patrick	216
Emile Francis	209
Phil Watson	124
Herb Brooks	113
Colin Campbell	108
Roger Neilson	104

Winning Percentage (minimum 100 games)

Emile Francis	.602
Roger Neilson	.566
Lester Patrick	.554
Herb Brooks	.532
Fred Shero	.522
Michel Bergeron	.519
Colin Campbell	.519

Rangers Record against All NHL Teams Since 1926

THROUGH 1999-2000 NHL SEASON

New York Rangers vs.

	GP	W	L	T	RT	GF	GA	PTS
OVERALL								
Chicago Blackhawks	566	230	239	97	0	1619	1662	557
Boston Bruins	584	220	267	97	0	1708	1880	537
Detroit Red Wings (a)	564	209	252	103	0	1558	1724	521
Toronto Maple Leafs	549	199	255	95	1	1569	1746	494
Montreal Canadiens	564	170	302	92	0	1463	1933	432
Philadelphia Flyers	198	80	81	37	0	604	615	197
Pittsburgh Penguins	180	87	71	22	0	700	635	196
New York Islanders	171	76	78	17	0	592	601	169
New Jersey Devils (K.C., Col.)	149	71	58	20	0	556	482	162
St. Louis Blues	118	72	31	15	0	433	308	159
Dallas Stars (Min.)	117	64	32	21	1	420	335	150
Vancouver Canucks	101	70	23	8	0	432	289	148
Washington Capitals	150	64	69	17	1	531	542	146
Los Angeles Kings	112	59	38	15	0	427	344	133
Buffalo Sabres	118	41	54	23	0	378	408	105
Calgary Flames (Atl.)	96	33	48	15	0	315	385	81
Ottawa Senators (b)	62	34	17	11	0	188	143	79
Carolina Hurricanes (Hfd.)	72	36	30	6	0	262	223	78
Colorado Avalanche (Que.)	62	31	24	7	0	245	222	69
Phoenix Coyotes (Wpg.)	55	30	19	6	0	222	195	66
Edmonton Oilers	54	21	24	9	0	192	200	51
Tampa Bay Lightning	36	17	14	5	0	128	124	39
Florida Panthers	33	14	14	5	0	91	88	33
San Jose Sharks	17	13	2	2	0	72	42	28
Anaheim Mighty Ducks	11	3	7	1	0	29	38	7
Nashville Predators	3	3	0	0	0	17	6	6
Atlanta Thrashers	4	4	0	0	0	22	10	8
Defunct Teams (c)	246	152	58	36	0	811	521	340
Totals	**4992**	**2103**	**2107**	**782**	**3**	**15584**	**15701**	**4991**
HOME								
Detroit Red WIngs (a)	282	134	89	59	0	862	726	327
Boston Bruins	294	127	112	55	0	895	831	309
Chicago Blackhawks	283	117	111	55	0	834	801	289
Toronto Maple Leafs	275	117	102	56	0	848	804	290
Montreal Canadiens	282	114	114	54	0	819	825	282
Philadelphia Flyers	100	43	34	23	0	322	289	109
New York Islanders	85	50	25	10	0	329	256	110
Pittsburgh Penguins	90	47	35	8	0	362	311	102
St. Louis Blues	58	44	8	6	0	240	134	94
New Jersey Devils (K.C., Colo.)	74	39	20	15	0	298	223	93
Dallas Stars (Min.)	59	34	14	11	0	205	161	79
Vancouver Canucks	52	37	10	5	0	232	133	79
Washington Capitals	74	34	32	8	1	280	260	77
Los Angeles Kings	55	34	15	6	0	224	156	74
Buffalo Sabres	58	24	19	15	0	189	155	63
Calgary Flames (Atl.)	49	23	21	5	0	174	174	51
Carolina Hurricanes (Hfd.)	37	23	11	3	0	147	100	49
Colorado Avalanche (Que.)	30	18	8	4	0	121	90	40
Ottawa Senators (b)	31	15	11	5	0	89	76	35
Phoenix Coyotes (Wpg.)	27	17	8	2	0	125	98	36
Edmonton Oilers	27	8	13	6	0	99	103	22
Tampa Bay Lightning	18	10	6	2	0	69	67	22
Florida Panthers	16	6	6	4	0	45	42	16
San Jose Sharks	8	6	1	1	0	37	23	13
Anaheim Mighty Ducks	5	2	2	1	0	14	14	5
Nashville Predators	2	2	0	0	0	10	2	4
Atlanta Thrashers	2	2	0	0	0	10	4	4
Defunct Teams (c)	123	80	26	17	0	425	258	177
Totals	**2496**	**1207**	**853**	**436**	**1**	**8304**	**7116**	**2851**

Rangers Record against All NHL Teams Since 1926

THROUGH 1999-2000 NHL SEASON

New York Rangers vs.

	GP	W	L	T	RT	GF	GA	PTS
ROAD								
Chicago Blackhawks	283	113	128	42	0	785	861	268
Boston Bruins	290	93	155	42	0	813	1049	228
Toronto Maple Leafs	274	82	153	39	1	721	942	204
Detroit Red Wings (a)	282	75	163	44	0	696	998	194
Montreal Canadiens	282	56	188	38	0	644	1108	150
Pittsburgh Penguins	90	40	36	14	0	338	324	94
Philadelphia Flyers	98	37	47	14	0	282	326	88
Dallas Stars (Min.)	58	30	18	10	1	215	174	71
Vancouver Canucks	49	33	13	3	0	200	156	69
New Jersey Devils (K.C.,Col.)	75	32	38	5	0	259	259	69
Washington Capitals	76	30	37	9	0	251	282	69
St. Louis Blues	60	28	23	9	0	193	174	65
Los Angeles Kings	57	25	23	9	0	203	188	59
New York Islanders	86	26	53	7	0	263	345	59
Ottawa Senators (b)	31	19	6	6	0	99	67	44
Buffalo Sabres	60	17	35	8	0	189	253	42
Calgary Flames (Atl.)	47	10	27	10	0	141	211	30
Phoenix Coyotes (Wpg.)	28	13	11	4	0	97	97	30
Colorado Avalanche (Que.)	32	13	16	3	0	124	132	29
Edmonton Oilers	27	13	11	3	0	93	97	29
Carolina Hurricanes (Hfd.)	35	13	19	3	0	115	123	29
Florida Panthers	17	8	8	1	0	46	46	17
San Jose Sharks	9	7	1	1	0	35	19	15
Tampa Bay Lightning	18	7	8	3	0	58	57	17
Nashville Predators	1	1	0	0	0	7	4	2
Anaheim Mighty Ducks	6	1	5	0	0	15	24	2
Atlanta Thrashers	2	2	0	0	0	12	6	4
Defunct Teams (c)	123	72	32	19	0	386	263	163
Totals	**2496**	**896**	**1254**	**346**	**2**	**7280**	**8585**	**2140**

(a) *includes records of Detroit Cougars and Detroit Falcons*

(b) *includes records of Ottawa Senators*

(c) *Brooklyn and New York Americans, Cleveland Barons (Calif.), Montreal Maroons, Philadelphia Quakers, Pittsburgh Pirates, and St. Louis Eagles*

Rangers Year-by-Year Scoring Leaders

Year	Goals		Assists		Points	
1926-27	33	Bill Cook	15	Boucher	37	Bill Cook
1927-28	23	Boucher	14	Bun Cook	35	Boucher
1928-29	15	Bill Cook	16	Boucher	26	Boucher
1929-30	29	Bill Cook	36	Boucher	62	Boucher
1930-31	30	Bill Cook	27	Boucher	42	Bill Cook
1931-32	33	Bill Cook	23	Boucher	47	Bill Cook
1932-33	28	Bill Cook	28	Boucher	50	Bill Cook
1933-34	18	Bun Cook	30	Boucher	44	Boucher
1934-35	25	Dillon	32	Boucher	45	Boucher
1935-36	18	Dillon	18	Boucher	32	Dillon
1936-37	22	Keeling	18	N. Colville	31	Dillon
1937-38	21	Dillon	25	Watson	39	Dillon
1938-39	24	Shibicky	23	Heller	41	C. Smith
1939-40	24	Hextall	28	Watson	39	Hextall
1940-41	26	Hextall	28	N. Colville	44	Hextall
					44	Lynn Patrick
1941-42	32	Lynn Patrick	37	Watson	56	Hextall
1942-43	27	Hextall	39	Lynn Patrick	61	Lynn Patrick
1943-44	21	Hextall	33	Hextall	54	Hextall
1944-45	24	DeMarco	30	DeMarco	54	DeMarco
1945-46	20	DeMarco	27	DeMarco	47	DeMarco
1946-47	27	Leswick	25	Laprade	41	Leswick
1947-48	24	O'Connor	36	O'Connor	60	O'Connor
	24	Leswick				
1948-49	18	Laprade	24	O'Connor	35	O'Connor
1949-50	22	Laprade	25	Leswick	44	Laprade
			25	Raleigh	44	Leswick
1950-51	20	Mickoski	24	Raleigh	39	Raleigh
					39	Sinclair
1951-52	26	Hergesheimer	42	Raleigh	61	Raleigh
1952-53	30	Hergesheimer	38	Ronty	59	Hergesheimer
1953-54	27	Hergesheimer	33	Ronty	46	Ronty
1954-55	29	Lewicki	32	Raleigh	53	Lewicki
1955-56	24	Prentice	47	Bathgate	66	Bathgate
	24	Hebenton				
1956-57	27	Bathgate	50	Bathgate	77	Bathgate
1957-58	32	Henry	48	Bathgate	78	Bathgate
1958-59	40	Bathgate	48	Bathgate	88	Bathgate
1959-60	32	Prentice	48	Bathgate	74	Bathgate
1960-61	29	Bathgate	48	Bathgate	77	Bathgate
1961-62	28	Bathgate	56	Bathgate	84	Bathgate
1962-63	37	Henry	46	Bathgate	81	Bathgate
1963-64	29	Henry	43	Bathgate	65	Goyette
1964-65	25	Gilbert	36	Gilbert	61	Gilbert
1965-66	29	Nevin	33	Nevin	62	Nevin
1966-67	28	Gilbert	49	Goyette	61	Goyette
1967-68	32	Ratelle	48	Gilbert	78	Ratelle
1968-69	32	Ratelle	49	Gilbert	78	Ratelle
1969-70	33	Balon	50	Tkaczuk	77	Tkaczuk
1970-71	36	Balon	49	Tkaczuk	75	Tkaczuk
1971-72	50	Hadfield	63	Ratelle	109	Ratelle
1972-73	41	Ratelle	59	Gilbert	94	Ratelle
1973-74	36	Gilbert	57	Park	82	Park
1974-75	41	Vickers	61	Gilbert	97	Gilbert
1975-76	36	Gilbert	53	Vickers	86	Gilbert
1976-77	34	Esposito	48	Gilbert	80	Esposito
1977-78	40	Hickey	48	Greschner	81	Esposito
1978-79	42	Esposito	45	Hedberg	78	Esposito
					78	Hedberg
1979-80	34	Esposito	50	Beck	78	Esposito
1980-81	30	Hedberg	41	Greschner	70	Hedberg
1981-82	40	Duguay	65	Rogers	103	Rogers
1982-83	37	Pavelich	53	Ruotsalainen	76	Rogers
1983-84	48	Larouche	53	Pavelich	82	Pavelich
1984-85	29	Sandstrom	45	Ruotsalainen	73	Ruotsalainen
1985-86	25	Sandstrom	43	Ridley	65	Ridley
1986-87	40	Poddubny	47	Poddubny	87	Poddubny
	40	Sandstrom				
1987-88	38	Poddubny	55	Kisio	88	Poddubny
1988-89	36	Granato	56	Sandstrom	88	Sandstrom
1989-90	43	Ogrodnick	45	Leetch	74	Ogrodnick
1990-91	49	Gartner	72	Leetch	88	Leetch
1991-92	40	Gartner	80	Leetch	107	Messier
1992-93	45	Gartner	66	Messier	91	Messier
1993-94	52	Graves	77	Zubov	89	Zubov
1994-95	17	Graves	39	Messier	53	Messier
	17	Verbeek				
1995-96	47	Messier	70	Leetch	99	Messier
1996-97	36	Messier	72	Gretzky	97	Gretzky
1997-98	23	Graves	67	Gretzky	90	Gretzky
	23	Gretzky				
	23	Kovalev				
	23	LaFontaine				
1998-99	38	Graves	53	Gretzky	62	Gretzky
1999-2000	26	York	49	Fleury	68	Nedved

Rangers All-Time Scoring List

	PLAYER	GP	Goals	Assists	Points	PIM
1	Rod Gilbert (RW)	1065	406	615	1021	508
2	Jean Ratelle (C)	862	336	481	817	192
3	Brian Leetch (D)	857	184	597	781	419
4	Andy Bathgate (RW)	719	272	457	729	444
5	Walt Tkaczuk (C)	945	227	451	678	556
6	Ron Greschner (D)	982	179	431	610	1226
7	Steve Vickers (LW)	698	246	340	586	330
8	Vic Hadfield (LW)	839	262	310	572	1036
9	Mark Messier (C)	421	183	335	518	474
10	Don Maloney (LW)	653	195	307	502	739
11	Adam Graves (LW)	690	270	211	481	733
12	Camille Henry (C)	637	256	222	478	78
13	James Patrick (D)	671	104	363	467	541
14	Dean Prentice (LW)	666	186	236	422	263
15	Frank Boucher (C)	533	152	261	413	114
16	Phil Esposito (C)	422	184	220	404	263
17	Anders Hedberg (RW)	465	172	225	397	144
18	Tomas Sandstrom (RW)	407	173	207	380	563
19	Brad Park (D)	465	95	283	378	738
20	Andy Hebenton (RW)	560	177	191	368	75
21	Bill Cook (RW)	475	228	138	366	386
22	Bryan Hextall, Sr. (RW)	449	187	175	362	227
23	Bill Fairbairn (RW)	536	138	224	362	161
24	Phil Watson (RW)	546	127	233	360	471
25	Harry Howell (D)	1160	82	263	345	1147
26	Bob Nevin (RW)	505	168	174	342	105
27	Ron Duguay (C)	499	164	176	340	370
28	Lynn Patrick (LW)	455	145	190	335	270
29	Phil Goyette (C)	397	98	231	329	51
30	Don Raleigh (C)	535	101	219	320	96
31	Mark Pavelich (C)	341	133	185	318	326
32	Pete Stemkowski (C)	496	113	204	317	379
33	Reijo Ruotsalainen (D)	389	99	217	316	154
34	Mike Rogers (C)	316	117	191	308	142
35	Kelly Kisio (C)	336	110	195	305	415
36	Jim Neilson (D)	810	60	238	298	766
37	Dave Maloney (D)	605	70	225	295	1113
38	Fred "Bun" Cook (LW)	433	154	139	293	436
39	Mike Gartner (RW)	322	173	113	286	231
40	Cecil Dillon (RW)	409	160	121	281	93
41	Edgar Laprade (C)	500	108	172	280	42
42	Don Marshall (LW)	479	129	141	270	40
43	Bill Gadsby (D)	457	58	212	270	411
44	Alexei Kovalev (RW)	388	116	152	268	447
45	Neil Colville (C)	464	99	166	265	213
46	Earl Ingarfield (C)	527	122	142	264	201
47	Pat Hickey (LW)	370	128	129	257	216
48	Darren Turcotte (C)	325	122	133	255	183
49	John Ogrodnick (LW)	338	126	128	254	106
50	Wayne Gretzky (C)	234	57	192	249	70
51	Brian Mullen (RW)	307	100	148	248	188
52	Rod Seiling (D)	644	50	198	248	425
53	Carol Vadnais (D)	485	56	190	246	690
54	Pierre Larouche (RW)	253	123	120	243	59
55	Barry Beck (D)	415	66	173	239	775
56	Ed Johnstone (RW)	371	109	125	234	319
57	Grant Warwick (RW)	293	117	116	233	179
58	Ott Heller (D)	647	55	176	231	465
59	Sergei Nemchinov (C)	418	105	120	225	151
60	Jan Erixon (LW)	556	57	159	216	167
61	Dave Balon (LW)	361	99	113	212	284
62	Red Sullivan (C)	322	59	150	209	300
63	Tony Leswick (LW)	368	113	89	202	420
64	Larry Popein (C)	402	75	127	202	150
65	Alex Shibicky (LW)	322	110	91	201	161
66	Clint Smith (C)	281	80	115	195	12

Rangers Career Leaders

GOALS	
Rod Gilbert (RW)	406
Jean Ratelle (C)	336
Andy Bathgate (RW)	272
Adam Graves (LW)	270
Vic Hadfield (LW)	262
Camille Henry (C)	256
Steve Vickers (LW)	246
Bill Cook (RW)	228
Walt Tkaczuk (C)	227
Don Maloney (LW)	195
Bryan Hextall, Sr. (RW)	187
Dean Prentice (LW)	186
Brian Leetch (D	184
Phil Esposito (C))	184
Mark Messier (C)	183
Ron Greschner (D)	179
Andy Hebenton (RW)	177
Mike Gartner (RW)	173
Tomas Sandstrom (RW)	173
Anders Hedberg (RW)	172
Bob Nevin (RW)	168
Ron Duguay (C)	164
Cecil Dillon (RW)	160
Fred "Bun" Cook (LW)	154
Frank Boucher (C)	152
Lynn Patrick (LW)	145
Bill Fairbairn (RW)	138
Butch Keeling (LW)	136
Mark Pavelich (C)	133
Don Marshall (LW)	129
Pat Hickey (LW)	128
Phil Watson (RW)	127
John Ogrodnick (LW)	126
Pierre Larouche (RW)	123
Earl Ingarfield (C)	122
Darren Turcotte (C)	122
Mike Rogers (C)	117
Grant Warwick (RW)	117
Alexei Kovalev (RW)	116

GAMES	
Harry Howell (D)	1160
Rod Gilbert (RW)	1065
Ron Greschner (D)	982
Walt Tkaczuk (C)	945
Jean Ratelle (C)	862
Brian Leetch (D)	857
Vic Hadfield (LW)	839
Jim Neilson (D)	810
Andy Bathgate (RW)	719
Steve Vickers (LW)	698
Adam Graves (LW)	690
James Patrick (D)	671
Dean Prentice (LW)	666
Don Maloney (LW)	653
Ott Heller (D)	647
Rod Seiling (D)	644
Camille Henry (C)	637
Dave Maloney (D)	605
Andy Hebenton (RW)	560
Jan Erixon (LW)	556
Phil Watson (RW)	546
Bill Fairbairn (RW)	536
Don Raleigh (C)	535
Frank Boucher (C)	533

GOALTENDER WINS	
Ed Giacomin	266
Mike Richter	252
Lorne Worsley	204
John Vanbiesbrouck	200
Dave Kerr	157
Chuck Rayner	123
Gilles Villemure	96
John Davidson	93
John Ross Roach	80
Glen Hanlon	56

ASSISTS	
Rod Gilbert (RW)	615
Brian Leetch (D)	597
Jean Ratelle (C)	481
Andy Bathgate (RW)	457
Walt Tkaczuk (C)	451
Ron Greschner (D)	431
James Patrick (D)	363
Steve Vickers (LW)	340
Mark Messier (C)	335
Vic Hadfield (LW)	310
Don Maloney (LW)	307
Brad Park (D)	283
Harry Howell (D)	263
Frank Boucher (C)	261
Jim Neilson (D)	238
Dean Prentice (LW)	236
Phil Watson (RW)	233
Phil Goyette (C)	231
Dave Maloney (D)	225
Anders Hedberg (RW)	225
Bill Fairbairn (RW)	224
Camille Henry (C)	222
Phil Esposito (C)	220
Don Raleigh (C)	219
Reijo Ruotsalainen (D)	217
Bill Gadsby (D)	212
Adam Graves (LW)	211
Tomas Sandstrom (RW)	207
Pete Stemkowski (C)	204
Rod Seiling (D)	198
Kelly Kisio (C)	195
Mike Rogers (C)	191
Andy Hebenton (RW)	191
Lynn Patrick (LW)	190
Carol Vadnais (D)	190
Mark Pavelich (C)	185

PENALTY MINUTES	
Ron Greschner (D)	1226
Jeff Beukeboom (D)	1157
Harry Howell (D)	1147
Dave Maloney (D)	1113
Vic Hadfield (LW)	1036
Nick Fotiu (LW)	970
Lou Fontinato (D)	939
Ching Johnson (D)	798
Barry Beck (D)	775
Jim Neilson (D)	766
Don Maloney (LW)	739
Brad Park (D)	738
Darren Langdon (LW)	735
Adam Graves (LW)	733
Kris King (LW)	733
Carol Vadnais (D)	690
Jack Evans (D)	670
Tomas Sandstrom (RW)	563
Tom Laidlaw (D)	561
Troy Mallette (LW)	557
Walt Tkaczuk (C)	556
Arnie Brown (D)	545
James Patrick (D)	541
Reg Fleming (LW)	540
Joe Kocur (RW)	537
Tie Domi (RW)	526
Rod Gilbert (RW)	508
Mark Messier (C)	474
Phil Watson (RW)	471
Ott Heller (D)	465
Alexei Kovalev (RW)	447

SHUTOUTS	
Ed Giacomin	49
Dave Kerr	40
John Ross Roach	30
Lorne Worsley	24
Chuck Rayner	24
Mike Richter	22
Lorne Chabot	21
John Vanbiesbrouck	16
Gilles Villemure	13
Andy Aitkenhead	11

Rangers Single Season Leaders

GOALS

Adam Graves	1993-94	52
Vic Hadfield	1971-72	50
Mike Gartner	1990-91	49
Pierre Larouche	1983-84	48
Mark Messier	1995-96	47
Jean Ratelle	1971-72	46
Mike Gartner	1992-93	45
Rod Gilbert	1971-72	43
John Ogrodnick	1989-90	43
Phil Esposito	1978-79	42
Jean Ratelle	1972-73	41
Steve Vickers	1974-75	41
Pat Verbeek	1995-96	41
Andy Bathgate	1958-59	40
Pat Hickey	1977-78	40
Ron Duguay	1981-82	40
Walt Poddubny	1986-87	40
Tomas Sandstrom	1986-87	40
Mike Gartner	1991-92	40

POINTS

Jean Ratelle	1971-72	109
Mark Messier	1991-92	107
Vic Hadfield	1971-72	106
Mike Rogers	1981-82	103
Brian Leetch	1991-92	102
Mark Messier	1995-96	99
Rod Gilbert	1971-72	97
Rod Gilbert	1974-75	97
Wayne Gretzky	1996-97	97
Jean Ratelle	1972-73	94
Jean Ratelle	1974-75	91
Mark Messier	1992-93	91
Wayne Gretzky	1997-98	90
Steve Vickers	1974-75	89
Sergei Zubov	1993-94	89
Andy Bathgate	1958-59	88
Walt Poddubny	1987-88	88
Tomas Sandstrom	1988-89	88
Brian Leetch	1990-91	88
Walt Poddubny	1986-87	87
Rod Gilbert	1975-76	86

ASSISTS

Brian Leetch	1991-92	80
Sergei Zubov	1993-94	77
Brian Leetch	1990-91	72
Mark Messier	1991-92	72
Wayne Gretzky	1996-97	72
Brian Leetch	1995-96	70
Wayne Gretzky	1997-98	67
Mark Messier	1992-93	66
Mike Rogers	1981-82	65
Jean Ratelle	1971-72	63
Rod Gilbert	1974-75	61
Rod Gilbert	1972-73	59
Mark Messier	1993-94	58
Brian Leetch	1996-97	58
Brad Park	1973-74	57
James Patrick	1991-92	57
Andy Bathgate	1961-62	56
Vic Hadfield	1971-72	56
Tomas Sandstrom	1988-89	56
Brian Leetch	1993-94	56
Jean Ratelle	1974-75	55
Kelly Kisio	1987-88	55
Rod Gilbert	1971-72	54
Jean Ratelle	1972-73	53
Steve Vickers	1975-76	53
Reijo Ruotsalainen	1982-83	53
Mark Pavelich	1983-84	53
Wayne Gretzky	1998-99	53
Mark Messier	1995-96	52
Andy Bathgate	1956-57	50
Walt Tkaczuk	1969-70	50
Rod Gilbert	1975-76	50
Walt Poddubny	1987-88	50

GOALS BY A DEFENSEMAN

Brad Park	1973-74	25
Brad Park	1971-72	24
Brian Leetch	1988-89	23
Brian Leetch	1993-94	23
Brian Leetch	1991-92	22
Ron Greschner	1977-78	21
Ron Greschner	1979-80	21
Ron Greschner	1980-81	20
Carol Vadnais	1975-76	20
Mike McEwen	1978-79	20
Reijo Ruotsalainen	1983-84	20
Brian Leetch	1996-97	20

GOALS BY A ROOKIE

Tony Granato	1988-89	36
Tony Amonte	1991-92	35
Mark Pavelich	1981-82	33
Don Murdoch	1976-77	32
Darren Turcotte	1989-90	32
Steve Vickers	1972-73	30
Tomas Sandstrom	1984-85	29
Ulf Dahlen	1987-88	29
Wally Hergesheimer	1951-52	26
Mike Allison	1980-81	26
Mike York	199-2000	26

PENALTY MINUTES

Troy Mallette	1989-90	305
Kris King	1989-90	286
Troy Mallette	1990-91	252
Tie Domi	1991-92	246
Barry Beck	1980-81	231
Michel Petit	1987-88	223
Jeff Beukeboom	1995-96	220
Ed Hospodar	1980-81	214
Lou Fontinato	1955-56	202
Rudy Poeschek	1988-89	199
Darren Langdon	1997-98	197
Jeff Beukeboom	1997-98	195
Darren Langdon	1996-97	195
Nick Fotiu	1978-79	190
Dave Maloney	1979-80	186
Tie Domi	1990-91	185
Larry Melynk	1986-87	182
Chris Nilan	1988-89	177
Darren Langdon	1995-96	175
Nick Fotiu	1976-77	174

GOALTENDER WINS

Mike Richter	1993-94	42
Ed Giacomin	1968-69	37
Ed Giacomin	1967-68	36
Ed Giacomin	1969-70	35
Mike Richter	1996-97	33
Lorne Worsley	1955-56	32
John Vanbiesbrouck	1985-86	31
Ed Giacomin	1966-67	30
Ed Giacomin	1973-74	30
Jim Henry	1941-42	29
John Bower	1953-54	29
Chuck Rayner	1949-50	28
Glen Hanlon	1983-84	28
John Vanbiesbrouck	1988-89	28

SHUTOUTS

John Ross Roach	1928-29	13
Lorne Chabot	1927-28	11
Lorne Chabot	1926-27	10
John Ross Roach	1931-32	9
Ed Giacomin	1966-67	9
Dave Kerr	1935-36	8
Dave Kerr	1937-38	8
Dave Kerr	1939-40	8
Ed Giacomin	1967-68	8
Ed Giacomin	1970-71	8

POWER PLAY GOALS

Vic Hadfield	1971-72	23
Marcel Dionne	1987-88	22
Mike Gartner	1990-91	22
Phil Esposito	1977-78	21
Adam Graves	1993-94	20
Pierre Larouche	1983-84	19
John Ogrodnick	1989-90	19
Brian Leetch	1993-94	17
Pat Verbeek	1995-96	17
Rod Gilbert	1973-74	16
Jean Ratelle	1974-75	16
Steve Vickers	1974-75	16
Phil Esposito	1975-76	16
Phil Esposito	1976-77	15
Darren Turcotte	1990-91	15
Mike Gartner	1991-92	15

SHORTHANDED GOALS

Don Maloney	1980-81	5
Mike Rogers	1982-83	5
Mike Gartner	1993-94	5
Mark Messier	1996-97	5
Ron Stewart	1969-70	4
Bill Fairbairn	1971-72	4
Greg Polis	1977-78	4
Tony Granato	1988-89	4
Adam Graves	1991-92	4
Mark Messier	1991-92	4
Adam Graves	1993-94	4
Steve Larmer	1993-94	4
Adam Graves	1996-97	4

Lifetime Rangers Shutouts

	Regular Season	Playoffs	Total
Giacomin	49	1	50
Kerr	40	7	47
Roach	30	5	35
Richter	22	9	31
Rayner	24	1	25
Worsley	24	0	24
Chabot	21	2	23
Vanbiesbrouck	16	2	18
Aitkenhead	11	3	14
Villemure	13	0	13
Davidson	7	1	8
Healy	7	0	7
Bower	5	0	5
Plante	5	0	5
Thomas	5	0	5
Henry	4	1	5

	Regular Season	Playoffs	Total
Baker	3	0	3
Maniago	2	0	2
Mio	2	0	2
Paille	2	0	2
Winkler	2	0	2
Hanlon	1	1	2
Beveridge	1	0	1
Froese	1	0	1
McAuley	1	0	1
McCartan	1	0	1
Sawchuk	1	0	1
Soetaert	1	0	1
Weeks	1	0	1
Miller	0	1	1
	302	**34**	**336**

Most Decisive Victories

HOME

12-1	vs. California	Nov. 21, 1971
10-0	vs. California	Nov. 17, 1974
9-0	vs. Montreal	Feb. 4, 1940
9-0	vs. Montreal	Jan. 30, 1949
9-0	vs. Boston	Feb. 23, 1969
9-0	vs. New Jersey	Mar. 31, 1986
11-2	vs. Detroit	Jan. 25, 1942
8-0	vs. Los Angeles	Jan. 9, 1972
9-1	vs. St. Louis	Jan. 5, 1972
9-1	vs. Pittsburgh	Dec. 17, 1972
10-2	vs. Chicago	Mar. 12, 1952
10-2	vs. Edmonton	Oct. 24, 1979
10-2	vs. Detroit	Dec. 23, 1985
11-3	vs. Hartford	Feb. 23, 1983

ROAD

11-2	at New Jersey	Oct. 25, 1984
11-3	at Pittsburgh	Nov. 25, 1992
10-2	at Tampa Bay	Nov. 10, 1998
7-0	at NY Americans	Jan. 29, 1928
7-0	at Montreal	Jan. 22, 1935
7-0	at NY Americans	Feb. 2, 1939
7-0	at Toronto	Mar. 22, 1958
8-1	at Oakland	Nov. 7, 1969
8-1	at California	Nov. 5, 1971
8-1	at Minnesota	Dec. 30, 1974
9-2	at Ottawa	Jan. 28, 1933
9-2	at Minnesota	Feb. 15, 1975
11-4	at Minnesota	Dec. 4, 1976
11-4	at Washington	Mar. 24, 1978

Most Decisive Defeats

HOME

3-13	vs. Boston	Jan. 2, 1944
0-9	vs. Detroit	Dec. 6, 1950
1-10	vs. Toronto	Mar. 21, 1965
0-8	vs. Toronto	Mar. 9, 1944
0-8	vs. Chicago	Apr. 2, 1967

ROAD

0-15	at Detroit	Jan. 23, 1944
1-14	at Toronto	Mar. 16, 1957
3-14	at Boston	Jan. 21, 1945
2-12	at Detroit	Feb. 3, 1944

Rangers Regular Season Records

MOST VICTORIES, ONE SEASON: 52, 1993-94. Home: **30,** 1970-71 (39 games). Road: **24,** 1993-94.

FEWEST VICTORIES, ONE SEASON: 6, 1943-44 (50-game schedule). Home: **4,** 1943-44 (25 games). Road: **2,** 1943-44 (25 games).

FEWEST VICTORIES, ONE SEASON (Minimum 70-game schedule): 17, 1952-53, 1954-55, 1959-60. Home: **8,** 1964-65 (35 games). Road: **6,** 1950-51, 1952-53, 1965-66 (35 games).

FEWEST LOSSES, ONE SEASON: 11, 1939-40 (48 games schedule). Home: **2,** 1970-71 (39 games). Road: **7,** 1928-29 (22 games), 1930-31 (22 games), 1939-40 (24 games).

FEWEST LOSSES, ONE SEASON (Minimum 70-game schedule): 17, 1971-72. Home: **2,** 1970-71 (39 games). Road: **10,** 1957-58 (35 games).

MOST LOSSES, ONE SEASON: 44, 1984-85 (80-game schedule); **41,** 1999-2000 (82-game schedule). Home: **17,** 1943-44 (25 games); **19,** 1964-65 (35 games). Road: **26,** 1975-76 (40 games); **26** 1984-85 (40 games).

MOST TIES, ONE SEASON: (Minimum 70-game schedule): 21, 1950-51 (70-game schedule). Home: **13,** 1954-55 (35 games). Road: **11,** 1950-51 (35 games).

FEWEST TIES, ONE SEASON: (Minimum 70-game schedule): 5, 1991-92 (80-game schedule). Home: **1,** 1983-84 (40 games). Road: **1,** 1991-92 & 1975-76 (40 games).

MOST POINTS, ONE SEASON: 112, 1993-94. Home: **67,** 1970-71 (39 games). Road: **50,** (twice) 1971-72, 1993-94.

FEWEST POINTS, ONE SEASON: 17, 1943-44 (50-game schedule). Home: **12,** 1943-44 (25 games). Road: **5,** 1943-44 (25 games).

FEWEST POINTS, ONE SEASON (Minimum 70-game schedule): 47, 1965-66. Home: **24,** 1964-65 (35 games). Road: **16,** 1965-66 (35 games).

MOST GOALS ONE SEASON: 321, 1991-92. Home: **186,** 1982-83 (40 games). Road: **155,** 1978-79, 1986-87 (40 games).

FEWEST GOALS , ONE SEASON: 72, 1928-29 (44-game schedule). Home: **32,** 1928-29 (22 games). Road: **40,** 1928-29 (22 games).

FEWEST GOALS, ONE SEASON (Minimum 70-game schedule): 150, 1954-55. Home: **86,** 1954-55 (35 games). Road: **63,** 1952-53 (35 games).

MOST ASSISTS, ONE SEASON: 540, 1988-89.

FEWEST ASSISTS, ONE SEASON: 45, 1926-27 (44-game schedule).

FEWEST GOALS AGAINST, ONE SEASON: 65, 1928-29 (44-game schedule). Home: **21,** 1928-29 (22 games). Road: **41,** 1926-27 (22 games).

FEWEST GOALS AGAINST, ONE SEASON (Minimum 70-game schedule): 177, 1970-71. Home: **71,** 1970-71 (39 games). Road: **95,** 1957-58 (35 games).

MOST GOALS AGAINST, ONE SEASON: 345, 1984-85 (80-game schedule). Home: **156,** 1986-87 (40 games). Road: **197,** 1975-76 (40 games).

MOST POWER PLAY GOALS, ONE SEASON: 111, 1987-88.

MOST POWER PLAY GOALS, ONE GAME: 6, 10/13/93 vs. Quebec at Madison Square Garden.

MOST POWER PLAY GOALS ALLOWED, ONE SEASON: 89, 1995-96.

MOST SHORTHANDED GOALS, ONE SEASON: 20, 1993-94.

MOST SHORTHANDED GOALS, ONE GAME: 3, 10/5/83 vs. New Jersey at Madison Square Garden.

MOST SHORTHANDED GOALS ALLOWED, ONE SEASON: 18, 1992-93.

MOST 20-GOAL SCORERS, ONE SEASON: 9, 1993-94.

MOST 30-GOAL SCORERS, ONE SEASON: 5, 1991-92.

MOST 40-GOAL SCORERS, ONE SEASON: 3, 1971-72.

MOST HAT TRICKS, ONE SEASON: 10, 1986-87.

MOST PLAYERS USED, ONE SEASON: 46, 1986-87.

MOST ROOKIES USED, ONE SEASON: 14, 1988-89.

MOST ROOKIES USED, ONE GAME: 9, 3/21/90, vs. Toronto and 3/27/90 vs. Quebec.

MOST SCORING POINTS (Goals and Assists), ONE SEASON: 854, 1978-79.

FEWEST SCORING POINTS, ONE SEASON: 140, 1926-27 (44-game schedule).

MOST PENALTY MINUTES, ONE SEASON: 2018, 1989-90.

FEWEST PENALTY MINUTES, ONE SEASON: 253, 1943-44 (50-game schedule).

MOST SHUTOUTS, ONE SEASON: 13, 1928-29 (44-game schedule). Home: **8,** 1928-29 (22 games). Road: **7,** 1926-27 (22 games).

MOST TIMES SHUT OUT, ONE SEASON: 10, 1928-29 (44-game schedule). Home: **5,** 1930-31 (22 games), 1938-39 (24 games). Road: **7,** 1952-53 (35 games).

LONGEST WINNING STREAK: 10, 1939-40. Began 12/19 with 5-2 victory over Montreal. Ended 1/14 when defeated by Chicago, 2-1. (Rangers then won next five games for overall record of 15 wins in 16 games). **10,** 1972-73. Began 1/19 with 6-0 victory over California. Ended 2/11 with 2-2 tie against Montreal.

LONGEST WINNING STREAK AT START OF SEASON: 5, 1983-84. Began 10/5 with 6-2 victory over New Jersey. Ended 10/15 when defeated by St. Louis, 6-5. (Rangers then won next four games for overall record of 9-1-0 in first 10 games of season.)

LONGEST HOME WINNING STREAK AT START OF SEASON: 8, 1990-91. Began 10/8 with 6-3 victory over Minnesota. Ended 11/2 when defeated by Islanders, 3-2.
LONGEST LOSING STREAK AT START OF SEASON: 11, 1943-44. Began October 30 with 5-2 loss to Toronto. Ended November 28 with a 2-2 tie with Montreal. (Rangers then lost next three games for overall record of 0-14-1 in first 15 games before defeating Boston 6-4 on December 12.)
LONGEST HOME WINNING STREAK: 14, 1939-40. Began 12/19 with 5-2 victory over Montreal. Ended 2/29 when defeated by Chicago, 2-1.
LONGEST HOME LOSING STREAK AT START OF SEASON: 4, 1940-41. Began 11/15 with 2-1 defeat to Boston. Ended with a 5-4 overtime victory over Chicago.
LONGEST ROAD WINNING STREAK: 7, 1934-35. Began 1/12 with a 3-1 victory over Americans. Ended 2/16 when defeated by Toronto, 5-1. **7** 1978-79. Began 10/28 with a 2-1 victory over Montreal. Ended 12/2 when defeated by Toronto, 5-2.
LONGEST UNDEFEATED STREAK: 19, 1939-40. Won 14 games and tied five. Began 11/23 with 1-1 tie against Montreal. Ended 1/14 when defeated by Chicago, 2-1. (Rangers then won next five games for overall record of 24 victories or ties in 25 games).
LONGEST HOME UNDEFEATED STREAK: 26, 1970-71. Won 19 games and tied seven. Began 3/29/70, with a 4-1 victory over Montreal. Ended 2/3/71, when defeated by Chicago, 4-2. The streak covered the final two games of the 1969-70 season and the first 24 games of the 1970-71 season.
LONGEST ROAD UNDEFEATED STREAK: 11, 1939-40. Won six games and tied five. Began 11/5 with 1-1 tie against Detroit. Ended 1/14 when defeated by Chicago, 2-1.
MOST CONSECUTIVE TIE GAMES: 4, 1929-30. Tied by Chicago, 1-1, on 2/27; by Toronto, 3-3, on 3/1; by Detroit, 2-2, on 3/2; by Chicago, 2-2, on 3/4. **4,** 1997-98. Tied by Islanders, 2-2, on 10/3; by Los Angeles, 2-2, on 10/5; by Edmonton, 3-3, on 10/8; by Calgary, 1-1, on 10/9. (All overtime games).
LONGEST LOSING STREAK: 11, 1943-44. Began 10/30 with 5-2 defeat by Toronto. Ended 11/28 with 2-2 tie against Montreal.
LONGEST HOME LOSING STREAK: 7, 1976-77. Began 10/20 with 4-2 defeat by Los Angeles. Ended 11/17 with 3-2 victory over Chicago. **7,** 1992-93. Began 3/26 with a 3-1 defeat by Chicago. Continued to end of season.
LONGEST ROAD LOSING STREAK: 10, 1943-44. Began 10/30 with 5-2 defeat by Toronto. Ended 12/25 with 5-3 victory over Toronto. **10,** 1960-61. Began 2/8 with 5-3 defeat by at Toronto. Continued to end of season.
LONGEST WINLESS STREAK, ONE SEASON: 21, 1943-44. Lost 17 games and tied four. Began 1/23 with 15-0 defeat by Detroit. Continued to end of season.
LONGEST HOME WINLESS STREAK, ONE SEASON: 10, 1943-44. Lost seven games and tied three. Began 1/30 with 5-3 defeat by Montreal. Continued to end of season.
LONGEST ROAD WINLESS STREAK, ONE SEASON: 16, 1952-53. Lost 12 games and tied four. Began 10/9 with 5-3 defeat by Detroit. Ended 12/25 with 2-1 victory over Boston.
MOST CONSECUTIVE SHUTOUTS: 4, 1927-28. Rangers were not scored upon for a total of 297 minutes and 42 seconds. Defeated Pittsburgh, 3-0; Chicago, 1-0; tied Detroit, 0-0 (10 minutes overtime); defeated Toronto, 1-0. Streak started on 2/23 and ran until 2/28.
MOST CONSECUTIVE TIMES SHUT OUT: 4, 1927-28. Rangers failed to score for 341 minutes and 42 seconds. Tied by Ottawa, 0-0 (twice); lost to Chicago, 3-0; Boston, 2-0. Streak ran 2/7-2/19.
LONGEST NON-SHUTOUT STREAK: 236, 1989-92. Began 12/20/89 with a 2-2 tie with Buffalo. Ended 12/15/92 vs. Calgary (Vernon).
MOST GOALS, ONE GAME: 12. Defeated California, 12-1, on 11/21/71, at Madison Square Garden.
MOST GOALS, ONE GAME, RANGERS AND OPPONENTS: 19. Defeated by Boston, 10-9, at Boston, 3/4/44.
MOST POINTS ONE GAME, RANGERS AND OPPONENTS: 46. Boston Bruins, at Boston, 3/4/44. Boston won, 10-9. Boston had 15 assists, Rangers 12.
MOST GOALS ALLOWED, ONE GAME: 15. Defeated by Detroit, 15-0, at Detroit, 1/23/44.
GREATEST WINNING MARGIN: 11. Defeated California, 12-1, 11/21/71, at Madison Square Garden.
GREATEST LOSING MARGIN: 15. Defeated by Detroit, 15-0 at Detroit, 1/23/44.
HIGHEST TIE SCORE: 7-7, tied Minnesota on 3/19/78 at Minnesota. **7-7,** tied Quebec on 3/22/81 at Madison Square Garden.
MOST ASSISTS, ONE GAME: 23, 11/21/71. Defeated California 12-1, at Madison Square Garden.

MOST POINTS, ONE GAME: 35, 11/21/71. 12 goals and 23 assists.

MOST GOALS, ONE PERIOD: 8, 11/21/71 (third period).

MOST POINTS, ONE PERIOD: 23, 11/21/71 vs. California (third period). Eight goals and 15 assists.

MOST ASSISTS, ONE PERIOD: 15, 11/21/71 vs. California (third period).

MOST GOALS, ONE PERIOD, RANGERS AND OPPONENTS: 10, 3/16/39 (third period). Rangers scored seven goals and Americans three, at Madison Square Garden. Rangers won game, 11-5.

MOST SHOTS, ONE GAME: 65, 4/5/70. Defeated Detroit, 9-5, at Madison Square Garden.

LARGEST HOME ATTENDANCE, ONE SEASON: 746, 200, 1995-96.

FASTEST TWO GOALS BY RANGERS: 4 sec. Kris King at 19:45 and James Patrick at 19:49 of the third period against the Islanders at Madison Square Garden, 10/9/91 Rangers won 5-3.

FASTEST TWO GOALS BY RANGERS AND OPPONENTS: 4 sec. Denis Savard of Chicago at 19:23 of third period and Mark Pavelich of Rangers at 19:27, 2/24/82 at Madison Square Garden, Rangers won, 6-4.

FASTEST THREE GOALS BY RANGERS: 28 sec. Doug Sulliman at 7:52, Eddie Johnstone at 7:57 and Warren Miller at 8:20 of first period against Colorado at Madison Square Garden, 1/14/80. Game ended in a 6-6 tie.

FASTEST THREE GOALS vs. RANGERS: 21 sec. Bill Mosienko of Chicago scored all three goals at 6:09, 6:20 and 6:30 of third period, 2/23/52, at Madison Square Garden. Chicago won, 7-6.

FASTEST THREE GOALS BY RANGERS AND OPPONENTS: 15 sec. Mark Pavelich of Rangers at 19:18 of second period and Ron Greschner at 19:27 and Willi Plett of Minnesota at 19:33, 2/10/83, at Minnesota. Minnesota won game, 7-5.

FASTEST FOUR GOALS BY RANGERS: 1 min. 38 sec. Mark Pavelich at 15:53, Mike Rogers at 16:18, Ron Greschner at 16:51 and Mike Rogers at 17:31 of first period against Edmonton at Madison Square Garden, 2/15/85. Rangers won, 8-7.

FASTEST FOUR GOALS vs. RANGERS: 1 min. 20 sec. Bill Thoms of Boston at 6:34 of second period, Frank Mario at 7:08 and 7:27, and Ken Smith at 7:54, 1/21/45, at Boston. Boston won 14-3.

FASTEST FOUR GOALS BY RANGERS AND OPPONENTS: 1 min. 1 sec. Doug Sulliman of Rangers at 7:52 of first period, Eddie Johnstone at 7:57, Warren Miller at 8:20 and Rob Ramage of Colorado at 8:53, 1/14/80, at Madison Square Garden. Game ended in 6-6 tie.

FASTEST FIVE GOALS BY RANGERS: 3 min. 22 sec. Mark Pavelich at 15:53, Mike Rogers at 16:18, Ron Greschner at 16:51, Mike Rogers at 17:31 and Grant Ledyard at 19:15 of first period against Edmonton at Madison Square Garden, 2/15/85. Rangers won, 8-7.

FASTEST FIVE GOALS vs. RANGERS: 2 min. 55 sec. Bobby Schmautz of Boston at 19:13 of first period, Ken Hodge at 0:18, Phil Esposito at 0:43, Don Marcotte at 0:58 and John Bucyk at 2:08 of second period, 12/19/74, at Boston. Boston won, 11-3.

MOST PENALTY MINUTES, ONE GAME BY RANGERS: 134. Rangers vs. Pittsburgh, 10/30/88 at Madison Square Garden.

MOST PENALTY MINUTES, ONE GAME BY RANGERS AND OPPONENT: 292. Rangers vs. Pittsburgh, 10/30/88 at Madison Square Garden.

MOST PENALTY MINUTES, ONE PERIOD BY RANGERS: 126. Rangers vs. Pittsburgh, 10/30/88 at Madison Square Garden (third period).

MOST PENALTY MINUTES, ONE PERIOD BY RANGERS AND OPPONENT: 272. Rangers vs. Pittsburgh, 10/30/88 at Madison Square Garden (third period).

INDIVIDUAL PLAYER RECORDS

MOST GOALS, ONE SEASON: 52, Adam Graves, 1993-94.
MOST ASSISTS, ONE SEASON: 88, Brian Leetch, 1991-92.
MOST POINTS, ONE SEASON: 109, Jean Ratelle, 1971-72.
MOST GOALS BY A CENTER, ONE SEASON: 48, Pierre Larouche, 1983-84.
MOST ASSISTS BY A CENTER, ONE SEASON: 72, Wayne Gretzky, 1996-97. Mark Messier, 1991-92.
MOST POINTS BY A CENTER, ONE SEASON: 109, Jean Ratelle, 1971-72.
MOST GOALS BY A LEFT WING, ONE SEASON: 52, Adam Graves, 1993-94.
MOST ASSISTS BY A LEFT WING, ONE SEASON: 56, Vic Hadfield, 1971-72.
MOST POINTS BY A LEFT WING, ONE SEASON: 106, Vic Hadfield, 1971-72.
MOST GOALS BY A RIGHT WING, ONE SEASON: 49, Mike Gartner, 1990-91.
MOST ASSISTS BY A RIGHT WING, ONE SEASON: 61, Rod Gilbert, 1974-75.
MOST POINTS BY A RIGHT WING, ONE SEASON: 97, Rod Gilbert, 1971-72, 1974-75.
MOST POWER PLAY GOALS, ONE SEASON: 23, Vic Hadfield, 1971-72.
MOST SHORTHANDED GOALS, ONE SEASON: 5, Mark Messier, 1996-97. Mike Gartner, 1993-94. Don Maloney, 1980-81. Mike Rogers, 1982-83.
HIGHEST SHOOTING PERCENTAGE, ONE SEASON: 29.6, Steve Vickers, 1979-80 (29 goals on 98 shots).
MOST GAME-WINNING GOALS, ONE SEASON: 9, Mark Messier, 1996-97. Don Maloney, 1980-81.

MOST POINTS BY A LINE, ONE SEASON*: 302, Vic Hadfield (97)-Jean Ratelle (109)-Rod Gilbert (96) 1971-72.
MOST GOALS BY A LINE, ONE SEASON*: 133, Vic Hadfield (45)-Jean Ratelle (46)-Rod Gilbert (42) 1971-72.
MOST GOALS, ONE GAME: 5, Don Murdoch, 10/12/76 against Minnesota at Minnesota; Mark Pavelich, 2/23/83 against Hartford at Madison Square Garden.
MOST POWER PLAY GOALS, ONE GAME: 3, Mark Messier, March 22, 1992 against New Jersey at Madison Square Garden.
MOST SHORTHANDED GOALS, ONE GAME: 2, Greg Polis, November 4, 1977 against Vancouver at Vancouver. Ron Duguay, January 22, 1980 against Los Angeles at Los Angeles. Don Maloney, February 21, 1981 against Washington at Madison Square Garden. Don Maloney, October 5, 1983 against New Jersey at Madison Square Garden. Don Maloney, January 14, 1987 against Calgary at Calgary.
MOST GOALS, ONE PERIOD: 3, Many: Last time: Adam Graves, November 25, 1992 in third period vs. Pittsburgh at Pittsburgh.
MOST ASSISTS, ONE PERIOD: 4, Wayne Gretzky. Second period on January 4, 1997 against Ottawa at Madison Square Garden. Phil Goyette. First period on October 20, 1963 against Boston at Madison Square Garden.
MOST ASSISTS, ONE GAME: 5, Walt Tkaczuk on Feb. 12, 1972 against Pittsburgh at Pittsburgh. Rod Gilbert on March 2, 1975 against Pittsburgh at Madison Square Garden, March 30, 1975 against Kansas City at Madison Square Garden and October 8, 1976 against Colorado at Colorado. Don Maloney on January 3, 1987 against Quebec at Quebec. Brian Leetch on April 18, 1995 against Pittsburgh at Pittsburgh.
MOST POINTS, ONE GAME: 7, Steve Vickers. Three goals and four assists on Feb. 18, 1976 against Washington at Madison Square Garden.
MOST HAT TRICKS, ONE SEASON: 4, Tomas Sandstrom, 1986-87.
MOST CONSECUTIVE HAT TRICKS: 2, Steve Vickers scored hat tricks against Los Angeles on November 12, 1972 and against Philadelphia on November 15, 1972.
MOST SHOTS ON GOAL, ONE GAME: 16, Rod Gilbert, February 24, 1968 against Montreal at Montreal.
MOST SHOTS ON GOAL, ONE SEASON: 344, Phil Esposito, 1976-77.

***These records computed on basis of having at least two members of line on ice at time of each goal.**

LONGEST CONSECUTIVE GOAL SCORING STREAK: 10, Andy Bathgate. Dec. 15, 1962 to Jan. 5, 1963 (11 goals during streak).
LONGEST CONSECUTIVE ASSIST SCORING STREAK: 15, Brian Leetch, Nov. 29 to December 31, 1991 (23 assists during the streak).
LONGEST CONSECUTIVE POINT SCORING STREAK: 17, Brian Leetch, Nov. 23 to December 31, 1991 (five goals and 24 assists during the streak).
FASTEST GOAL AT START OF GAME: 9 sec. Ron Duguay, April 6, 1980 at Philadelphia and Jim Wiemer, March 27, 1985, at Buffalo.
FASTEST TWO GOALS: 8 sec. Pierre Jarry, scored at 11:03 and 11:11 of third period against California on November 21, 1971 at Madison Square Garden. Don Maloney, scored at 12:48 and 12:56 of third period against Philadelphia on March 12, 1987 at Philadelphia.
FASTEST THREE GOALS: 2 min. 30 sec. Don Maloney scored at 16:41, 18:37 and 19:11 of second period on February 21, 1981 against Washington at Madison Square Garden.
FASTEST THREE ASSISTS: 1 min. 21 sec. Don Raleigh at 5:23; 5:43 and 6:44 of first period on November 16, 1947 against Montreal at Madison Square Garden.
MOST PENALTY MINUTES, ONE GAME: 35, Chris Nilan, October 8, 1989 against Chicago at Chicago.
MOST PENALTY MINUTES, ONE SEASON: 305. Troy Mallette, 1989-90.
MOST GOALS WITH THE RANGERS: 406, Rod Gilbert.
MOST ASSISTS WITH THE RANGERS: 615, Rod Gilbert.
MOST POINTS WITH THE RANGERS: 1,021, Rod Gilbert.
MOST PENALTY MINUTES WITH THE RANGERS: 1,226, Ron Greschner.
MOST GAMES WITH THE RANGERS: 1,160, Harry Howell.
MOST SEASONS WITH THE RANGERS: 18, Rod Gilbert, 1960-61–1977-78.
MOST CONSECUTIVE GAMES WITH THE RANGERS: 560, Andy Hebenton. Including playoff games, 22, Hebenton appeared in 582 consecutive games with the Rangers (1955-56–1962-63).
MOST 20-GOAL SEASONS WITH THE RANGERS: 12, Rod Gilbert.
MOST 20-ASSIST SEASONS WITH THE RANGERS: 13, Walt Tkaczuk, Rod Gilbert.
MOST 30-POINT SEASONS WITH THE RANGERS: 14, Rod Gilbert.
MOST 30-GOAL SEASONS WITH THE RANGERS: 6, Jean Ratelle.

INDIVIDUAL ROOKIE RECORDS

MOST GOALS, ONE SEASON: 36, Tony Granato, 1988-89.
MOST ASSISTS, ONE SEASON: 48, Brian Leetch, 1988-89.
MOST POINTS, ONE SEASON: 76, Mark Pavelich, 1981-82.
MOST GOALS BY A DEFENSEMAN, ONE SEASON: 23, Brian Leetch, 1988-89.
MOST ASSISTS BY A DEFENSEMAN, ONE SEASON: 48, Brian Leetch, 1988-89.
MOST POINTS BY A DEFENSEMAN, ONE SEASON: 71, Brian Leetch, 1988-89.
MOST GOALS, ONE GAME: 5, Don Murdoch, October 12, 1976 against Minnesota at Minnesota.
MOST ASSISTS, ONE GAME: 4, Brad Park, February 2, 1969 against Pittsburgh at Madison Square Garden; Walt Tkaczuk, February 26, 1969 against Chicago at Madison Square Garden; Mark Heaslip, March 12, 1978 against Washington at Madison Square Garden; Brian Leetch, February 17, 1989 against Toronto at Madison Square Garden.
MOST POINTS ONE GAME: 5, Rick Middleton, November 17, 1974 against California at Madison Square Garden; Don Murdoch, October 12, 1976 against Minnesota at Minnesota; Brian Leetch, February 17, 1989 against Toronto at Madison Square Garden.
LONGEST GOAL SCORING STREAK: 7, Darren Turcotte, October 15, 1989–October 28, 1989 (Scored eight goals during streak.)
MOST POWER PLAY GOALS, ONE SEASON: 15, Camille Henry, 1953-54.
MOST SHORTHANDED GOALS, ONE SEASON: 4, Tony Granato, 1988-89.
MOST SHOTS, ONE SEASON: 268, Brian Leetch, 1988-89.
MOST HAT TRICKS, ONE SEASON: 3, Tony Granato, 1988-89.
MOST PENALTY MINUTES, ONE SEASON: 305, Troy Mallette, 1989-90.

INDIVIDUAL DEFENSEMEN RECORDS

MOST GOALS, ONE SEASON: 25, Brad Park, 1973-74.
MOST ASSISTS, ONE SEASON: 80, Brian Leetch, 1991-92.
MOST POINTS, ONE SEASON: 102, Brian Leetch, 1991-92.
MOST GOALS, ONE GAME: 3 (many). Last time: Reijo Ruotsalainen, March 17, 1982 against Philadelphia at Madison Square Garden.
MOST ASSISTS, ONE GAME: 5, Brian Leetch, April 18, 1995 against Pittsburgh at Pittsburgh.
MOST POINTS, ONE GAME: 5 (twice), Brian Leetch, February 17, 1989 against Toronto at Madison Square Garden and April 18, 1995 at Pittsburgh.
MOST POWER PLAY GOALS, ONE SEASON: 17, Brian Leetch, 1993-94.
MOST SHORTHANDED GOALS, ONE SEASON: 3, Brian Leetch, 1988-89.
MOST SHOTS, ONE SEASON: 328, Brian Leetch, 1993-94.
MOST SHOTS, ONE GAME: 13, Brian Leetch, January 4, 1989 against Washington at Madison Square Garden.
MOST PENALTY MINUTES, ONE SEASON: 231, Barry Beck, 1980-81.
LONGEST CONSECUTIVE ASSIST SCORING STREAK: 15, Brian Leetch, Nov. 29 to December 31, 1991 (23 assists during the streak).
LONGEST CONSECUTIVE POINT SCORING STREAK: 17, Brian Leetch, Nov. 23 to December 31, 1991 (5 goals and 24 assists).

INDIVIDUAL GOALTENDER RECORDS

MOST GAMES, ONE SEASON: 72, Mike Richter, 1997-98.
MOST WINS, ONE SEASON: 42, Mike Richter, 1993-94.
MOST WINS, ONE SEASON (Including Playoffs): 58, Mike Richter, 1993-94.
LOWEST GOAL-AGAINST AVERAGE: 1.48, John Ross Roach, 1928-29.
MOST SHUTOUTS, ONE SEASON: 13, John Ross Roach, 1928-29.
MOST ASSISTS, ONE SEASON: 5, John Vanbiesbrouck, 1984-85 and 1987-88. Mike Richter, 1992-93.
MOST PENALTY MINUTES, ONE SEASON: 56, Bob Froese, 1986-87.
HIGHEST SAVE PERCENTAGE, ONE SEASON: .917, Mike Richter, 1996-97.
MOST SAVES, ONE GAME: 59, Mike Richter, January 31, 1991 vs. Vancouver at Vancouver. Game ended in 3-3 tie.
MOST ASSISTS ONE GAME: 2, Ed Giacomin, March 19, 1972 vs. Toronto at Madison Square Garden. John Vanbiesbrouck, January 8, 1985 vs. Winnipeg at Winnipeg. Mike Richter, February 23, 1990 vs. Washington at Washington, and October 29, 1992 vs. Quebec at MSG.
MOST ASSISTS, CAREER: 22, John Vanbiesbrouck.
MOST SHUTOUTS, CAREER: 49, Ed Giacomin.
MOST WINS, CAREER: 266, Ed Giacomin.

Rangers All-Time Register

Number	Name & Position ....Yrs. Played
	A
4	Taffy Abel (D) 1926-27–1928-29
19	Doug Adam (LW) 1949-50
17	Lloyd Ailsby (D) 1951-52
1	Andy Aitkenhead (G) 1932-33–1934-35
15	Clint Albright (C) 1948-49
17	George Allen (D) 1938-39
14	Mike Allison (C) 1980-81–1985-86
18	Bill Allum (D) 1940-41
31, 33	Tony Amonte (RW) 1991-92–1993-94
36	Glenn Anderson (RW) 1993-94
1	Lorne Anderson (G) 1951-52
24	Kent-Erik Andersson (RW) ..1982-83–1983-84
5	Peter Andersson (D) 1992-93–1993-94
25	Steve Andrascik (RW) 1971-72
18	Paul Andrea (RW) 1965-66
17	Lou Angotti (C) 1964-65–1965-66
20	Hub Anslow (LW) 1947-48
6	Syl Apps (C) 1970-71
10	Dave Archibald (C) 1989-90
18	Derek Armstrong (C) 1998-1999–current
16	Oscar Asmundson (C) 1932-33–1933-34
31	Hardy Astrom (G) 1977-78
9	Walt Atanas (RW) 1944-45
24	Ron Attwell (C) 1967-68
10	Oscar Aubuchon (LW) 1943-44
6	Don Awrey (D) 1977-78
2	Thomas Ayres (D) 1935-36
	B
15	Pete Babando (LW) 1952-53
21	Mike Backman (RW) 1981-82–1983-84
6	Bill Baker (D) 1982-83
35	Steve Baker (G) 1979-80–1982-83
8, 11, 17, 22	Dave Balon (LW) 1959-60–1962-63; 1968-69–1971-72
25	Jeff Bandura (D) 1980-81
11	Dave Barr (C) 1983-84
14, 17, 22	Jimmy Bartlett (LW) 1955-56; 1958-59–1959-60
–	Cliff Barton (RW) 1939-40
9, 10, 12, 16	Andy Bathgate (RW) 1952-53–1963-64
16	Frank Bathgate (C) 1952-53
21	Frank Beaton (LW) 1978-79–1979-80
3, 5	Barry Beck (D) 1979-80–1985-86
23	John Bednarski (D) 1974-75–1976-77
19	Danny Belisle (RW) 1960-61
29	Bruce Bell (D) 1987-88
1	Gordie Bell (G) 1955-56
2	Harry Bell (D) 1946-47
5, 20	Joe Bell (LW) 1942-43; 1946-47
15	Lin Bend (C) 1942-43
20	Curt Bennett (C) 1972-73
17, 27	Ric Bennett (LW) 1989-90–1991-92
14	Doug Bentley (LW) 1953-54
10, 22	Max Bentley (C) 1953-54
24	Gordon Berenson (C) 1966-67–1967-68
18	Bill Berg (LW) 1995-96–1997-98
23	Jeff Beukeboom (D) 1991-92–1998-99
1	Bill Beveridge (G) 1942-43
25	Nick Beverley (D) 1974-75–1976-77
6	Bob Blackburn (C) 1968-69
23	Don Blackburn (LW) 1969-70–1970-71
18	Mike Blaisdell (RW) 1983-84–1984-85
38	Jeff Bloemberg (D) 1988-89–1991-92
30, 32, 38	Sylvain Blouin (LW) 1996-97–1997-98
3, 6	Tim Bothwell (D) 1978-79–1981-82
21	Dick Bouchard (RW) 1954-55
7, 17	Frank Boucher (C) 1926-27–1937-38; 1943-44
2, 12	Leo Bourgault (D) 1926-27–1930-31
29	Phil Bourque (LW) 1992-93–1993-94
27	Paul Boutilier (D) 1987-88
1	Lionel Bouvrette (G) 1942-43
1	Johnny Bower (G) 1953-54–1954-55; 1956-57
2, 15	Jack Bownass (D) 1958-59–1959-60; 1961-62
8	William Boyd (RW) 1926-27–1928-29
15	Doug Brennan (D) 1931-32–1933-34
12	Rich Brennan (D) 1998-99
8	John Brenneman (LW) 1964-65–1965-66
32	Stephane Brochu (D) 1988-89
13	Bob Brooke (C) 1983-84–1986-87
37	Paul Broten (RW) 1989-90–1992-93
4	Arnie Brown (D) 1964-65–1970-71
16	Harold Brown (RW) 1945-46
4, 21	Larry Brown (D) 1969-70–1970-71
14	Stanley Brown (LW) 1926-27
17, 24	Jeff Brubaker (LW) 1987-88
12	Glenn Brydson (RW) 1935-36
19	Bucky Buchanan (C) 1948-49
4	Hy Buller (D) 1951-52–1953-54
14	Kelly Burnett (C) 1952-53
24, 27	Gary Burns (LW) 1980-81–1981-82
15	Norman Burns (C) 1941-42
17, 20	Jerry Butler (RW) 1972-73–1974-75
1	Steve Buzinski (G) 1942-43
15	Jerry Byers (LW) 1977-78
	C
2, 5	Larry Cahan (D) 1956-57–1958-59; 1961-62–1964-65
29	Eric Cairns (D) 1996-97–1997-98
14	Patsy Callighen (D) 1927-28
14	Angus Cameron (C) 1942-43
38	Terry Carkner (D) 1986-87
11	Bob Carpenter (C) 1986-87
9, 20	Gene Carr (C) 1971-72–1973-74
11	Lorne Carr (RW) 1933-34
14	Gene Carrigan (C) 1930-31
18	Bill Carse (C) 1938-39
–	Gerald Carson (C) 1928-29
26	Jay Caufield (RW) 1986-87
1	Lorne Chabot (G) 1926-27–1927-28
–	Bill Chalmers (C)............1953-54
36	Todd Charlesworth (D) 1989-90
11	Rick Chartraw (D) 1982-83–1983-84
6	Bob Chrystal (D) 1953-54–1954-55
22	Shane Churla (LW) 1995-96–1996-97
15	Hank Ciesla (C) 1957-58–1958-59
6, 18	Joe Cirella (D) 1990-91–1992-93
32	Dan Clark (D) 1978-79
6	Bruce Cline (RW) 1956-57
34, 39	Dan Cloutier (G) 1997-98–1998-99
15	Bill Collins (RW) 1975-76
5, 16	Mac Colville (RW) 1935-36–1941-42; 1945-46–1946-47
6	Neil Colville (C) 1935-36–1941-42; 1944-45–1948-49
16	Les Colwill (RW) 1958-59
6, 16	Charles Conacher, Jr. (LW) ...1954-55–1955-56
5, 15	Jim Conacher (C) 1951-52–1952-53
28	Pat Conacher (C)...........1979-80; 1982-83
15	Bert Connolly (LW) 1934-35–1935-36
20	Cam Connor (RW) 1979-80–1982-83
5	Bill Cook (RW) 1926-27–1936-37
6	Fred "Bun" Cook (LW) 1926-27–1935-36

No.	Player	Seasons
10	Hal Cooper (RW)	1944-45
11, 12	Joe Cooper (D)	1935-36–1937-38; 1946-47
2, 17	Art Coulter (D)	1935-36–1941-42
21	Russ Courtnall (RW)	1996-97
18	Danny Cox (LW)	1933-34
32	Bob Crawford (RW)	1985-86–1986-87
16	Dave Creighton (C)	1955-56–1957-58
14	Brian Cullen (C)	1959-60–1960-61
17	Ray Cullen (C)	1965-66
19	Bob Cunningham (C)	1960-61–1961-62
2	Ian Cushenan (D)	1959-60
22	Paul Cyr (LW)	1987-88–1988-89

D

No.	Player	Seasons
9, 16	Ulf Dahlen (LW)	1987-88–1989-90
12	Alexandre Daigle (RW)	1999-2000–current
5	Hank Damore (C)	1943-44
4	Gordon Davidson (D)	1942-43–1943-44
00, 30, 35	John Davidson (G)	1975-76–1982-83
8	Ken Davies (C)	1947-48
22	Jason Dawe (RW)	1999-2000–current
16	Billy Dea (LW)	1953-54
23, 32, 35	Lucien DeBlois (RW)	1977-78–1979-80; 1986-87–1988-89
1	Bob DeCourcy (G)	1947-48
16	Val Delory (LW)	1948-49
24	Ab DeMarco, Jr. (D)	1969-70–1972-73
15	Ab DeMarco, Sr. (D)	1943-44–1946-47
5	Tony Demers (RW)	1943-44
14	Jean Paul Denis (RW)	1946-47; 1949-50
11	Victor Desjardins (C)	1931-32
2	Tommy Dewar (D)	1943-44
14	Herb Dickenson (LW)	1951-52–1952-53
4	Bob Dill (D)	1943-44–1944-45
8, 15	Cecil Dillon (RW)	1930-31–1938-39
9, 11	Wayne Dillon (C)	1975-76–1977-78
16	Rob DiMaio (RW)	1999-2000–current
16	Marcel Dionne (C)	1986-87–1988-89
44	Per Djoos (D)	1991-92–1992-93
3	Gary Doak (D)	1971-72
25	Jason Doig (D)	1999-2000–current
28	Tie Domi (RW)	1990-91–1992-93
22	Mike Donnelly (LW)	1986-87–1987-88
2, 27, 33	Andre Dore (D)	1978-79–1982-83; 1984-85
8	Jim Dorey (D)	1971-72
33	Bruce Driver (D)	1995-96–1997-98
1	Dave Dryden (G)	1961-62
19	Christian Dube (C)	1996-97–1998-99
16	Jim Drummond (D)	1944-45
9	Dick Duff (LW)	1963-64–1964-65
6	Marc Dufour (RW)	1963-64–1964-65
10, 44	Ron Duguay (C)	1977-78–1982-83; 1986-87–1987-88
19	Craig Duncanson (RW)	1992-93
25	Andre Dupont (D)	1970-71
18	Duke Dutkowski (D)	1933-34
20	Radek Dvorak (RW)	1999-2000–current
–	Henry Dyck (LW)	1943-44

E

No.	Player	Seasons
28	Dallas Eakins (D/LW)	1996-97
32	Mike Eastwood (C)	1996-97–1997-98
2	Frank Eddolls (D)	1947-48–1951-52
6	Pat Egan (D)	1949-50–1950-51
20	Jack Egers (RW)	1969-70–1971-72; 1973-74
20	Jan Erixon (LW)	1983-84–1992-93
12	Bob Errey (RW)	1997-98
5, 12, 77	Phil Esposito (C)	1975-76–1980-81
3, 5, 30	Jack Evans (D)	1948-49–1951-52; 1953-54–1957-58
5	Bill Ezinicki (RW)	1954-55

F

No.	Player	Seasons
24	Trevor Fahey (LW)	1964-65
10, 14	Bill Fairbairn (RW)	1968-69–1976-77
3	Dave Farrish (D)	1976-77–1978-79
6	Glen Featherstone (D)	1994-95
37	Brent Fedyk (LW)	1998-99
32	Tony Feltrin (D)	1985-86
25, 42	Paul Fenton (LW)	1986-87
14	Chris Ferraro (C)	1995-96–1996-97
14, 17, 21	Peter Ferraro (RW)	1995-96–1997-98
21	Ray Ferraro (C)	1995-96
26	Jeff Finley (D)	1997-98–1998-99
41	Peter Fiorentino (D)	1991-92
12	Dunc Fisher (RW)	1947-48–1950-51
6	Sandy Fitzpatrick (C)	1964-65
8	Pat Flatley (RW)	1996-97
9	Reg Fleming (LW)	1965-66–1968-69
14	Theoren Fleury (RW)	1999-2000–current
18	Gerry Foley (RW)	1956-57–1957-58
14	Val Fonteyne (LW)	1963-64–1964-65
8	Lou Fontinato (D)	1954-55–1960-61
4	Harry "Yip" Foster (D)	1929-30
18	Herb Foster (LW)	1940-41; 1947-48
22	Nick Fotiu (LW)	1976-77–1978-79; 1980-81–1984-85
1, 16	Emile Francis (G)	1948-49–1951-52
1	Jimmy Franks (G)	1942-43
6	Archie Fraser (C)	1943-44
21	Scott Fraser (RW)	1998-99
33	Bob Froese (G)	1986-87–1989-90
8, 38	Robbie Ftorek (C)	1981-82–1984-85

G

No.	Player	Seasons
4	Bill Gadsby (D)	1954-55–1960-61
9	Dave Gagner (C)	1984-85–1986-87
8	Dutch Gainor (C)	1931-32
4	Maxim Galanov (D)	1997-98
1	Bruce Gamble (G)	1958-59
1	Bert Gardiner (G)	1935-36; 38-39
12, 17	Cal Gardner (C)	1945-46–1947-48
15	Dudley Garrett (D)	1942-43
22	Mike Gartner (RW)	1989-90–1993-94
9	Fern Gauthier (RW)	1943-44
7, 10	Guy Gendron (LW)	1955-56–1957-58; 1961-62
5	Bernie Geoffrion (RW)	1966-67–1967-68
12	Ken Gernander (C)	1995-96–1996-97
1, 30	Ed Giacomin (G)	1965-66–1975-76
17	Greg Gilbert (LW)	1993-94
7, 16	Rod Gilbert (RW)	1960-61–1977-78
6	Curt Giles (D)	1986-87–1987-88
16	Randy Gilhen (C)	1991-92–1992-93
6	Jere Gillis (LW)	1980-81–1981-82
8	Howie Glover (RW)	1963-64
19	Pete Goegan (D)	1961-62
12	Bill Goldsworthy (RW)	1976-77–1977-78
14	Leroy Goldsworthy (D)	1929-30
11	Hank Goldup (LW)	1942-43–1945-46
16, 36, 39	Daniel Goneau (LW)	1996-97–current
16	Billy Gooden (LW)	1942-43–1943-44
16, 19	Jack Gordon (RW)	1948-49–1950-51
11	Benoit Gosselin (LW)	1977-78
9, 20	Phil Goyette (C)	1963-64–1968-69; 1971-72
18, 39	Tony Granato (RW)	1988-89–1989-90
33	Gilles Gratton (G)	1976-77
23	Norm Gratton (LW)	1971-72
9, 11	Adam Graves (LW)	1991-92–current
2	Alex Gray (RW)	1927-28
4	Ron Greschner (D)	1974-75–1989-90
99	Wayne Gretzky (C)	1996-97–1998-99
5	Jari Gronstrand (D)	1987-88
2	Jocelyn Guevremont (D)	1979-801
12, 20	Aldo Guidolin (D)	1952-53–1955-56

H

No.	Player	Seasons
11	Vic Hadfield (LW)	1961-62–1973-74
19	Wayne Hall (LW)	1960-61
6, 25	Allan Hamilton (D)	1965-66; 1967-68–1969-70
6	Ken Hammond (D)	1988-89
22	Ted Hampson (C)	1960-61–1962-63
1	Glen Hanlon (G)	1982-83–1985-86
2, 6	John Hanna (D)	1958-59–1960-61
6	Pat Hannigan (RW)	1960-61–1961-62
14	Mark Hardy (D)	1987-88–1992-93
3	Ron Harris (D)	1972-73–1975-76
17	Ed Harrison (LW)	1950-51
18	Mike Hartman (RW)	1992-93–1994-95
2	Doug Harvey (D)	1961-62–1963-64
20	Todd Harvey (RW)	1998-99
4	Kevin Hatcher (D)	1999-2000–current
12	Gordie Haworth (C)	1952-53
30	Glenn Healy (G)	1993-94–1995-96
19	Mark Heaslip (RW)	1976-77–1977-78
26, 40	Randy Heath (LW)	1984-85–1985-86
12	Andy Hebenton (RW)	1955-56–1962-63
15	Anders Hedberg (RW)	1978-79–1984-85
23	Bill Heindl (LW)	1972-73
3, 14	Ott Heller (D)	1931-32–1945-46
23	Raimo Helminen (C)	1985-86–1986-87
21	Camille Henry (C)	1953-54–1954-55; 1956-57–1964-65; 1967-68
1, 20	Jim Henry (G)	1941-42–45-46; 1947-48
18	Wally Hergesheimer (RW)	1951-52–1955-56; 1958-59
15	Orville Heximer (LW)	1929-30
6	Bryan Hextall, Jr. (C)	1962-63
12, 19	Bryan Hextall, Sr. (RW)	1936-37–1943-44; 1945-46–1947-48
21	Dennis Hextall (C)	1967-68–1968-69
12, 17	Bill Hicke (RW)	1964-65–1966-67
28	Greg Hickey (LW)	1977-78
14, 16, 24	Pat Hickey (LW)	1975-76–1979-80; 1981-82
14	Ike Hildebrand (RW)	1953-54
8, 18	Dutch Hiller (LW)	1937-38–1940-41; 1943-44
16	Jim Hiller (RW)	1993-94
2	Wayne Hillman (D)	1964-65–1967-68
27	Jan Hlavac (LW)	1999-2000–current
31	Corey Hirsch (G)	1992-93
32, 33	Milan Hnilicka (G)	1999-2000–current
88	Ken Hodge (RW)	1976-77–1977-78
22	Jerry Holland (LW)	1974-75–1975-76
17	Greg Holst (C)	1975-76–1977-78
6	Miloslav Horava (D)	1988-89–1990-91
3	Tim Horton (D)	1969-70–1970-71
6, 11	Bronco Horvath (C)	1955-56–1956-57; 1962-63
23	Ed Hospodar (D)	1979-80–1980-81
11, 16	Vic Howe (RW)	1950-51; 1953-54–1954-55
3	Harry Howell (D)	1952-53–1968-69
5, 21	Ron Howell (D-F)	1954-55–1955-56
27	Willie Huber (D)	1983-84–1987-88
15	Mike Hudson (C)	1993-94
28	John Hughes (D)	1980-81
21	Jody Hull (RW)	1990-91–1991-92
5	Fred Hunt (RW)	1944-45
25	Larry Huras (D)	1976-77
32	Mike Hurlbut (D)	1992-93
11	Ron Hutchinson (C)	1960-61

I

No.	Player	Seasons
10	Earl Ingarfield (C)	1958-59–1966-67
4	Ron Ingram (D)	1963-64–1964-65
27	Ted Irvine (LW)	1969-70–1974-75
2	Ivan Irwin (D)	1953-54–1955-56; 1957-58

J

No.	Player	Seasons
29	Don Jackson (D)	1986-87
14	Jeff Jackson (LW)	1986-87
1	Percy Jackson (G)	1934-35
14	Jimmy Jamieson (D)	1943-44
15, 27, 47	Mark Janssens (C)	1987-88–1991-92
28	Doug Jarrett (D)	1975-76–1976-77
8	Pierre Jarry (LW)	1971-72
10, 17	Larry Jeffrey (LW)	1967-68–1968-69
15, 39	Chris Jensen (RW)	1985-86–1987-88
2	Joe Jerwa (D)	1930-31
6, 5	Don Johns (D)	1960-61; 1962-63–1964-65
3	Ching Johnson (D)	1926-27–1936-37
24	Jim Johnson (C)	1964-65–1966-67
3	Kim Johnsson (D)	1999-2000–current
14, 17	Ed Johnstone (RW)	1975-76; 1977-78–1982-83
6	Bob Jones (LW)	1968-69
16	Bing Juckes (LW)	1947-48; 1949-50
19	Bill Juzda (D)	1940-41–1941-42; 1945-46–1947-48

K

No.	Player	Seasons
11, 15	Bob Kabel (C)	1959-60–1960-61
17	Alex Kaleta (LW)	1948-49–1950-51
13	Valeri Kamensky (LW)	1999-2000–current
26	Sheldon Kannegiesser (D)	1972-73–1973-74
25	Alexander Karpovtsev (D)	1993-94–1998-99
12	Mike Keane (RW)	1997-98
21	Mike Keating (LW)	1977-78
10, 11	Butch Keeling (LW)	1928-29–1937-38
6	Ralph Keller (D)	1962-63
38	Chris Kenady (RW)	1999-2000–current
6	Dean Kennedy (D)	1988-89
16	Bill Kenny (D)	1930-31
1	Dave Kerr (G)	1934-35–1940-41
12	Tim Kerr (RW)	1991-92
12, 19	Kris King (LW)	1989-90–1992-93
25	Steven King (RW)	1992-93
16	Bobby Krik (RW)	1937-38
6	Bob Kirkpatrick (C)	1942-43
11, 16	Kelly Kisio (C)	1986-87–1990-91
3	Scot Kleinendorst (D)	1982-83–1983-84
44	Terry Kleisinger (G)	1985-86
1	Julian Klymkiew (G)	1958-59
22	Mike Knuble (RW)	1998-99
26	Joe Kocur (RW)	1990-91–1995-96
23	Chris Kontos (C)	1982-83–1984-85
6	Mike Korney (RW)	1978-79
16	Dick Kotanen (D)	1948-49; 1950-51
24	Chris Kotsopoulos (D)	1980-81
27	Alexei Kovalev (RW)	1992-93–1998-99
6	Steve Kraftcheck (D)	1951-52–1952-53
12	Joe Krol (LW)	1936-37; 1938-39
22	Jim Krulicki (LW)	1970-71
15	Dolph Kukulowicz (C)	1952-53–1953-54
18	Stu Kulak (RW)	1986-87
14, 19	Eddie Kullman (RW)	1947-48–1948-49; 1950-51–1953-54
17	Alan Kuntz (LW)	1941-42; 1945-46
17	Jarri Kurri (RW)	1995-96
25	Orland Kurtenbach (C)	1960-61; 1966-67–1969-70
–	Larry Kwong (RW)	1947-48
19	Bill Kyle (C)	1949-50–1950-51
6, 15	Gus Kyle (D)	1949-50–1950-51
19	Nick Kypreos (LW)	1993-94–1995-96

L

No.	Player	Seasons
15	Michel Labadie (RW)	1952-53
31	J. F. Labbe (G)	1999-2000–current
18, 19	Gordon Labossiere (C)	1963-64–1964-65
17	Max Labovitch (RW)	1943-44

20 Guy Labrie (D) 1944-45
32, 37 Daniel Lacroix (C) 1993-94–1995-96
28 Eric Lacroix (LW) 1998-99–current
22 Nathan LaFayette (C) 1994-95–1995-96
10 Guy Lafleur (RW)...........1988-89
16 Pat LaFontaine (C) 1997-98
15 Jason Lafreneiere (C) 1988-89
2 Tom Laidlaw (D) 1980-81–1986-87
14 Lane Lambert (RW) 1986-87
16, 21, 22 Jean Paul Lamirande (D) 1946-47–1947-48; 1949-50
16 Jack Lancien (D) 1946-47–1947-48; 1949-50–1950-51
12 Myles Lane (D).............1928-29
15, 19 Darren Langdon (LW) 1994-95–current
4 Al Langlois (D).............1961-62–1963-64
22 Ian Laperriere (C) 1995-96
10 Edgar Laprade (C)..........1945-46–1954-55
28 Steve Larmer (RW).........1993-94–1994-95
20 Claude Larose (LW) 1979-80–1981-82
10, 24 Pierre Larouche (RW).......1983-84–1987-88
39 Steve Larouche (C).........1995-96
19 Norm Larson (RW) 1946-47
44 Jim Latos (RW) 1988-89
18 Phil Latreille (RW)..........1960-61
39 Peter Laviolette (D) 1988-89
17 Brian Lawton (C)...........1988-89
2 Hal Laycoe (D).............1945-46–1946-47
24 Jim Leavins (D) 1986-87
18 Al Lebrun (D) 1960-61; 1965-66
18 Albert Leduc (D) 1933-34
30 Grant Ledyard (D)..........1984-85–1985-86
2 Brian Leetch (D) 1987-88–current
5 Roger Leger (D) 1943-44
4 Randy Legge (D) 1972-73
28 Mikko Leinonen (C) 1981-82–1983-84
9, 14 Real Lemieux (LW) 1969-70; 1973-74
18 Tony Leswick (LW) 1945-46–1950-51
14 Joe Levandoski (RW) 1946-47
11 Alex Levinsky (D) 1934-35
22 Danny Lewicki (LW) 1954-55–1957-58
27 Dale Lewis (LW)............1975-76
26 Igor Liba (LW) 1988-89
6 Doug Lidster (D) 1993-94; 1997-98
21 Johan Lindbom (RW) 1997-98
28 Bill Lochead (LW) 1979-80
14 Troy Loney (LW) 1994-95
25 Jim Lorentz (C) 1971-72
4 Kevin Lowe (D) 1992-93–1995-96
19 Odie Lowe (C) 1948-49–1949-50
14 Don Luce (C) 1969-70–1970-71
9 Pentti Lund (RW) 1948-49–1950-51
1 Harry Lumley (G) 1943-44

M

2, 8, 14 Kilby MacDonald (LW) 1939-40–1940-41; 1943-44–1944-45
14 Parker MacDonald (LW) 1956-57–1957-58; 1959-60
17, 19 Hub Macey (LW) 1941-42–1942-43
12, 14 Bruce MacGregor (RW) 1970-71–1973-74
14 Mickey MacIntosh (F) 1952-53
37 Norm Maciver (D) 1986-87–1988-89
15 John MacLean (RW) 1998-99–current
26 Brian MacLellan (LW) 1985-86
11 Bill MacKenzie (D) 1934-35
2 Reg Mackey (D) 1926-27
12 Bob MacMillan (RW) 1974-75
6 Al MacNeil (D) 1966-67
14 Craig MacTavish (C) 1993-94
2 John Mahaffy (C) 1943-44
6 Manny Malhotra (C) 1998-99–current
16, 26 Troy Mallette (LW) 1989-90–1990-91
26 Dave Maloney (D) 1974-75–1984-85
12 Don Maloney (LW)..........1978-79–1988-89
26 Mike Maneluk (RW).........1998-99
5 Felix Mancuso (RW) 1942-43
30 Cesare Maniago (G) 1965-66–1966-67
16 Jack Mann (C) 1943-44–1944-45
19 Ray Manson (LW) 1948-49
14 Henry Maracle (F) 1930-31
39 Todd Marchant (C) 1993-94
42 Dave Marcinyshyn (D) 1992-93
29 Ray Markham (C) 1979-80
25 Mario Marois (D) 1977-78–1980-81
6 Gilles Marotte (D) 1973-74–1975-76
4 Bert Marshall (D)...........1972-73
22 Don Marshall (LW)..........1963-64–1969-70
17 Clare Martin (D).............1951-52
16 Charles Mason (RW) 1934-35–1935-36
32 Stephane Matteau (LW) 1993-94–1995-96
26 Brad Maxwell (D) 1986-87
34 Jim Mayer (RW)............1979-80
12 Sam McAdam (LW) 1930-31
1 Ken McAuley (G)...........1943-44–1944-45
20 Dunc McCallum (D) 1965-66
1 Jack McCartan (G) 1959-60–1960-61
28 Dan McCarthy (C) 1980-81
9, 39 Rob McClanahan (LW) 1981-82–1983-84
39 Shawn McCosh (C) 1994-95
21 Bill McCreary (LW) 1953-54–1954-55
19 Bill McDonagh (LW) 1949-50
14 Bob McDonald (RW) 1943-44
6 Bucko McDonald (D) 1943-44–1944-45
11 John McDonald (RW) 1943-44
22, 28 Mike McDougal (RW)........1978-79; 1980-81
31 Peter McDuffe (G)...........1972-73–1973-74
6, 27 Mike McEwen (D) 1976-77–1979-80; 1985-86
18 Sandy McGregor (RW) 1963-64
14 John McIntyre (C) 1992-93
25 Tony McKegney (RW) 1986-87
17 Don McKenney (C) 1962-63–1963-64
14 John McKenzie (RW) 1965-66
30 Kirk McLean (G) 1999-2000–current
12, 14, 18, 19 Jack McLeod (RW) 1949-50–1952-53; 1954-55
4, 6 Mike McMahon (D) 1963-64–1965-66; 1971-72
21, 37 George McPhee (LW) 1982-83–1986-87
16 Brian McReynolds (C) 1990-91
36, 55 Marty McSorley (D).........1995-96
12 Dick Meissner (RW).........1963-64–1964-65
30 Larry Melnyk (D) 1985-86–1987-88
8 Jan Mertzig (D) 1998-99
28, 29 Joby Messier (D) 1992-93–1994-95
11 Mark Messier (C) 1991-92–1996-97
9, 12, 18 Larry Mickey (RW) 1965-66–1967-68
11 Nick Mickoski (LW) 1947-48–1954-55
9 Rick Middleton (RW) 1974-75–1975-76
12 Jim Mikol (D) 1964-65
4 Hib Milks (LW) 1931-32
23, 32 Corey Millen (C)............1989-90–1991-92
1 Joe Miller (G)...............1927-28
10, 40 Kelly Miller (RW) 1984-85–1986-87
26, 32 Kevin Miller (RW) 1988-89–1990-91
24 Warren Miller (RW) 1979-80
41 Ed Mio (G).................1981-82–1982-83
21 Bill Moe (D) 1944-45–1948-49
5 Lloyd Mohns (D) 1943-44
24 Randy Moller (D) 1989-90–1991-92
16 Larry Molyneaux (D) 1937-38–1938-39
32 Sergio Momesso (LW) 1995-96–1996-97
15 Hartland Monahan (RW) 1974-75
21, 40 Jayson More (D) 1988-89; 1996-97

11 Howie Morenz (C) 1935-36
8 Elwin Morris (D) 1948-49
2 Jim Morrison (D) 1960-61
21 Mark Morrison (C) 1981-82; 1983-84
19 Brian Mullen (RW) 1987-88–1990-91
14 Don Murdoch (RW) 1976-77–1979-80
9 Murray Murdoch (LW) 1926-27–1936-37
14 Mike Murphy (RW)..........1972-73–1973-74
10, 15 Ron Murphy (LW) 1952-53–1956-57
31 Jason Muzzatti (G).......... 1997-98
18 Vic Myles (D) 1942-43

N

36 Rumun Ndur (D) 1998-99
3 Stan Neckar (D)............1998-99
34 Vaclav Nedomansky (RW) 1982-83
10, 93 Petr Nedved (C) 1994-95, 1998-99–current
15 Jim Neilson (D) 1962-63–1973-74
13 Sergei Nemchinov (C) 1991-92–1996-97
47 Steve Nemeth (C) 1987-88
21 Lance Nethery (C)..........1980-81–1981-82
8 Bob Nevin (RW) 1963-64–1970-71
24 Dan Newman (LW) 1976-77–1977-78
9 Bernie Nicholls (C) 1989-90–1991-92
25 Graeme Nicolson (D) 1982-83
36 Jeff Nielsen (RW) 1996-97
30 Chris Nilan (RW) 1987-88–1989-90
11, 19 Ulf Nilsson (C) 1978-79–1982-83
16, 28 Brian Noonan (RW).........1993-94–1994-95; 1996-97
5, 14 Mattias Norstrom (D) 1993-94–1995-96
14 Warren Oatman (F) 1928-29
5 Buddy O'Connor (C) 1947-48
25 John Ogrodnick (LW) 1987-88–1991-92
12 Eddie Olczyk (LW)..........1992-93–1994-95
1 Dan Olesevich (G)........... 1961-62
26 David Oliver (RW) 1996-97
19, 20 Mark Osborne (LW).........1983-84–1986-87; 1994-95

P

11 Wilf Paiement (RW).........1985-86
1, 23 Marcel Paille (G)............ 1957-58–1962-63; 1964-65
14 Aldo Palazzari (RW) 1943-44
2 Brad Park (D)...............1968-69–1975-76
27 Joe Paterson (LW) 1987-88–1988-89
6 Larry Patey (C) 1983-84–1984-85
3 James Patrick (D)..........1983-84–1993-94
16 Lester Patrick (G)........... 1927-28
9, 18 Lynn Patrick (LW)..........1934-35–1942-43; 1945-46
2, 15 Muzz Patrick (D) 1937-38–1940-41; 1945-46
11 Stephen Patrick (RW)........1984-85–1985-86
16, 40 Mark Pavelich (C) 1981-82–1985-86
18 Jim Pavese (D) 1987-88
12, 16 Mel Pearson (LW) 1959-60; 1961-62; 1962-63–1964-65
– Marcel Pelletier (G).......... 1962-63
3 Fern Perreault (LW).........1947-48; 1949-50
4 Frank Peters (D) 1930-31
21 Gary Peters (C) 1965-66
17, 24 Michel Petit (D) 1987-88–1988-89
11 Gordon Pettinger (C) 1932-33
32 Dave Pichette (D) 1987-88
2, 16 Alf Pike (C)................1939-40–1942-43; 1945-46–1946-47
47 Rich Pilon (D)..............1999-2000–current
2, 25 Bob Plager (D) 1964-65–1966-67
1 Jacques Plante (G).......... 1963-64–1964-65
24 Pierre Plante (RW) 1978-79
8 Walt Poddubny (C) 1986-87–1987-88
29, 41 Rudy Poeschek (RW) 1987-88–1989-90
14 Bud Poile (RW) 1949-50
19 Johnny Polich (RW) 1939-40–1940-41
20 Greg Polis (LW) 1974-75–1978-79
19 Larry Popein (C) 1954-55–1960-61
34 Peter Popovic (D) 1998-99
2, 11 Babe Pratt (D) 1935-36–1942-43
17 Dean Prentice (LW) 1952-53–1962-63
18 Wayne Presley (RW)........1995-96
15 Noel Price (D) 1959-60–1960-61
47 Pat Price (D) 1986-87
32 Sean Pronger (C) 1998-99
45 Dale Purinton (D) 1999-2000–current
17 Jean Pusie (D) 1933-34

Q

12 Leo Quenneville (F)..........1929-30
5 Stephane Quintal (D) 1999-2000–current

R

7, 9 Don Raleigh (C) 1943-44; 1947-48–1955-56
34 Jamie Ram (G).............. 1995-96
14, 19 Jean Ratelle (C) 1960-61–1975-76
1 Chuck Rayner (G) 1945-46–1952-53
5 Mel Read (C) 1946-47
11 William Regan (D) 1929-30–1930-31
11 Oliver Reinikka (F) 1926-27
5 Leo Reise, Jr. (D) 1952-53–1953-54
2 Leo Reise, Sr. (D) 1929-30
10 Steven Rice (RW) 1990-91
18 Dave Richardson (LW) 1963-64–1964-65
29 Barry Richter (D) 1995-96
35 Mike Richter (G) 1989-90–current
41 Steve Richmond (D) 1983-84–1985-86
35 Curt Ridley (G).............. 1974-75
18 Mike Ridley (C) 1985-86–1986-87
4 Vic Ripley (LW) 1933-34–1934-35
19 Alex Ritson (LW) 1944-45
21 Wayne Rivers (RW) 1968-69
1 John Ross Roach (G) 1928-29–1931-32
5 Doug Robinson (LW)........1964-65–1966-67
20 Luc Robitaille (LW) 1995-96–1996-97
24, 25 Mike Robitaille (D) 1969-70–1970-71
16 Leon Rochefort (RW) 1960-61; 1962-63
5 Normand Rochefort (D) 1988-89–1991-92
12 Edmond Rodden (F) 1930-31
17, 27 Mike Rogers (C)............1981-82–1985-86
5 Dale Rolfe (D) 1970-71–1974-75
1 Al Rollins (G)............... 1959-60
19 Len Ronson (LW)...........1960-61
9 Paul Ronty (C).............1951-52–1954-55
2, 15 Jim Ross (D) 1951-52–1952-53
22 Bobby Rousseau (RW) 1971-72–1974-75
15 Ronnie Rowe (LW) 1947-48
8 Jean-Yves Roy (RW) 1994-95
44 Lindy Ruff (D) 1988-89–1990-91
29 Reijo Ruotsalainen (D) 1981-82–1985-86
19 Duane Rupp (D) 1962-63
16 Church Russell (LW) 1945-46–1947-48

S

21 Simo Saarinen (D)..........1984-85
2, 3, 4, 5 Larry Sacharuk (D) 1972-73–1973-74; 1975-76–1976-77
8, 26 Kjell Samuelsson (D) 1985-86–1986-87
5 Ulf Samuelsson (D) 1995-96–1998-99
4, 16 Derek Sanderson (C) 1974-75–1975-76
5 Chuck Sands (C) 1943-44
28 Tomas Sandstrom (RW) 1984-85–1989-90
6 Glen Sather (LW)...........1970-71–1973-74
10, 33 Marc Savard (C) 1997-98–1998-99
30 Terry Sawchuk (G) 1969-70
1 Joe Schaefer (G)............ 1959-60–1960-61
17 Chuck Scherza (C) 1943-44–1944-45
18 Ken Schinkel (RW) 1959-60–1963-64; 1966-67

25 Mathieu Schneider (D) 1998-99–current
11 Lawrence Scott (F) 1927-28
31, 35 Ron Scott (G)...............1983-84–1987-88
2, 21 Earl Seibert (D) 1931-32–1935-36
16 Rod Seiling (D) 1963-64–1974-75
16 George Senick (LW) 1952-53
36 Pierre Sevigny (LW) 1997-98
5, 6 Eddie Shack (RW) 1958-59–1960-61
18 Joe Shack (LW) 1942-43; 1944-45
21, 27 David Shaw (D) 1987-88–1991-92
6 Bobby Sheehan (C) 1978-79
23 Ray Sheppard (RW) 1990-91
– Johnny Sherf (LW) 1937-38
3 Fred Shero (D) 1947-48–1949-50
4 Alex Shibicky (LW) 1935-36–1941-42; 1945-46
4 Albert Siebert (LW) 1932-33–1933-34
16 Dave Silk (RW) 1979-80–1982-83
41 Mike Siltala (RW) 1986-87–1987-88
30 Don Simmons (G) 1965-66; 1967-68–1968-69
21 Reg Sinclair (RW) 1950-51–1951-52
20 Brian Skrudland (C) 1997-98
11, 20 Ed Slowinski (RW) 1947-48–1952-53
10, 14, 20 Clint Smith (C) 1936-37–1942-43
15 Dallas Smith (D) 1977-78
21 Don Smith (RW) 1949-50
19 Floyd Smith (RW) 1960-61
14 Geoff Smith (D) 1997-98–1998-99
17 Stan Smith (C) 1939-40–1940-41
8 Brad Smyth (RW) 1997-98
1, 31 Doug Soetaert (G)...........1975-76–1980-81
12 Art Somers (LW) 1931-32–1934-35
16 Glen Sonmor (LW) 1953-54–1954-55
15, 16, 21 Irv Spencer (D) 1959-60–1961-62
19 Red Staley (C) 1948-49
8 Allan Stanley (D) 1948-49–1954-55
4 Wally Stanowski (D) 1948-49–1950-51
4 Harold Starr (D) 1934-35–1935-36
21 Bud Stefanski (C) 1977-78
21 Pete Stemkowski (C) 1970-71–1976-77
5 Ulf Sterner (LW) 1964-65
17 Kevin Stevens (LW) 1997-98–1999-2000
1 Doug Stevenson (G) 1944-45
16 Gaye Stewart (LW) 1951-52–1952-53
12 Ron Stewart (RW) 1967-68–1972-73
20, 28, 32 P.J. Stock (C) 1997-98–current
13 Jack Stoddard (RW) 1951-52–1952-53
21 Blaine Stoughton (RW) 1983-84
21 Neil Strain (LW) 1952-53
10, 15 Art Stratton (C) 1959-60
10 Art Strobel (LW) 1943-44
9 Doug Sulliman (RW) 1979-80–1980-81
7 Red Sullivan (C) 1956-57–1960-61
38 Ronnie Sundin (D) 1997-98
24 Niklas Sundstrom (RW/LW) ...1995-96–1998-99
25 Peter Sundstrom (RW) 1983-84–1985-86
5 Bill Sweeney (C) 1959-60
37 Tim Sweeney (RW) 1997-98

T

19 Dean Talafous (RW) 1978-79–1981-82
4 Chris Tamer (D) 1998-99
26, 35 Ron Talakoski (RW) 1986-87–1987-88
25 Dave Tataryn (G)............1976-77
15 Bill Taylor (C) 1947-48
19 G. Bill Taylor (C) 1964-65
12 Ralph Taylor (D) 1929-30
5, 18 Ted Taylor (LW) 1964-65–1965-66
26 Tim Taylor (C) 1999-2000–current
17 Spence Thatchell (D) 1942-43
1 Wayne Thomas (G) 1977-78–1980-81
8, 10 Paul Thompson (LW) 1926-27–1930-31
14 Fred Thurier (C) 1944-45
10 Esa Tikkanen (LW) 1992-93–1993-94; 1996-97; 1998-99
6 Mark Tinordi (D) 1987-88
17, 18 Walt Tkaczuk (C) 1967-68–1980-81
12 Zellio Toppazzini (RW) 1950-51–1951-52
14 Wes Trainor (RW) 1948-49
14 Guy Trottier (RW) 1968-69
4 Rene Trudell (RW) 1945-46–1947-48
8 Darren Turcotte (C) 1988-89–1993-94
6 Dean Turner (D) 1978-79
17 Norm Tustin (LW) 1941-42

V

2, 5 Carol Vadnais (D) 1975-76–1981-82
11 Sparky Vail 1928-29–1929-30
34 John Vanbiesbrouck (G) 1981-82; 1983-84–1992-93
37 Ryan VandenBussche (RW) ...1996-97–1997-98
36 Alexei Vasiliev (D) 1999-2000–current
16, 17 Pat Verbeek (RW) 1995-96
40 Dennis Vial (D) 1990-91
8 Steve Vickers (LW) 1972-73–1981-82
1, 30 Gilles Villemure (G)..........1963-64–1967-68; 1970-71–1975-76
32 Terry Virtne (D) 1999-2000–current
39 Vladimir Vorobiev (RW) 1996-97–1997-98
11 Carl Voss (C) 1932-33

W

15 Frank Waite (F) 1930-31
14, 36 Gord Walker (LW) 1986-87–1987-88
25 Peter Wallin (RW) 1980-81–1981-82
– Eddie Wares (RW) 1936-37
14 Billy Warwick (LW) 1942-43–1943-44
8 Grant Warwick (RW) 1941-42–1947-48
7, 15 Phil Watson (RW) 1935-36–1942-43; 1944-45–1947-48
21 John Webster (LW) 1949-50
31 Steve Weeks (G) 1980-81–1983-84
39 Doug Weight (C) 1991-92–1992-93
24 Jay Wells (D) 1991-92–1994-95
12 Len Wharton (D) 1944-45
41 Simon Wheeldon (C) 1987-88–1988-89
17, 39 Rob Whistle (D) 1985-86
19 Sherman White (C) 1946-47; 1949-50
14 Doug Wickenheiser (C) 1988-89
20 Juha Widing (C) 1969-70
6, 24 Jim Wiemer (D) 1984-85–1985-86
17 Tom Williams (LW) 1971-72–1973-74
14 Bert Wilson (LW) 1973-74–1974-75
17 Carey Wilson (C) 1988-89–1989-90
1, 31 Dunc Wilson (G).............1974-75–1975-76
16 Johnny Wilson (LW) 1960-61–1961-62
1 Hal Winkler (G) 1926-27
14, 29 Johan Witehall 1998-99
4 Bob Wood (D) 1950-51
1 Lorne Worsley (G)...........1952-53–1962-63
14 Bill Wylie (C) 1950-51

Y

32 Harry York (C) 1997-1998
18 Mike York (C) 1999-2000–current
19, 39 Tom Younghans (RW) 1981-82

Z

31 Rob Zamuner (C) 1991-92
24 Joe Zanussi (D) 1974-75
21 Sergei Zubov (D) 1992-93–1994-95

Index

Bold face page numbers indicate pictured items

Photography Credits

Bruce Bennett/Bruce Bennett Studios
38, 47, 48–49, 52b, 66, 72b, 89, 132, 138, 142, 140, 141, 147a, 152–53, 157

Bruce Bennett Studios
42b, 43, 44–45, 70, 97, 108, 115, 133, 144a, 145, 148, 149, 151, 153a

Bettmann/CORBIS
26

Collection of William J. Martin
13

Corbis/Bettmann-UPI
23, 24, 71, 79

Melchior DiGiacomo/Bruce Bennett Studios
116a, 117a, 120, 127, 128–29

J. Giamundo/Bruce Bennett Studios
122b, 143

Ray Grabowski
116–117

Graphic Artists/Hockey Hall of Fame
86a, 99a, 104–105

John Halligan Collection
2–3, 14, 22, 34–35, 53, 58, 63, 65a, 65b, 68–69, 70b, 70c, 73b, 74a, 76, 84–85, 92b, 92c, 94–95, 101a, 101b, 106b, 111, 122a, 124a

Hockey Hall of Fame
12c, 16, 18, 40, 50a, 56–57, 81b, 85, 160b, 161

Hulton-Deutsch Collection/CORBIS
25

Imperial Oil-Turofsky/Hockey Hall of Fame
15a, 80a, 81a, 74b, 87b, 90–91

Bob Koller/*New York Daily News*
96

Scott Levy/Bruce Bennett Studios
142b

R. Lewis/Bruce Bennett Studios
150b

London Life-Portnoy/Hockey Hall of Fame
98, 110, 124b, 126a, 130, 131, 136–37

Doug MacLellan/Hockey Hall of Fame
12b, 25b, 42a, 75, 121a–d, 121f, 147b, 160a, 160c–g, 161a–g

Jim McIsaac/Bruce Bennett Studios
12d, 12–13, 32, 32–33, 50, 50–51, 74, 74–75, 92, 92–93, 117b, 118, 122b, 142c, 158–59

B. Miller/Bruce Bennett Studios
139

New York Rangers
6–7, 10, 17, 19, 20, 27, 28–29, 30, 32c, 37, 39, 41, 46, 46, 47, 47, 48a, 48b, 50b, 55, 57, 59, 60, 62–63, 64, 67, 72a, 73a, 73c, 77, 80b, 82–83, 88a, 88b, 100a, 107a, 107b, 109, 112a, 112c–i, 113b, 113c, 114, 125, 135, 142a, 144b, 146, 148b, 154–55, 156b

O-Pee-Chee/Hockey Hall of Fame
90

Frank Prazak/Hockey Hall of Fame
102–3, 103, 116b

Dave Sandford/Hockey Hall of Fame
1, 12a, 15b, 18a, 22, 30, 32a, 32b, 33, 36, 42, 51, 54, 70a, 76, 78, 86b, 90, 91a, 91b, 92a, 93, 99b, 100b, 103, 106a, 112b, 113a, 121e, 123, 126b, 134, 138, 148a, 150a, 153b–d, 156a

Nancy Siesel/NYT Pictures
4–5

© 1938 Time Inc. Reprinted by permission
52

Letters indicate image placement, clockwise from top